ired. There is a process of change just as there is a process of
r for growing wheat. How to change is the problem.'

eming

akes place project-by-project and in no other way.'

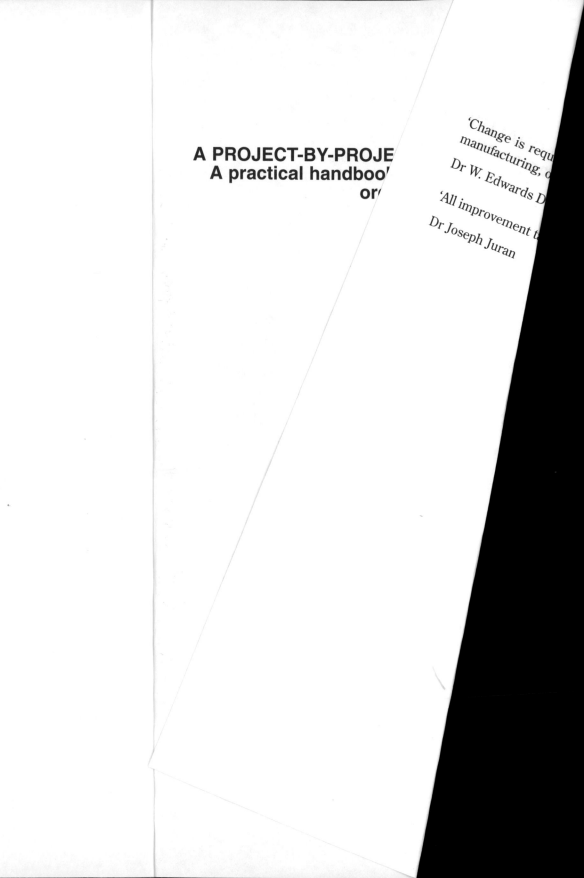

A PROJECT-BY-PROJE
A practical handbook
or

'Change is requ
manufacturing, o

Dr W. Edwards D

'All improvement t

Dr Joseph Juran

A PROJECT-BY-PROJECT APPROACH TO QUALITY

A PRACTICAL HANDBOOK FOR INDIVIDUALS, TEAMS AND ORGANIZATIONS

Richard Capper

Gower

Published by
Gower Publishing Limited
Gower House
Croft Road
Aldershot
Hampshire GU11 3HR
England

Gower
Old Post Road
Brookfield
Vermont 05036
USA

British Library Cataloguing in Publication Data
Capper, Richard
  A project-by-project approach to quality: a practical
  handbook for individuals, teams and organizations
  1. Total quality management
  I. Title
  658.4'013

  ISBN 0566079259

Library of Congress Cataloging-in-Publication Data
Capper, Richard, 1961–
  A project-by-project approach to quality: a practical handbook
for individuals, teams and organizations / Richard Capper.
      p. cm.
  Includes bibliographical references and index.
  ISBN 0–566–07925–9 (cloth)
  1. Total quality management. 2. Teams in the workplace.
3. Industrial project management. I. Title.
HD62.15.C353 1997
658.4'013—dc21   97–20129
                    CIP

Typeset in Century Old Style by Bournemouth Colour Press and printed in Great Britain by Biddles Limited, Guildford.

Contents

Preface

Many organizations set up improvement projects of one form or another. These projects may be undertaken by individuals or teams, may be large or small, may be chosen by the managers or the workforce, may be established as part of a quality initiative, may be identified through the business plan, customer satisfaction data or may simply be 'a good idea'. The people involved nearly always begin the project with enthusiasm and commitment. However, only rarely are they given adequate support or guidance regarding how the project should be carried out. The result is that they start from scratch, often spending much time in unproductive meetings, unclear about the remit, and uncertain of what to do next. This is not due to a lack of ability but simply because the people are ill-equipped for their task. They generally receive no training and most books about quality are too theoretical with no link to practical application. Books about project management are at the other extreme. They are often too technical and don't offer general guidelines or best practice about running a project. Thus, there is no structured approach to the project, little use is made of quality tools and techniques and the group do not function well as a team. Some will conclude with no results. Others will drag on for long periods of time until they peter out. Those that do reach a conclusion do not produce optimum results, often having poor proposals with inadequate data and implementation plans.

This book addresses these issues and presents some guidelines based on best practice about how to set up and run improvement projects. The ideas behind the book are firmly rooted in quality management. Where many books about quality are written at an ideological and philosophical level, this book is intended to be a practical 'how to' guide. But it's not just a book about running better projects. You can use it to make profound changes and bring about a transformation in your work, your team and your organization.

THE STRUCTURE

The book is divided into five parts. *Part I, The project-by-project approach*, introduces the thinking behind the approach, why it is needed and its roots in the ideas of quality management. There have been many projects over the years to try to improve quality. You will find a chapter about what goes wrong with these projects when they are approached in a traditional manner. This part also considers the various roles in a project: Champion, Project Leader, team members and Quality Adviser.

Part II, Managing the strategy, takes a step back and looks at strategic issues such as organizational goals, understanding customers, and how to determine strategies for improvement. Next it looks at how to convert fine intentions into practical actions using projects. This part deals with how to identify, set up, coordinate, support and implement improvement projects in a coherent manner.

Part III, Project methodologies, focuses on how to run efficient and effective projects. It provides a number of approaches depending on the exact nature of the topic and these are laid out as step-by-step guidelines. Also included are details of how to pilot, review and implement changes and how to collect and use data.

Part IV, Tools and techniques, brings together the tools and techniques that will never let you down. Included here are tools for planning, analysis, decision making and data display. There are also techniques for working with groups of people and project teams to ensure that you get the most out of those involved. This is not a list of all the tools I have ever heard of – only the ones I have used and have found to work.

Part V, More about Quality Advisers, covers the role in detail – although you will find many references to Quality Advisers throughout the book. Those organizations that have adopted this approach have found that the training and use of Quality Advisers is a crucial stage and vital element.

'IN ACTION' CHAPTERS

At the end of each part there is an 'in action' chapter. Whereas the other chapters tell you how to do it, the 'in action' chapters provide some stories about how people have done it.

HOW THE FIVE PARTS FIT TOGETHER

This book is not about business planning or quality philosophy. It is a highly practical guide to implementation at both a strategic and tactical level. It assumes that your organization knows broadly where it wants to go. Parts I and II are about strategy and how to manage this. Parts III, IV and V provide the tactics to implement your strategies. You will be able to see the link between identifying and setting up a project in Parts I and II through to running the project in Part III and the tools and techniques you can bring to bear in Part IV. You will also be able to follow through the examples in the 'in action' chapters in the same way.

Your organization does not need to have a quality initiative for you to be able to use this book. Your job will be easier if it does but as an individual you can still use these ideas to greatly improve the way you yourself work. Good luck! And please let me know how you do.

Richard Capper

Acknowledgements

These are people who have made a contribution to the book, either by contributing, reading my drafts or helping my thinking. Andy Barrett, Phil Bennett, Pat Byrne, Sylvia Cotton, Carol Crawford, Audrey Davidson, Tony Finnegan, Keith Handy, Andrew Q. Harvey, Andrea Higginbottom, Maggi Howard, Ronnie Hughes, Steve Jones, Leonie Lupton, John MackMersh, Bali Maman, Jayne Mason, Sue Ormrod, Dave Power, Steve Robinson, Carew Satchwell, Spider, Peter Strachan, Ray Tasker, Janet Taylor, Bill Wynn.

RC

List of figures

How you can use this book

WHERE TO START

You don't have to read the whole book before you can start using it. Indeed, it is not the sort of book to read from cover to cover in one sitting. It is a practical guide. Here are some suggestions as to how you might get into it:

- First, have a flick through. Familiarize yourself with the structure of the five parts and have a look at the subheadings in each chapter.

- If you're a manager in charge of an organization or department and you want to create some sort of order in its projects and the way you set tasks for individuals and teams, then turn to Part II.

- If you're responsible for a specific project whether it's something you're doing on your own or if you're leading a team, go to Part III to see what approach might apply.

- If you want to try some new tools and techniques in your day-to-day work or in meetings of any sort, have a look through Part IV and see if anything interests you.

- If you're the sort of person who likes reading real-life examples about how people have done it, try the 'in action' chapters at the end of each part. They might spark off some ideas.

- If you attend numerous meetings and they could do with being more productive or with livening up, try Chapters 21, 17 and 22.

- If you've simply had enough of being involved in projects that go nowhere and the thought of more projects fills you with dread, turn to Chapters 2 and 3.

- If you like reading books like this from cover to cover, I think you will find Parts I, II and V pretty easy going. Parts III and IV are laid out as step-by-step instructions so you might find these a little more difficult – they are not intended to be read; they are intended to be used.

HOW NOT TO USE THIS BOOK

Don't just read this book. You need to try out ideas, no matter how small.

CROSS-REFERENCING

Use the cross-referencing to bounce about between the various parts. Where a lot of books and training fall down is that they provide many tools in isolation, but you need to know how all these fit together and how they can be used as a coherent whole rather than here and there. The cross-referencing will help with this. For example, you will find cross-references to the various tools and techniques in each of the project methodologies in Part III. When you come to one of these you need to refer to the specific tool or technique in Part IV.

Part I
The Project-by-Project Approach

1 Taking a project-by-project approach

PROJECT-BY-PROJECT: WHAT, WHY AND HOW?

WHAT IS THE PROJECT-BY-PROJECT APPROACH?

The project-by-project approach applies at two levels: strategic and tactical. At a strategic level, it represents a way of establishing a coherent, aligned and properly resourced improvement plan. It can be used to refocus existing initiatives, manage new initiatives, implement a business plan, achieve specific business objectives or structure the daily running of an organization or department. At its most powerful, the project-by-project approach can do all of the above and ensure that all activities are brought together under the same umbrella.

At a tactical level, the project-by-project approach is a means by which individual projects can be run in the most effective manner. It ensures that they have a clear remit, involve the right people, follow a clearly defined methodology and use appropriate tools and techniques.

WHY IS A PROJECT-BY-PROJECT APPROACH NECESSARY?

Repetitive strain injury, or RSI, is now a recognized problem in the workplace. People performing the same manual tasks can have physical problems as a result. What is not so well recognized is RIS – repetitive initiative syndrome – a problem suffered in silence by many organizations. There is a desire to change and improve but a lack of constancy of purpose. Organizations have flirted with customer care, management by objectives, performance related pay, BS5750 or ISO9000/1, Total Quality Management, Charter Mark, business process re-engineering, National Vocational Qualifications and competencies, Investors in People, the learning organization and so on. In large organizations this can often involve several million pounds and endless training. Frequently, project teams or working groups with various aims are set up. These begin with a big bang and die

3

with a whimper. Where these initiatives usually fail is in the link between strategic intent and practical application.

All of the above initiatives have similar if not identical aims:

- improved customer satisfaction
- improved cost effectiveness and thus profitability
- improved internal processes
- a happier and more skilled workforce.

There is another set of organizational initiatives with an equally good pedigree, but they are not launched in a blaze of publicity with free mugs for all the workforce. These initiatives are cost cutting, reorganization, downsizing (now known as rightsizing) and management by fear. What would you print on a mug to launch one of these? A happier and more skilled workforce is rarely the result. Improved customer satisfaction is sometimes stated as the reason for the introduction of these initiatives, as is improved internal processes. Such management styles are often the default position when times are tough: 'We need to sharpen up and reduce our costs to maintain our competitive position.' Most managers are good at these techniques and the activity of reorganization in particular creates the illusion of improvement. Real improvement for front-line staff or the customers is not usually an outcome.

Often running parallel to, but in isolation from, both these types of initiatives are business planning processes. Every organization with any credibility has a business plan. These are religiously updated once a year, but once again there is often failure in the link between intent and implementation. More sophisticated organizations develop 'performance indicators' which are presented at monthly management meetings. The response to the information? 'Do you think we could have these in colour next month?'

Why is this? There are a number of problems:

1. Line managers, particularly at the sharp end in production or operational functions, see these initiatives as extra work with little relevance to the real job.
2. New initiatives are bolted on rather than integrated into the way the organization runs.
3. There is no coordination between activities. New initiatives, business planning, personal objective setting, sorting out operational problems and a multitude of other activities all take place in isolation of each other.
4. Even when specific projects are established they are given insufficient support and guidance. In addition, those involved often have little knowledge of the tools and techniques necessary to bring about a successful result.

HOW DOES THE PROJECT-BY-PROJECT APPROACH HELP?

The project-by-project approach at its simplest is the tightening up of some of these issues. It introduces a structured approach to change and improvement and embraces a number of critical elements:

1. A sweep up of all existing activities and an evaluation of their status – in progress (if so, at what stage?), stalled (if so, why?) or not started (if so, why not?).
2. A listing of all the other goals it is hoped will be achieved. This list might be drawn from many sources such as the business plan or customer satisfaction data.
3. Prioritization of all these – which really are important?
4. Establishment of well-defined projects to achieve those objectives at the top of the list. For each project the following are clearly understood:
   - the reason why the work is being undertaken
   - the remit
   - the approach being taken (the methodology)
   - who is responsible
   - who is involved
   - what resources are being used.
5. Support and guidance from the senior managers, and regular monitoring and reporting to the senior management team.

This result is a powerful combination of strategic and tactical action. Senior managers establish, coordinate and support projects, which are then conducted in an efficient and effective manner.

PROJECTS, PROJECTS EVERYWHERE

WHAT IS A PROJECT?

Since we are talking about using projects as the means by which organizational change can be brought about it might be a good idea to spend some time thinking about what a project might look like. The definition of a project used in this book is as follows:

> *A project is any piece of work apart from routine operation in an organization.*

Projects come in all shapes and sizes. At the top end of the range, for example, is the construction of the Channel Tunnel. At the other extreme might be the

5

project given to the work experience student, such as the reorganization of the filing system. Projects can have different aims – to improve a process, introduce a new service, introduce a new product, remove a problem and so on. Projects may be undertaken by individuals or teams.

Many managers would not regard much of the work they carry out as a project. If asked 'What approach do you take to a piece of work?', they will reply 'I just do it.' If asked 'How was that particular task selected?', they may look at you askance or say 'It's one of my objectives.' In fact, much of the work carried out by managers can be broken down into discrete pieces which could be called a project and would benefit from some of the discipline which can go with this.

'Project management' has traditionally been the realm of professional project managers and is probably most often associated with large-scale civil engineering projects. Most other managers today have been exposed to some of the disciplines and techniques of project management and will be familiar with some of the so-called quality tools. What is often lacking, however, is the big picture – how these tools and techniques fit together as a coordinated approach. The project-by-project approach is a powerful union of the ideas, tools and techniques of quality management with some of the well-founded disciplines of project management.

PROJECTS AND CHANGE

You may hear the term 'change initiative' bandied around in organizations. Often you will hear much rhetoric but see little change. Change only comes about as a result of alteration to working practices. Generally speaking, if no change is taking place, the organization will stay the same and be buffeted by external factors. Routine operation of the organization will be carried out in the same way. Projects are the means by which change comes about in an organization. Projects alter routine operations by changing the way in which existing processes work, introducing new services, products or processes and removing problems.

WHERE CAN THE PROJECT-BY-PROJECT APPROACH BE APPLIED?

AT AN ORGANIZATIONAL LEVEL

The approach is most powerful at an organizational level when used to implement business objectives. The methodologies and tools are firmly rooted in the philosophy of quality management and if you are considering or are engaged in a quality initiative this is an excellent way to move from fine ideals to practical actions. If you are not thinking about a quality initiative, you probably still have a business plan of some sort. The steering group methodology (see Chapter 6) will enable you to break down the business plan into its component parts and set up projects to achieve each of these. If you have neither a quality initiative nor a business plan, all is not lost. You can still use the steering group methodology to get a grip on what is going on in the organization and take it from there. Start from where you are, not where you'd like to be!

AT A DEPARTMENTAL LEVEL

If you are responsible for a department, you can use the steering group methodology to list, prioritize and monitor all of your project activities. This includes taking elements of the business plan for which your department is responsible and converting them into team or individual objectives. These are then managed as a series of projects through your regular management meetings and performance reviews. The project methodologies (Part III), tools and techniques (Part IV) will help your department to transform the effectiveness of its projects.

AT A PERSONAL LEVEL

Even if you are a lone voice in your organization, you can use the project methodologies, tools and techniques to radically improve the effectiveness of the projects as well as the efficiency of your day-to-day work for which you are responsible. If you begin to work in this more efficient and effective way, people will notice. They will start to wonder what you are doing differently and will want to be involved.

PRINCIPLES UNDERPINNING THE PROJECT-BY-PROJECT APPROACH

Although this is intended to be a practical book, it is important for users to understand where the ideas come from and more importantly some of the principles you are buying into if you choose to adopt these ideas. I have already said that the principles are deeply rooted in the ideas of quality management. You will find most of them fall under the heading of common sense. There are others, however, that may require a change in some of your views and in your management style and practices. (If you want to know more, see the recommendations for further reading at the end of the book.)

'Change is required. There is a process of change just as there is a process of manufacturing, or for growing wheat. How to change is the problem.'

This quotation is from Dr W. Edwards Deming who was an authority in the field of quality and inspired me greatly. This sums up nicely the fact that change in organizations does not come about as the result of good intentions or wishing for it. A process of change is required. The project-by-project approach provides this.

'All improvement takes place project by project and in no other way.'

This second quotation comes from Dr Joseph Juran. Dr Juran defined a project as a 'problem scheduled for solution', a definition which is much narrower than that used in this book. However, the quotation provides a clue as to what the process of change might look like. Intent is converted into change through a series of projects and there is no other way.

'Workers work in the system. The job of the manager is to work on the system and improve it with their help.'

This completes the hat-trick of quotations and originates from a third eminent quality thinker, Myron Tribus. Tribus suggests a principle by which the projects might work. The job of the manager is to identify, set up and support projects. The projects themselves need to involve the workforce as these are the people who best understand the way things work in the organization. This is the most important element of the project-by-project approach. You must directly involve the people who do the job.

UNDERSTAND THE OLD AND NEW WAYS OF VIEWING AN ORGANIZATION

The old way to view an organization is through the departmental bunkers of the hierarchy chart. The project-by-project approach recognizes a number of important truths about the way work is done. This is the new way to view the organization.

- The customer does not feature on the hierarchy chart. In many organizations most customer contact will take place at the 'lower' levels.
- The most important processes in any organization cross several departments and therefore require cooperation. As a consequence there is not usually a specific senior manager responsible for a process – it will usually cross the domain of several.

The project-by-project approach helps address these two issues by:

- Setting up interdepartmental project teams consisting of the people who actually do the job irrespective of grade, seniority, position or department. A key task is to gather data about the customer.
- Every project has a Champion drawn from the senior management team. The Champion works interdepartmentally with the cooperation of other senior managers.

8

DON'T BE AFRAID TO DIRECT

Many organizations spend much time talking about empowerment without understanding what it means or how to achieve it. The 'e' word is banned from this book because you don't need it. If you have a structured approach to improvement and running the organization which involves the workers, platitudes are not necessary.

On the contrary, nearly everybody I have ever worked with has not wanted empowerment but direction. The job of senior managers and directors is to direct. They do this by being directly involved in the work of only the most strategically important projects and by championing others. Championing does not mean interfering. It means providing direction, guidance and support.

REMEMBER THE 85–15 RULE

What is the 85–15 rule? It could be paraphrased as 'Don't just concentrate on the people, understand the processes by which work is accomplished.' Many improvement initiatives are motivationally based – work harder, work smarter, be nice to the customers. These work on the assumption that if only the workers would do their jobs properly then everything would be all right. Performance related pay backs this up – do a good job and get rewarded for it. This approach ignores a couple of important facts. First, there is very little that is 100 per cent within the control of the worker. In fact, a comprehensive study undertaken by Dr Juran put the figure within worker control at only 15 per cent. Put another way, 85 per cent is outside worker control. Second, the most important processes cross several departments and will therefore involve several or more likely many people. To make significant improvements it is therefore not enough to try to motivate individuals, who will not thank you for this anyway. Far better to analyse the whole chain of events – the process and all the factors affecting this.

Customer care initiatives can sometimes fall into this trap too. In the early 1980s I worked in the ticket office on Nottingham station and became involved as a part-time trainer in a customer care initiative. The skills were great but something else was needed above and beyond this. On one course I ran I had a cleaner from the station platforms attend. His job involved emptying the litter bins which he had to do by hand piece by piece. He said, 'Richard, it would really help me to have bin bags, it would be much easier to empty the bins, I could do it faster and then I could spend my time doing more useful work.' I duly reported this to the local manager. Every time I saw John after the course he asked me 'any progress?'. I kept asking, but no bin bags appeared. One day I saw John and he didn't ask. It was at that moment that I realized customer care as an organizational philosophy was flawed – something more is needed.

PLAN-DO-STUDY-ACT

Plan-do-study-act is the Shewhart cycle, named after Walter Shewhart, the American statistician who inspired Deming's early work. You will see the Shewhart cycle at work throughout this book both at a strategic and tactical level. It tells us to:

1. Spend some time carefully planning an action or project.
2. Do it – carry it out preferably first as a pilot or on a small scale.
3. Study the results – what worked, what didn't? Did you achieve what you set out to do?
4. Act on your conclusions. This might mean adopt the change on a permanent basis, modify it and pilot it again or abandon it altogether.
5. Go around the cycle again.

You will notice this principle built into the structure of the methodologies later in the book.

A BRIEF HISTORY

Who are all these people I have been quoting and what is the story behind them? The story behind quality is strange but true.

Quality is a word used by many different organizations to mean many different things. When you see the word 'quality' used in this manual, it refers to the ideas of Walter Shewhart in America in the 1930s, developed in American industry during the war and taken to Japan by eminent management thinkers such as Deming and Juran in the early 1950s. Thirty years later these ideas found their way back to Western industry.

Like some of the approaches mentioned earlier in this chapter, this version of quality has its own set of techniques. The difference is that these are bound together by a philosophy with a strong pedigree, and this is the story behind it.

SURELY QUALITY HAS ALWAYS EXISTED?

Quality has always been an issue, even in early industry. The success of the craft worker depended upon the ability to sell a decent product. However, in earlier days the craft worker tended to be responsible for the whole process from the purchase of raw materials, production and sale on to the customer. The industrial revolution changed all that. People were employed in factories and were responsible for only a very small part of the overall process. A new function was born and became known as 'management'. The job of the managers was to tell workers to do their job and pass it on. This style of management flourished with thinkers such as Frederick Taylor focusing on task analysis and the ideas of mass production taking hold in the late nineteenth and early twentieth century.

However, problems with this style of management soon became apparent. Consistency and reliability could not be guaranteed. Quality control inspectors were employed to weed out bad from good but faulty goods continued to reach the customer.

TELEPHONES, CROP EXPERIMENTATION AND THE CENSUS

The story of quality as we understand it today starts with Walter Shewhart. Born in 1891 in Canton, Illinois, Shewhart became a statistician and in 1918 was hired by the Western Electric Company, a subsidiary of AT&T. In the early 1920s, Shewhart worked at the Hawthorne Plant in Chicago and later moved to the Bell Telephone Laboratories in New Jersey. His job was to investigate poor quality in telephone apparatus and improve consistency and reliability. It is worth pointing out that at this point in the twentieth century, the telephone industry was revolutionizing the way business was done and the way the world worked. This was the cutting edge of technology much as computers are today.

Shewhart discovered the importance of variation. If it was possible to eliminate all variation in incoming materials, in the production processes employed, in the machinery and equipment used, in the working environment and in the way people did their jobs, then complete uniformity and reliability could be guaranteed. How to go about doing this was the question that laid the foundations for quality management. Shewhart's ideas about how to do this extended far beyond statistics into leadership and customer satisfaction. He also discovered that product defects were rarely attributable to the workers. Other factors accounted for the main causes. Much of Shewhart's work was influenced by Sir Roland A. Fisher, a Briton who applied statistical techniques in agriculture to greatly improve crop experiments.

The next name to appear in this story is another statistician, Dr W. Edwards Deming. Introduced to Shewhart in the mid-1930s, Deming took a year of absence to study under Roland Fisher. Deming began to build on Shewhart's work and also transferred these techniques to service industry. In 1939 Deming joined the US census bureau and the following census set new standards for accuracy, efficiency and cost effectiveness.

THE WAR, JAPAN, RADIOS AND A WORLD FAMOUS ORGANIZATION

The Second World War emphasized the importance of the quality of manufactured product. Production lines were converted to munitions and equipment to support the war effort. Unfortunately, existing quality problems did not disappear. Between 1936 and 1944 Shewhart worked as a consultant for the War Department on ammunition specifications. At the outbreak of the war, Deming was asked to teach statistical quality control to companies supplying the armed forces.

Following the war, Japan had been devastated. General MacArthur began to consider reconstruction of the country. Homer Sarasohn, the next name in our story, was a product development engineer at the Massachusetts Institute of Technology. In 1945 Sarasohn received a telegram from General MacArthur's Headquarters asking him to go to Japan. This he ignored as he thought it was a practical joke. Luckily MacArthur's HQ followed up by telephone and Sarasohn ended up in Japan for five years. His first task was to establish how to supply the population with radios so that they could receive communications from the Occupation HQ. Many of the senior managers had been removed from their positions so Sarasohn set about training the new managers and established a training programme which eventually reached the majority of managers. The Japanese were taken with statistical quality control and in 1950 Sarasohn invited Shewhart to come out to Japan but he was unable to do so because of poor health.

Luckily Shewhart's protégé was available. Deming, who had already visited Japan in 1947 to help with the census, was initially invited back by the world famous Japanese Union of Scientists and Engineers. Although he accepted the invitation, he refused the fee. In 1950 Deming embarked upon a series of lectures to Japanese managers. At one gathering, he addressed 21 leaders representing 80 per cent of the financial capital of the country. His lectures were translated into Japanese and published as a book. Deming refused the royalties and asked JUSE to use the money for any purpose it wanted. JUSE decided to start a quality award and, as a mark of respect, named this the Deming Prize. This remains the most coveted award in the country. Deming returned to Japan often during the 1950s. In 1954 JUSE also invited Dr Joseph Juran and he also greatly helped the Japanese, in particular with the strategy and techniques for improving quality. Deming told the Japanese that if they followed the principles of quality, they could dominate many of the world's markets. They listened.

QUALITY COMES HOME

Post-war America had eight times the manufacturing capacity of the rest of the world combined. Quality was no longer an issue. If you could make it, you could sell it, but the mid-1970s saw a change. Cheap Japanese imports began to flood many markets. Worse still, as time progressed, the quality of these imports improved and began to outstrip home produced goods. Not only America suffered. The British motor cycle industry was also an early casualty. The initial response to this influx of competition thought to be built on the back of cheap labour was to erect trade barriers and import quotas. When this did not work, the West began to wake up to the threat and Deming, largely ignored in his own country for many years, became a sought-after consultant. Right up until his death in 1993 he ran four-day seminars around the world which were attended by many thousands of managers.

QUALITY TODAY AND TOMORROW

Quality in Britain first started under the banner of Total Quality Management in manufacturing industry responding to competition from abroad, particularly from Japan. In the late 1980s and early 1990s it began to be adopted by large public sector organizations and the service industry. In the late 1990s, the spread continued into the voluntary sector. Today many different organizations have tried quality initiatives in one form or another. Many have suffered because the ideas have been bought 'off the shelf' from another organization or industry. Relatively few organizations have attempted quality as Shewhart intended. The few that have can document progress and improvement.

A key ingredient of this approach is involvement of the workforce in making improvements. Many tools and techniques have been developed over the years to help with this involvement. An unexpected benefit has been in the field of community participation. The principle of 'involve the workers' has a direct parallel with 'involve the community' and the tools and techniques are directly transferable. To quote Peter Scholtes, another authority on the subject, 'The next generation of quality initiatives will be community based.'

There is a final twist to the story that I am reminded of by the radio playing in the background as I write. I have just listened to a story on the news about Nissan at Sunderland expanding production and creating more jobs. This is a feature of the late 1990s – Japanese companies building new production facilities where traditional industry once stood. What many people don't realize is that these 'foreign' plants often outperform their equivalents 'at home' in Japan. Why might this be? One theory is that the Japanese style of participative management suits the British worker very well. British workers are full of good ideas and Japanese management style lets them have their say whereas traditional Western management style is 'do your job'. I like this theory and believe that the project-by-project approach is a good way to make the most of this latent talent.

2 What goes wrong with projects?

The project-by-project approach advocates setting up projects to improve your organization. You have just read Chapter 1 and are itching to set up a few projects. You select someone to lead your first project and enthusiastically tell them about it. 'Oh good' is not what they will say.

Why is this? Sadly many people have less than positive experiences of being involved in projects. There are several reasons for this and this chapter examines some of them.

'YOU ARE NOW A PROJECT LEADER. GO AWAY, SET UP A TEAM AND IMPROVE QUALITY.'

Unfortunately, many projects are set up in the way this heading suggests. Project Leaders are not given any guidance, training or support. Despite this and some initial trepidation, projects usually begin their life with enthusiasm and commitment, but this is often lost along the way.

This chapter reviews the areas of project work where problems most commonly arise. You may well recognize some of them!

THE APPROACH TAKEN

In my early days of working with improvement teams, we used the following approach:

1. Call a meeting.
2. Sit down.
3. What shall we do?
4. What shall we do next?
5. Repeat (4) until the end of the meeting, then go back to (1).

This wasn't very effective. Second, there was no common approach from project to project – each would be tackled in a different way. Thus it was start from scratch in every case. Lessons were not learned and best practice not adopted.

TRAINING

As a general rule there is no training. However, many organizations have put their managers and staff through quality training of one sort or another. Here is what two of these people said:

'The training received was too theoretical and there was no link to practical application.'

'A series of tools and techniques were taught but not how these fit together or when to use them in a project.'

THE REMIT

Here are some more quotes from leaders and members of real project teams:

- 'Unclear.'
- 'Given as a verbal instruction.'
- 'Too broad.'
- 'Additional bits of work got added on to the project.'
- 'No timescales were given.'
- 'The timescales were unrealistic.'
- 'The team members did not really understand it.'

USE OF TOOLS AND TECHNIQUES

A typical comment:

'Little if any use was made of the available tools.'

This sums up this issue nicely and is the case in the vast majority of review exercises I have carried out. Brainstorming is the tool most commonly cited as being used in a project. However, the rules of brainstorming are rarely adhered to and it is often used in inappropriate situations such as for analysis.

USE OF DATA AND MEASUREMENT

There is no use made of data and measurement. Decisions are made using 'experience', 'judgement', hunches and personal preferences.

TEAM COMPOSITION

Typical problems relating to team composition are:

- no systematic approach to team selection
- 'He's a good bloke' policy adopted
- 'I rang up a few colleagues'
- duplication of people from the same work area
- key individuals missing
- people who do the job not represented
- teams made up of the managers above the people who do the job
- a few individuals involved in all the projects.

TEAMWORK

Teamwork is what saves many projects. Despite a lack of nearly all the other elements, projects will often survive on the good will and hard work of those involved. In fact, some people will try to sell you this as the organizational approach to quality. Set up teams and improve teamwork and everything will be all right. Teamwork on its own is no substitute for a bit of structure and people will struggle, often finding the experience an unpleasant rather than enjoyable one. Typical problems are:

- The Project Leader takes on too much of the work.
- The Project Leader is not properly prepared for the role of team leader.
- The project is carried through on good will rather than good planning.
- Decisions are made through debate or arguing rather than with the help of tools or data.
- People who liked each other at the start of the project never want to be in the same room ever again.

SET UP, SUPPORT AND GUIDANCE

- Projects are not linked to the management structure of the organization.

- Projects that should have an input from several departments are tackled departmentally.
- There is no coordination between different projects.
- There are overlaps between projects.
- Project Leaders and team want, but don't get, clear direction.
- There is no support from the day the Project Leader is asked to do the project to the day they make their proposals.
- There is no appropriate forum for proposals to be debated at.
- When proposals are made, the senior managers say 'that's not quite what we had in mind'.

RESULTS

It is fair to say that the results are determined by all of the above. Again, here are some comments:

- 'There were some positive results.'
- 'The project was reasonably successful.'
- 'Some of the smaller, more focused remits have produced better results.'
- 'There comes a stage when enthusiasm isn't enough.'
- 'The goal posts moved...'

RESOURCES

Even when a project does produce good ideas, it then hits the 'no resources' wall. Time after time organizations set up working groups to solve a problem without even considering that the solution might involve spending some money or taking on a new member of staff. If there is no money to spend this needs making clear from the start.

HOW THE PROJECT-BY-PROJECT APPROACH ADDRESSES THESE ISSUES

The project-by-project approach addresses these issues by making sure there are a number of elements present:

1. Every project has a clear remit.
2. Every project follows a well-defined methodology.
3. There are four clearly defined roles. The project is not dumped on one

unfortunate individual. Responsible for the project is the Project Leader. Strategic support and guidance is provided by a Champion. Team-based projects have a number of carefully selected team members. Support in methodologies, tools, techniques and teamwork is provided by a Quality Adviser. Each of these roles and the division of responsibilities is well defined and understood.

4. Tools and techniques are used. Rather than rely on sitting in meetings discussing anecdotes and making decisions based on gut feel or who shouts loudest, a set of tools and techniques is applied. It is clear in each of the methodologies which tools and techniques are appropriate and when to apply them.

5. Appropriate training is provided when needed for individuals and teams.

Chapter 3 explains these elements in more detail.

3 Elements of the project-by-project approach

The project-by-project approach contains a number of important elements. First, a steering group of senior managers is needed to set up, direct and support activities. Second, each project needs to follow a clear methodology taking a step-by-step approach. Next some well-defined roles are required: a Champion from the steering group to take strategic responsibility for each individual project; a Project Leader to get on with the work of the project; team members for team-based projects responsible to the Project Leader and a Quality Adviser to help the Project Leader with the way the project is run. This includes the use of tools, techniques and data. The final element is the provision of suitable training on a just-in-time basis.

THE STEERING GROUP

The steering group is the senior management team in an organization or department who identify, prioritize, set up and support improvement projects. One member of the steering group acts as a Champion to each project. The steering group fulfils a number of vital functions. These include selecting the Project Leader and appropriate team members and producing a clear remit for the project. (See Part II for more about steering groups.)

THE METHODOLOGIES

WHAT IS A METHODOLOGY?

At its simplest using a methodology means starting with the end in sight. A methodology is a step-by-step approach to a project. It follows a sequential structure from start up to finish. There are a number of methodologies appropriate to different situations.

WHAT ARE THE METHODOLOGIES?

Steering group methodology

Steering group methodology is the mother of all projects. It is used by the senior management team in an organization or department to identify, set up and support projects tackling specific issues. Steering group methodology is also appropriate for a project team when the area under study is large or complex and requires a number of sub-projects to tackle it.

Planning methodology

Planning methodology is the blank sheet of paper approach. It is used to plan and implement new services, products and processes. It is applicable to projects of all sizes, small or large, and may be undertaken by an individual or team.

Quality improvement team methodology

Quality improvement team methodology is about improving processes and areas of work that already exist. It is particularly applicable when the process to be improved crosses the remits of a number of sections or departments.

Problem-solving methodology

The name gives it away: problem-solving methodology is appropriate when investigation needs to be carried out to determine and eliminate the causes of a problem or failure. It may be undertaken by an individual or team.

Network methodology

Network methodology is appropriate when identical or similar activities exist in different locations or parts of the organization. It brings the individuals concerned together to tackle common issues, identify and adopt best practice.

WHERE DO THE METHODOLOGIES COME FROM?

The methodologies were developed when working with many different groups and project teams. Each team was starting from scratch and there was no common approach. The methodologies resulted from documenting best practice for project teams. These evolved into step-by-step instructions. It was also apparent that the approach taken needed to vary depending upon the nature of the project although many of the constituent parts remained the same.

THE METHODOLOGIES – KEY PRINCIPLES

- Produce a clear remit.
- Involve the right people.
- Follow a step-by-step check-list approach.
- Use appropriate tools and techniques.
- Use data not opinion.
- Systematic, logical, meticulous and exhaustive.

THE METHODOLOGIES – SIMILARITIES

- Common sense.
- Check-list structure.
- Many stages are the same particularly in the latter part of a project.

THE METHODOLOGIES – DIFFERENCES

- Different sequence and approach depending on the nature of the project.
- Some difference in the detail of what happens at each stage.

SOME COMMON CRITICISMS

As with all new ideas, the methodologies sometimes meet criticism and resistance. This seems to fall into three categories. 'Up front' resistance occurs before people have tried using a methodology and consists of statements like:

- 'What do I need a methodology for? – I've never needed one in the past.'
- 'I know intuitively what to do in a project.'
- 'Do we really need all this bureaucracy?'
- 'Surely this stifles creativity?'

If you yourself need any convincing of the need, re-read the list of what goes wrong with projects and think about how a methodology might help remove these.

The second sort of resistance might be described as 'methodology fatigue'. I have much sympathy for this as it occurs especially in Project Leaders and Quality Advisers who are some way into their projects. As noted, methodologies are intended to be exhaustive, they leave no stone unturned and cover all the options. Especially in the early days of the project-by-project approach, the subjects chosen are issues that have been floating around for years. The problems have not been solved in the past because they are not simple. The adoption of a methodology does not always make a project easy, just easier.

'Methodology fatigue' sets in because projects can still be a grind. As Project Leaders and Quality Advisers become more experienced, they become more able to manipulate and adopt the methodologies to their specific projects.

The third type of resistance is 'told you so'. This can break out amongst senior managers and people not involved in the projects some way into a project. Typical criticism here is that the projects are taking too long and that the methodology is slowing it down – it's long winded and time consuming. 'Told you so' is often linked to amnesia. This amnesia affects those parts of the brain containing information about all the other attempts to crack this particular issue.

TRACK RECORD

Despite these criticisms the methodologies have a proven track record and projects that have been set up and run using them have a near 100 per cent survival and success rate. Compare this to other projects you may have been involved in or seen. These too have followed a methodology, but the difference is that this particular methodology will probably have been a one-off, not stated, planned or well understood. (See Part III for details of the methodologies.)

Let us now examine each of the 'roles' more closely.

ROLE 1: THE CHAMPION

WHAT'S IN A NAME?

Different organizations adopt different names for this role. Some like 'Sponsor' and some prefer 'Champion'. My own preference is for Champion as, to me, this implies a greater commitment than Sponsor. However, the choice usually depends on organizational culture and history. Both of these terms have been bandied around for many years and unfortunately may be tainted by previous poor experience.

THE ROLE

Every project needs a Champion. The Champion is a senior manager who directs and supports the Project Leader. The Champion does not 'do' the project, that is the job of the Project Leader. Where there is a project team, the Champion is not a team member, nor are they actively involved in the day-to-day work of the project. The Champion is a member of the steering group, management team or other body that set up the project. On some occasions the Champion may be the line manager of the Project Leader, on others the Project Leader may come from a different department. The Champion works cross-functionally with the support of their other colleagues and is not constrained by departmental boundaries. The Champion must be sufficiently senior in the organization to move things along and remove blockages to the project.

RESPONSIBILITIES

The Champion fulfils the following functions:

1. *Explains and agrees the remit with the Project Leader.* This is the briefing of the Project Leader and provides an opportunity for clarification on both parts. Use of the remit ensures a good structure to the briefing.
2. *Talks regularly with the Project Leader.* This might vary from a formal review meeting to a brief chat on the telephone. The important thing is that this is done regularly as it is the opportunity for the Project Leader to update the Champion on progress and for the Champion to provide support and guidance.
3. *Provides strategic direction and guidance.* This too covers a variety of situations. Some good examples of this are advising what other projects are doing to ensure there is coordination and ensuring that the direction the project is taking is in line with business objectives. If there are a range of expenditure options, advising which suits the current financial situation.
4. *Ensures that the necessary resources are provided for the project.* This is resources in terms of running the project such as staff release to participate in meetings, training where necessary and any budgetary considerations.
5. *Provides help in case of difficulty.* Common difficulties are lack of cooperation on the part of some departments or failure to release people from their jobs to participate. These are good examples of where Champions have to use their authority.
6. *Reports project progress to the steering group at regular intervals.* This is to update other managers as to progress and ensure their continued cooperation. This also ensures that the work of one project does not overlap or clash with the work of another that might have a different Champion.

ROLE 2: THE PROJECT LEADER

The Project Leader is usually a manager or supervisor in the work area under study. The Project Leader may work alone or lead a project team. For major projects the Project Leader may be a professional project manager. The Project Leader is selected by the Champion, sometimes taking advice from their colleagues, and is responsible for the 'doing' of the project.

RESPONSIBILITIES

The Project Leader fulfils the following functions:

1. *Leads the project team if there is one.* This is a responsibility that should not be underestimated. The responsibility for the content of a project is often a large one. If a project team is involved, then the Project Leader must also lead this and ensure a balanced contribution from each team member.
2. *Arranges and chairs meetings.* The Project Leader plans meetings at suitable intervals and chairs these. It is worth pointing out that while you are concentrating on chairing a meeting, it is difficult to concentrate on the content of the project, so the Project Leader has to maintain a fine balancing act. The Quality Adviser helps with this.
3. *Delegates tasks to team members.* A common pitfall for Project Leaders is taking on too much of the work between meetings. They should strive for a good balance of work between team members.
4. *Coordinates activities between meetings.* This might be as simple as chasing up team members to ensure they have carried out their action items. At the other end of the scale, this might involve leading a data collection exercise.
5. *Is the contact point with the Champion.* This might be an active or passive role depending on the Champion. Some Champions are very proactive in their role and will be in regular contact with the Project Leader. Others work on the principle of offering help when it is asked for. The Project Leader will need to judge about what and when they wish to consult the Champion.
6. *Maintains records.* The importance of this responsibility is often underestimated. Minutes from meetings are an obvious source of records but there are some specific areas where a Project Leader would be very wise to keep records. These include decisions made and why, data collected and how. There are a number of circumstances in which these records might be important, such as explaining decisions to the Champion or steering group or, if there is a change of Project Leader during the life of the project, briefing new or replacement team members.
7. *Works closely with the Quality Adviser.* The role of the Quality Adviser is discussed later. However, it can already be seen that the Project Leader has a number of potentially conflicting responsibilities such as the need to contribute to the content of the project while chairing a meeting and leading the team. The Quality Adviser is there to help in these situations.

ROLE 3: TEAM MEMBERS

Team members are chosen by the Project Leader with help from the Champion and Quality Adviser. The team is made up of people who have a contribution to make through their knowledge of, or close association with, the subject under study. Grade and position play no part in determining membership. Team members may come from several different departments.

RESPONSIBILITIES

A team member fulfils the following functions:

1. *Shares knowledge about the subject under study.* This is the key responsibility of a team member. Team members are chosen because of their knowledge about how things really work. They may well be in customer contact positions and know what will work and what will go wrong with new ideas.
2. *Attends each meeting.* This is how team members make their input. Although this might seem obvious, it is important to list it as a responsibility. Team members are often drawn from the operational levels of an organization and their absence to attend meetings needs covering by their colleagues. Proper arrangements therefore need to be made for this.
3. *Progresses the project in the workplace.* This includes the carrying out of assignments between meetings and the responsibility covers a number of activities such as keeping colleagues informed, asking their opinions, research, visiting other departments and data collection.

ROLE 4: THE QUALITY ADVISER

WHAT'S IN A NAME?

Once again, different organizations adopt different names for this role. The name Quality Adviser is normally used only by those organizations who have adopted this role as part of a quality initiative. Other organizations know this role as the Facilitator. My own preference is for Quality Adviser. This is because a Quality Adviser is usually an integral part of an organizational strategy and this is far more powerful than individuals in a specific role working in isolation.

THE ROLE

Every team-based project should have a Quality Adviser who attends each meeting. The Quality Adviser is specially trained to help the team, and particularly the Project Leader, with their project. The Quality Adviser is interested in the effectiveness of the methodology and not the content of the project and therefore does not need any knowledge of the subject being addressed. A few organizations have full-time Quality Advisers. Most, however, take a part-time approach. Quality Advisers take on this role in addition to their ordinary job. The number of projects that can be undertaken by a Quality Adviser depends on the nature of their 'proper' job but is usually no more than one or two.

RESPONSIBILITIES

A Quality Adviser fulfils the following functions:

1. *Helps the Project Leader and team plan and follow the methodology by which they will work.* At a high level this involves planning to follow an appropriate methodology from start to finish of a project. At a lower level, this is the planning of individual agendas for meetings. During a meeting, the Quality Adviser will help the Project Leader to adhere to the planned structure and agenda.
2. *Advises which tools and techniques are appropriate at each stage of the project and helps apply these.* For example, if a team is going to use a tool such as brainstorming or clustering, the Quality Adviser will ensure that everyone understands why the tool is being used, ensures everyone understands how it works, leads in the use of the tool so that everyone including the Project Leader can participate and ensures that everyone gets an equal say. A slightly different example might be if the team is about to make a presentation to the steering group. The Quality Adviser will help the team to plan and practise this.
3. *Observes and helps with team dynamics and the effectiveness of meetings.* The Quality Adviser will be looking for things such as level of contribution, conflict, good and bad meeting behaviours. They will then work with the Project Leader according to pre-arranged ground rules. This might involve making a direct intervention during a meeting or sharing observations with the Project Leader afterwards.

HOW A QUALITY ADVISER WORKS IN PRACTICE

The Quality Adviser will work with the Project Leader in three stages before, during and after a meeting:

1. Before a meeting the Quality Adviser will help to plan the agenda, suggest tools and techniques and agree how they will work with the Project Leader.
2. During a meeting the Quality Adviser will help the Project Leader to run the meeting, keep the team on track and at the right level of detail and help with the use of tools and techniques. At the end of a meeting they will hold a review with the team.
3. After a meeting the Quality Adviser will hold a review with the Project Leader and start thinking about what happens next.

'WE CAN MANAGE WITHOUT THEM'

This is a common response. Senior managers in particular can sometimes see Quality Advisers as an unnecessary luxury and believe that the Project Leader can look after everything with a bit of help from the Champion. If you're thinking 'we can manage without them', you're quite right, but at best all you will do is manage and more than likely you will struggle. The fiercest supporters of the Quality Adviser concept are Project Leaders who have had to manage a project without one. In the early days of some projects the Quality Adviser can be almost a co-leader. This allows the Project Leader to concentrate on getting the project plan and methodology organized and then assume full leadership of the team. The need for and importance of Quality Advisers is a point which cannot be emphasized enough to an organization embarking on a quality initiative. They are your real change agents and you must have them.

TOOLS AND TECHNIQUES

Although most managers will probably be familiar with many of the tools and techniques detailed in the book, they will probably have learned them at different times and in isolation. The project-by-project approach puts these tools and techniques into an overall context and it is clear in each methodology which tools are appropriate and when. The tools and techniques fall into a number of categories although it is worth pointing out that many of the tools have a number of different applications.

The tools for planning and organizing start with brainstorming to generate lists. The other tools then help to make sense of the resulting list. Clustering for grouping, must-should-could for prioritization, the planning grid for producing a project plan and TPN analysis to determine how much control a group has over an issue. The second set of tools are for analysis: deployment flowcharting to understand and plan processes, Ishikawa diagrams to identify underlying causes, the Kano model to understand and break down customer needs and measles diagrams for analysis by location. The third set of tools are helps and hinders, 3-2-1 voting, traffic light assessment and the evaluation matrix. These are the tools for evaluation and decision making. The final set of tools are for the display and analysis of numerical data: bar charts, histograms, Pareto analysis, run charts and pie charts.

There are also a series of techniques for group work. These are designed to optimize the effectiveness of meetings and get the best out of groups. They also eliminate the trap of always sitting round a table as a whole group and talking about things.

All these tools and techniques are detailed individually in Part IV. Additionally, each of the methodologies suggests when they should be used in the context of a project. Training in and use of tools and techniques is a vital ingredient when the project-by-project approach is used in the context of a quality initiative. These tools and techniques are not only useful in projects but invaluable in day-to-day work and meetings.

USE OF DATA

The project-by-project approach requires a radical change in the way data is collected and used. First, each of the methodologies requires that data is collected in a rigorous and systematic manner about customers and process performance. This data is then used as the basis for identifying improvements and making decisions. The spin off benefit at an organizational level is that, as people become more adept at collecting, understanding and using data, the inadequacy of existing data in the organization becomes apparent. It is not long before serious questions are being asked about what is being measured, what if anything the results mean and how the information is used.

JUST-IN-TIME TRAINING

The issue of training is one that first needs putting in context. Those organizations which have embarked on a quality initiative will usually have some sort of training for managers and workers as an element of this. The form this training can take is quite varied. Normally it involves buying in a quality consultancy who deliver their standard package. I have come across 'awareness training' where everyone is introduced to the key principles of quality, 'skills training' where various tools and techniques are taught to selected people and 'cascade training' where everyone is 'sheep dipped' with a mixture of principles, tools and techniques. Other organizations take a do-it-yourself route, buying various books and perhaps a video series, and leave the training to people inside the organization.

If there is no quality initiative, then perhaps your organization has a management development programme. There will normally be a module or two covering project management or tools and techniques. Alternatively, MBAs are popular with senior managers. These often have a module on quality.

WHAT'S WRONG WITH TRADITIONAL TRAINING?

What all of these approaches lack is application and focus. The ideas discussed are often couched in general terms; they do not deal with specific examples nor tell you when or how to do it. There is little or no link to practical application. Specific tools and techniques might be taught but they lack context. It is not explained when to use them or how they relate to each other.

Second, training is rarely timely. Training courses work on the just-in-case principle, teaching a cocktail of ideas, tools and techniques just-in-case they are ever needed.

THE BOLD ALTERNATIVE: JUST-IN-TIME TRAINING

You may well be familiar with the concept of just-in-time manufacturing, which originated in Japan and is known there as Kanban. This was pioneered by Toyota and is based on the principle of delivering component parts immediately before assembly thus eliminating unnecessary stages in a process along with the associated inventory. This principle can also be applied to training. Specific skills are provided when they are needed and not before.

In the early 1990s some of my colleagues in the railway industry were arguing for 'sheep dip' awareness training for all staff. I believed in a much more focused approach, providing training only when it was needed and for a specific purpose. So, for example, if a member of staff was to be involved in a quality improvement team, the team would receive tailor-made training appropriate to the individuals and the situation. I called this approach the Bold Alternative. At the time, new three-in-one Bold washing powder was being advertised on the television offering a detergent, softener and fabric conditioner all rolled into one. Just-in-time training also offered a 'bold' three-in-one alternative: quality training, an opportunity to start work on the real project in hand during the training and transferability of new learning, tools and techniques into the workplace.

JUST-IN-TIME TRAINING IN WHAT?

Some examples of just-in-time training are as follows:

Steering group training

Steering group training is training of the whole management team in the steering group methodology. Participants apply each stage of the methodology to existing and proposed projects during the training. This includes selection of Champions and training in how to champion a project.

Quality Adviser training

Participants in Quality Adviser training learn the role, responsibilities, methodologies, tools and techniques. This new learning is put into practice as soon as possible with project teams.

Quality improvement team training

Quality improvement teams are trained as a team once the project has been identified and Project Leader, Quality Adviser and team members have been chosen. Participants learn the quality improvement team methodology and associated tools and techniques. The team works on the real project during the course and completes some of the early stages. The project is then completed back in the workplace. Experience has shown that this kick-start approach has the added benefit of saving lots of time as it eliminates the necessity for many of the early meetings in a project.

Project planning events

Key players identified as important in planning projects are brought together for a project planning event. The main purpose of the event is to work on the project but participants closely follow the planning methodology and use appropriate tools and techniques, input being given as and when necessary.

Data collection, display and analysis

Data collection, display and analysis is best done once some project teams have had some experience in collecting and using data.

4 Project-by-project in action

The project-by-project approach has been successfully used by organizations, departments and individuals. In this chapter we will examine some actual examples: Liverpool Housing Trust and Greater Manchester Waste. Both of these organizations have been using the project-by-project approach for a while and have experience of what works and what does not. I spent some time speaking to key people in both organizations and the format is a mixture of commentary and question and answer. Next you will find how I applied project-by-project at a departmental level with my own team.

PROJECT-BY-PROJECT IN LIVERPOOL HOUSING TRUST

BACKGROUND TO LIVERPOOL HOUSING TRUST

Liverpool Housing Trust (LHT) is a registered housing association founded in 1965 which owns and manages about 8 900 homes in Liverpool and Runcorn. LHT works in a series of partnerships with Local Authorities, the Housing Corporation, Health Authorities and voluntary organizations to invest in housing and the local community. LHT tenants have a low income or are unemployed and half of new lettings go to lone parents or single people. LHT employs just over 200 staff mainly based at four offices. The staff fall into five categories:

1. maintaining and managing houses
2. developing and acquiring new homes
3. specialists, for example supported housing for vulnerable people, tenant participation
4. finance
5. support services.

Although LHT employs a range of people, the staff are typified by a commitment to working in the not-for-profit sector, to help people living in poverty by maximizing their housing rights. Dave Power is the Director of Planning and Quality at LHT and he provided the answers to my questions.

How and why did LHT become interested in quality in general and the project-by-project approach in particular?

DAVE:

LHT interest in quality and the project-by-project approach was largely driven by external factors. We started looking at quality in the early 1990s. We'd been doing corporate planning and management by objectives since 1987 but it was the 1988 Housing Act that gave us a real drive. The main change as a result of the act was the need to use private finance. Government grants would reduce, competition would increase and this meant we would have to be much more flexible and innovative. Many of the staff and senior managers also knew we had to reorganize and re-energize. Many of the senior managers had been here a long time, were comfortable and maybe a little complacent. We needed to look outside for new ideas. We'd been doing quite a lot of customer research. This told us we were pretty good at what we were doing but we didn't use it to concentrate on improvement, although we wanted to be a better landlord.

We actually made several false starts. First, we tried Investors in People. That didn't work! Then, inspired by another housing association who had a quality initiative, the Senior Management Group had a few days' training and we set up a number of improvement projects. These didn't work either, mainly because they had no methodology and no view about where they were heading. We also tried using performance indicators. This gave us measures of how we were doing but didn't tell us how to improve.

At this stage I was seconded from my own job to set up a quality programme. We had a corporate plan but needed the quality programme to make it work. We identified four key outputs for the programme. We wanted people to work in a much more organized way; we wanted them to apply new techniques to eliminate old problems; we wanted people to look outside and not get hung up on internal solutions; and we wanted to re-engage people in the organization and its future. Alongside these outputs we were looking to change the culture. The key elements of this were to get people to have an appreciation of the 'real world', an acceptance that things and their jobs were and would continue to change and for them to view the organization as a whole as opposed to 'my job'. You might call it 'an organization appreciation society'. The project-by-project approach provided all these elements.

What appealed about the project-by-project approach?

DAVE:

It was a way of getting started quickly with immediate benefit and would involve the right staff immediately rather than train everyone and see some results in two years' time, which is what our first consultants suggested. At that stage we were keen on the methodologies and tactics rather than quality philosophy. We wanted to involve people at various levels from managers to administrative assistants. We also had in mind various targets that we wanted to hit in key parts of the organization. We wanted to look at a key process, that of a tenant reporting a repair through to the job being completed. We wanted to look at an interface with customers, our reception services. We wanted to look at the integrity of the data we had on our computer systems, key to running the organization. Finally, we wanted to look at development standards, vital in building new properties. All these needed to be addressed so we wanted to focus on tactics rather than strategy. Also, bearing in mind our existing false starts, we had to demonstrate that the methodologies actually worked before buying wholesale into the project-by-project approach.

What were your first steps?

DAVE:

Getting the Senior Management Group to manage the programme. Not just saying 'we're going to do it' but actually managing it. Part of my secondment was to take part in and improve Senior Management Group meetings and we reordered these to focus on more strategic matters. Next, I set up a one-day training event for Senior Management Group which introduced the project-by-project approach and the steering group methodology. We already had a fair idea about some of the ideas behind it as a result of our previous experience. Following on from this we split our meetings into two parts, Quality Steering Group followed by the regular meeting. We also confirmed our choice of initial projects – five or six out of a short-list of about ten. I did a series of presentations to the Senior Management Group about quality – what is a customer, processes, specifications and so on.

The next main step was to select our Quality Advisers. It was an easy decision to have them. Dave Bebb the Chief Executive said 'every book I've read and everyone I've spoken to says you've got to have them so we'll have them'. Next we used your person specification which we adapted slightly, agreed this at Senior Management Group and each member nominated people from their departments. The Quality Advisers were hand picked. We aimed at middle or potential middle managers. Next we trained 15 Quality Advisers including myself. If we hadn't done that we wouldn't have got anywhere. Having a group of 15 people trained makes a big difference in an organization like ours. Immediately after this we trained our first two quality improvement teams. We actually trained the Quality Advisers on Monday, Tuesday and Wednesday and then trained the QITs with their Quality Advisers on Thursday and Friday of the same week!

How have you approached training?

DAVE:

Don't train everyone at once. Initially we concentrated on the Quality Advisers and project teams. At the same time we ran a series of one-day introductions for anyone who wanted to attend. The next wave was quality skills for all managers. We did this gradually and it took us about a year to complete. We also made sure that all staff had been on at least the one-day introduction. We still have a hard core of individuals who have resisted all attempts to get them on this but they are now a very small minority.

What changes have you seen as a result?

DAVE:

Problem-solving skills in the organization have been transformed. We used to get people in a room, sit down and sort it out, more or less. Now we have a much more focused and structured way of doing things. People now generally have a set of rapid, usable skills. The use of tools and techniques in all sorts of situations is probably the most demonstrable result.

As far as the first projects are concerned, these are all finished. They've all come up with recommendations most of which have been adopted and most of which have led to other things. Some were more effective than others but they happened and they involved the right people. They also gave people the confidence that the process works and we are now doing it on the big things that really matter to LHT. Initially we had no comprehensive review of LHT's systems and processes but we're doing that now.

Taking part in the projects or being trained as a Quality Adviser has also brought people on by leaps and bounds. It's been a real developmental opportunity.

PROJECT-BY-PROJECT IN GREATER MANCHESTER WASTE

BACKGROUND TO GREATER MANCHESTER WASTE

Greater Manchester Waste Limited (GMW) was formed in 1995 as a privatized company with origins first in Greater Manchester Council and then the Greater Manchester Waste Disposal Authority. The company receives household waste from district councils in the Greater Manchester area along with trade waste. It also runs civic amenity sites where the public can bring rubbish for disposal. Some recyclable materials are extracted and then the waste is either burned or pulverized for transport to landfill sites by road or rail. The company is actively progressing new initiatives and technology such as aluminium extraction and conversion of waste to energy. GMW is a multi-site operation. The headquarters and workshops are at Bolton with seven major sites (refuse treatment plants, incinerator and transfer loading stations) and about twenty civic amenity sites spread around the Greater Manchester area. The company owns and operates around 50 rail wagons, 60 heavy goods vehicles and 1 000 containers. Turnover is around £40 million per annum and 400 staff are employed. Workers fall into a number of categories:

- Waste disposal operatives.
- Heavy goods vehicle drivers.
- Civic amenity site attendants.
- Craft workers such as fitters, electricians, plumbers, welders and painters.
- Administration, finance, business systems and personnel.

Many of the staff have been with GMW and its predecessors since they left school and are steeped in the 'old way' of doing things. When the company came into being there was a traditional local authority ethos driven by maximization of employment rather than business needs and efficiency. Sue Ormrod is the Human Resources Manager at GMW who has driven their quality initiative and she answered my questions. Bill Wynn, Business Systems Manager, chipped in.

How and why did GMW become interested in quality in general and the project-by-project approach in particular?

SUE:

We needed to do it. There was and is lots of change going on. We got into the project-by-project approach not because we wanted to have a quality initiative but because we wanted to manage change properly. Quality and the project-by-project approach was not the reason for change but the tool to bring it about. We needed delivery in a manner that the staff would accept and that would get the top people on board. I knew other people had used the project-by-project approach before and I had a belief in its ability to deliver.

What appealed about the project-by-project approach?

SUE:

Simplicity. A common sense approach. That we could do it, not for the sake of the quality banner, but because of business need. We could work on live issues that would have a specific outcome and we would be able to quickly see the fruits of our labour. A good example of this was one of our transport projects. We set it up, the team made recommendations, these went into the capital expenditure budget and you can now see the new vehicles because of this.

What were your first steps?

SUE:

To sell it to Management Executive, in particular Stephen Jenkinson the Managing Director and Graham Johnson the Finance Director. I needed their support to lead the other senior managers.

We knew we'd have a problem with the trade unions if we didn't do it right. GMW is heavily unionized and the full-time officials in particular might see it as impinging on their roles especially when you're putting project teams together and the members are not trade union representatives. So we had to take away that fear and demystify the process. I explained the process thoroughly to all the shop stewards, invited key shop stewards on the initial Quality Adviser training and have supplemented this since then. Nearly all the shop stewards have been involved in some form either through training as a Quality Adviser or as a project team member. Full involvement, participation and training has led to a full awareness that has removed doubts about the process. This and subsequent developments have taken away the impression that this is just another management initiative.

Next the Quality Adviser training was a key step. My selection of people to attend this training was not based just on people who would actually become Quality Advisers but also key influencers who would be able to sell the process back in the organization. I also took a conscious decision to hold the training off-site, in a nice hotel, to show the people that this was something special and so that they could start to knit together as a group. These decisions were well thought out with identifiable benefits.

How have you approached training?

SUE:

As and when it's been needed. We've had training for the steering group, Quality Advisers, project teams and we've also done a series of one-hour briefing sessions at the plants. I believe that the Quality Adviser training in particular is useful, not only for people's jobs but also for developing their potential. We've had several examples of them using their skills outside work as well. After our first 15 Quality Advisers, we've put other people through this training. I don't think we've done enough training for the steering group – we need to review progress and consolidate in the near future.

What changes have you seen as a result?

SUE:

The biggest change has been in the way that meetings are held. People who have had the training get exasperated with the old way of doing things. Examples are the finance team meeting and the health and safety committee. These have really changed because of the Quality Adviser training.

BILL:

Some of the more junior people who once might not have said anything aren't afraid to contribute now. Quality Advisers have earned a certain status and people respect their opinions.

SUE:

Trade union meetings have also changed and the officials are also using the tools elsewhere. We had a massive task of writing job descriptions recently and the tools for planning and organizing came in really useful. Staff who haven't had the training are impressed by what they see. People are changing the whole way of their working life and are beginning to question a lot of the things they have been doing.

BILL:

We've had a period of constant change that has led to an insecure environment. The quality way of doing things is much more acceptable. Change in local authorities was very slow – we've seen more change in 12 months than there's probably been in the last 12 years. It's noticeable the issues that the staff have had an input to have been more successful.

PROJECT-BY-PROJECT IN THE BUSINESS QUALITY GROUP

THE BUSINESS QUALITY GROUP

Despite its grand title, the Business Quality Group was a small team led by myself and comprising around half a dozen people. I was Quality Manager for InterCity West Coast Limited and my team had a dual objective. First, we had to provide support and training within the organization. Typically, we trained Facilitators, acted as Facilitators to key meetings in the organization, provided consultancy and support to line managers and ran training courses in various aspects of quality. The second objective was to be as self-sufficient in cost terms as was possible by selling our services outside the organization.

THE APPROACH

The approach had to be project-by-project. I appointed a Project Leader to each of our 'products'. Thus, for example, there was a Project Leader for each of Facilitator training, training for quality improvement teams and team events. This did not mean that these people did everything connected to these products or ran all the training courses. Everybody needed to be able to run the courses and had a contribution to make. The responsibilities of the Project Leader were to design and then develop the course itself, produce and update support materials and be responsible for the budget. Running alongside this, I also had a Project Leader for each of our customers. The idea of this was that each senior manager inside the organization or paying customer outside the organization would have a 'one stop shop' for all their quality needs. For the enthusiastic managers, the Project Leader would hold regular one-to-one reviews, attend and facilitate their management team meetings and follow up any training requirements. For the not very enthusiastic managers, the Project Leader would provide whatever services we could interest them in.

MANAGING THE TEAM

One area I found extremely difficult was regular team meetings. With a team of people who were trying to bend their diaries around those of busy line managers, I simply could not get everyone along on a regular basis without compromising the service to our customers. Instead I tried to be available for one-to-ones as often as possible and also programmed proper review sessions at about six-monthly intervals when we would get away from the workplace for two days and conduct a mixture of team building, update, review and planning. This worked well. The second element to managing the team was an annual performance review. Although this was required by the company, I followed the format only from the point of view of what was useful and completing the paperwork. I called these PDSA days (plan-do-study-act) after the Shewhart cycle. Each individual team member got a day of my time once a year. Although we had a formal agenda, they could take me anywhere to do it. We would work on the train going, once we had got there and on the return journey. This took me bird-spotting to the Wirral and to the Tate Gallery in Liverpool among other destinations. The agenda would include a project-by-project review for each product and customer, the planning of next steps, a personal development review (not just 'I'd like to go on this training course') and setting objectives for the next twelve months. Most objectives were set by the people themselves rather than me.

HOW IT WORKED

As a team we went through ups and downs just like any other but we made solid progress at a difficult time in the industry. Projects we were involved in went well and individuals we trained found new skills. Just as important, everyone who worked for me has gone on to bigger and better things.

Part II
Managing the Strategy

5 Strategic issues

The project-by-project approach relates to organizing your strategy and the conversion of strategic intentions into actual change. There is, however, a bit of chicken and egg here – which comes first? Without a good grip on some key strategic issues, there is little point in applying the project-by-project approach. Although the rest of the book is about implementation, this chapter examines some strategic issues which will need to be dealt with sooner or later. My experience is that these are dealt with in no particular order. The order eventually adopted will depend on several factors including what other work or initiatives have been going on and where the greatest interest lies. However, the establishment of a structure for quality improvement has to be the first step and the foundation upon which all other change can be built. This takes the form of the foundation of a high-level steering group. This steering group needs to look after the strategic issues discussed in this chapter.

A STRUCTURE FOR IMPROVEMENT – STEERING GROUPS

Many organizations set up top-level steering groups to manage major initiatives. Organizations engaged in quality initiatives will often establish a special body to manage the initiative, sometimes called a Quality Council. What this approach lacks is integration and application. Steering groups established outside the existing managerial structure are very likely to fail because they only deal with a small part of the whole. Additionally, even the most enthusiastic steering group may well become a talking shop, full of good intentions but lacking a methodology to apply and implement these.

The project-by-project approach provides a structure to combat this. It proposes the establishment of steering groups in two distinct places:

1. *A high-level steering group.* This is composed of the leader of the organization, the Chief Executive or Director and the top tier of senior managers. The

purpose of this group is to produce and manage all organizational strategies. It identifies, sets up, coordinates and supports interdepartmental projects and initiatives that are vital to the future of the organization.

2. *Departmental steering groups.* These are established in each department and are composed of the leader and section heads in that department. The purpose of a departmental steering group is to manage departmental strategies. They identify, set up, coordinate and support projects within their individual departments.

WHY ARE STEERING GROUPS NEEDED?

Organizational change is all too often left to chance. Projects are frequently set up without much thought and receive little support during their lives. If an organization is serious about change it needs to organize to bring this about. The vehicles for change are individual projects all pulling towards the goals of the business plan. Steering groups are needed because no one individual can manage policies, plans and the projects that will achieve these. Steering groups bring together managers so that they can:

- identify opportunities
- determine priorities
- decide how and by whom projects will be tackled
- direct, monitor, coordinate and support projects
- ensure that the projects deliver what the organization wants
- ensure successful implementation.

HOW DO STEERING GROUPS WORK?

Steering groups work at two levels: strategic and tactical.

Strategic development

This chapter covers those responsibilities which concern strategy and policy at an organizational level. Analysis of these issues should result in the identification of a series of actions which will then require projects to be established to bring about the desired change.

Tactical operation

Tactical operation is covered in Chapter 6. The conversion of strategies to tactical actions is where many initiatives flounder. The steering group methodology provides a step-by-step approach for converting strategic intent into a series of well-managed projects.

ISSUE 1: ORGANIZATIONAL PURPOSE AND GOALS

Many organizations have a mission or vision statement: 'We aim to be the world leader in widget production.' These should be viewed with caution, particularly where they are written by an individual or working party, framed and hung in reception or used as a screen saver on the computer system. It is, however, important that everybody in an organization understands its purpose and where it is going. Simple though this might seem, it is not a common feature in many organizations.

The steering group needs to to articulate clearly the purpose of the organization or department and have a set of clearly defined strategic objectives, preferably brought together in a business plan.

ISSUE 2: THE CUSTOMERS

The second responsibility for a steering group is to understand the customers and plan to increase customer satisfaction. If an organization does not keep the customers happy it will go out of business, some more quickly than others. Specifically, this means ensuring that research is carried out on a regular basis, that answers the following questions:

1. Who are our customers? (Companies; individuals; demographic profile; how often they use our organization; market segments.)
2. What are the key interfaces between the organization and the customers?
3. What do we already know about them and what they think?
4. What do they want? What are the key quality characteristics by which they judge the organization? (These are features of the product or service such as timely delivery, reliability, ease of use and so on.)
5. How important is each key quality characteristic and how satisfied are the customers with current delivery? What are the gaps between expectation and delivery?
6. Who are our potential customers? Are they a non-user or going to one of our competitors? Why?

This information will provide clues as to where improvement efforts and resources should be concentrated. It feeds into the steering group methodology as possibilities for projects.

ISSUE 3: PROCESSES AND PERFORMANCE

The third responsibility is to understand and improve how work is done. Customers judge an organization by what they see. If real improvement is to be achieved, effort must also be focused on how this is achieved – the internal processes of an organization. The questions to ask are:

1. What are our key processes?
2. What do we already know about these processes and how they are performing?
3. What are the key performance indicators, high-level measures which show how the process is performing?
4. What do we need to find out? (This might include the speed of processing and whether this changes over time. Are there errors or is there waste?)
5. What are the gaps between the performance of our processes and customer expectations and requirements?

Again this information will provide ideas for possible projects.

ISSUE 4: THE WORKFORCE

The fourth responsibility is to involve the workforce and improve worker satisfaction. Securely locked away deep in the workforce of any organization is a source of new ideas, information about customers and ways in which processes can be improved. Most people enjoy being asked what they think and being involved in improvement projects. Just as customer satisfaction surveys are important, so are surveys that measure how contented the workforce is with the way they are managed. The questions to ask are:

1. What do our employees think about the organization, customers and processes?
2. What ideas do they have?
3. What are their requirements from us as an employer and how happy are they with the way the organization delivers these?
4. How good is their understanding of the organization, how it works and its objectives?
5. How satisfied are they with their jobs and the way they are managed?
6. What is the rate of sickness and absenteeism?
7. What is the rate of turnover?
8. How many people are involved in improvement projects?

ISSUE 5: LEADERSHIP

Closely linked to worker satisfaction is the issue of leadership. If organizations are to survive and grow, new leadership styles are required. A change from directive management, 'do as you are told', to process management involving workers in improving the way work gets done is required. The project-by-project approach will help increase the level of worker participation but this must be backed up by an improvement in management practice and leadership style. This is particularly important in the early days of any new initiative as all eyes will be focused on the managers looking for commitment and behaviour that either supports or goes against it.

Another responsibility for the steering group is to consider existing leadership practices and consider what training and development is necessary for managers at all levels in the organization.

ISSUE 6: COMPETITORS AND THE ENVIRONMENT

Yet another consideration is competitors and the environment. It is also worth bearing in mind that customers do not always judge an organization by its direct competition. Service received at your reception or on the telephone for example will be compared against similar experience in any manner of organization. Questions to be asked here include:

1. Who are our competitors?
2. How do we compare to our competitors?
3. What differentiates us from our competitors?
4. Are our competitors doing anything that we are not?
5. What factors are there in the environment in which we operate that might affect us? (This includes things such as market trends, new legislation and so on.)
6. What might our customers spend their money on if they don't spend it with us?

ISSUE 7: SUPPLIERS

An organization is heavily dependent upon suppliers. There is a strong tendency at the present moment in time to manage suppliers through competitive tender, contracts and penalty clauses. The project-by-project approach advocates closer working relationships, cooperation and involving suppliers in the projects. The questions to be asked here are:

1. Who are our suppliers and what do they supply?
2. How many do we have?
3. How good are our interfaces?
4. What problems do they cause us?
5. What problems do we cause them?
6. How can we improve relationships?

QUALITY IMPROVEMENT STRATEGY

All of the above factors need to be brought together into a quality improvement strategy to be implemented by the steering group. The steering group methodology addresses the mechanics by which this will actually be achieved. These are some additional considerations:

1. How will we pilot this new approach?
2. How quickly do we want to change?
3. How many projects should we have at once?
4. What education and training will be necessary?
   - for steering group members
   - for managers
   - for the workforce
   - for project teams.
5. What technical support will be required?
   - someone to coordinate the initiative
   - Quality Advisers
   - external help such as consultants.
6. What are the budgetary implications of (3), (4) and (5)?
7. How do we link projects into the financial processes of the organization?
8. How will intention and activity be communicated throughout the organization?
9. How will progress be measured and regularly reviewed? (One option here is to use the European Business Excellence Model as a self-assessment tool. The detail of this is outside the scope of this book but you will find a reference in the suggestions for further reading.)

6 Steering group methodology

WHERE CAN THE METHODOLOGY BE USED?

The steering group methodology can be used in three different situations:

1. By a high-level steering group composed of the senior managers of an organization, to set up, coordinate and support interdepartmental projects and initiatives that are vital to the future of the organization. The purpose of steering group methodology at this level is to manage organizational strategy.
2. By the managers of a particular department to set up, coordinate and support projects within that department. The purpose of steering group methodology at this level is to manage departmental strategy.
3. By project teams when a project is particularly complex and needs breaking down into a number of smaller, more manageable sub-projects.

In the first two situations, there is usually an existing meeting that can take on these responsibilities. There will be more about this in the next chapter.

THE STEERING GROUP METHODOLOGY

This chapter outlines a step-by-step approach for a steering group to follow to help establish, support and implement projects (see Figure 6.1). Unlike most of the project methodologies, the steering group methodology is not strictly linear. Stages 1 and 2 are concerned with selecting projects and need to take place regularly but not at every meeting. Stages 3 to 8 relate to setting up individual projects and will happen for every project selected. Stage 9 is what happens when a project is up and running and will be where most projects are at any one time. Stages 10, 11 and 12 are concerned with recommendations, implementation and the conclusion for each individual project.

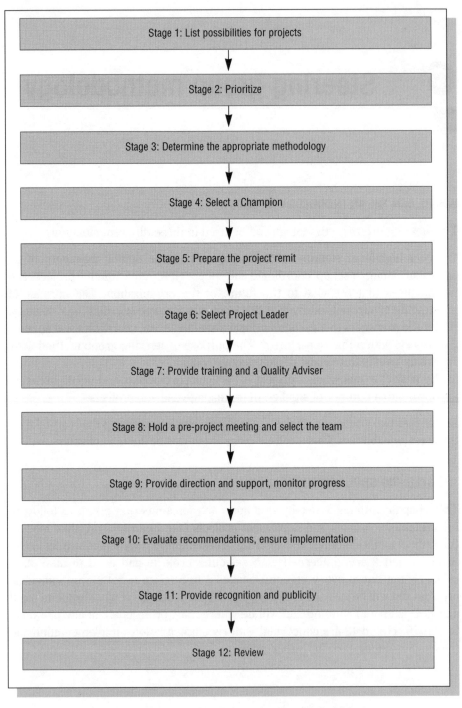

Figure 6.1 Overview of the steering group methodology

STAGE 1 – LIST POSSIBILITIES FOR PROJECTS

Possibilities for projects can come from several sources:

- The business plan.
- Customer satisfaction data.
- Ideas from managers and workers.
- Changing circumstances such as new legislation or developments in technology.

The reality for most management teams in the early days of the project-by-project approach is that the availability of the above sort of information is often patchy. A best guess will therefore need to be adopted. Once issues such as the strategic direction of the organization have been established, the identification of projects will become much more sophisticated. The drivers will become organizational goals, customer data and performance data linked through the business plan.

EXISTING PROJECTS

Before embarking on a whole new set of projects, it is sensible to start by evaluating current projects. A good set of test questions is:

- What is the remit?
- Who is in the lead?
- Status? In progress, stalled, not started.
- Progress and results to date.

Evaluate each current project against the steering group methodology and make whatever interventions are necessary. These might be:

- redefine the remit
- allocate a Champion or Quality Adviser
- review progress against a particular methodology
- change the Project Leader or team composition
- close it down.

STAGE 2 – PRIORITIZE

The list of possible projects in any organization will usually be vast. In the words of Dr Juran, 'If we have done a good job of working up nominations for projects, the resulting list is long and may be beyond the digestive capacity of the managers.' Steering group methodology helps identify the vital few projects to take forward. Decisions about priorities in an organization are often made using one of the following criteria:

- seems like a good idea
- easy to do
- boss's pet subject
- went wrong last week.

Better decisions can be made using corporate goals, customer data, performance data and employee data. If such data is not available or does not immediately point to projects, some discussion will need to take place to agree the criteria by which the classification will be made. A useful approach is to classify each possible project using one of the following:

- Urgency – must, should or could.
- Priority – high, medium or low.

An evaluation matrix (see Chapter 19) can also help at this stage.

EARLY PROJECTS

The choice of projects early in an initiative is vital. Make sure you choose something that will succeed.

Don't choose

✖   An area already being worked on.

✖   Something very complex – 'solve world hunger'.

✖   A process that might adversely affect something else.

✖   Something jinxed – pieces of work where projects have already failed several times.

✖   Communications!

Do choose

✔   Something you feel has a reasonable chance of success.

✔   Something worthwhile and likely to produce visible improvement.

✔   Projects requiring contributions from several departments.

✔ The more 'sympathetic' parts of the organization – departments where a clear commitment has been shown.

DEPARTMENTAL STEERING GROUPS

Departmental steering groups may need to also use TPN analysis (see Chapter 17) at this stage to determine if a proposed project is totally, partially or not within the control of the department. Projects requiring a small involvement from other departments can still be established but consideration should be given to escalating more complex issues to the high-level steering group.

STAGE 3 – DETERMINE THE APPROPRIATE METHODOLOGY

There are a number of options as to the most suitable methodology. The choice should be determined by the nature of the project.

1. *Planning methodology.* Used to plan and implement new services, products and processes. Applicable to projects of all sizes, small or large. May be undertaken by an individual or team.
2. *Quality improvement team methodology.* Improves existing processes and areas of work. Appropriate when the process crosses the remits of a number of sections or departments.
3. *Problem-solving methodology.* Appropriate when investigation needs to be carried out to determine and eliminate the causes of a problem or failure. May be undertaken by an individual or team.
4. *Network methodology.* Appropriate when identical or similar activities exist in different locations or parts of the organization. Brings the individuals concerned together to tackle common issues, identify and adopt best practice.
5. *Steering group methodology.* Appropriate for a project team when the area under study is large or complex and requires a number of sub-projects to tackle it.
6. *Individual action.* This is not really a methodology but is put here as a reminder not to go project team crazy. Good old individual action is appropriate when the project falls within the remit of one individual. The individual may well use one of the above methodologies and should certainly use the tools and techniques. Also appropriate when you need to say: 'Oi you – sort it.'

WHAT HAPPENS IF THE APPROPRIATE METHODOLOGY ISN'T CLEAR?

The methodology may not be clear when the steering group itself isn't clear on what it wants from the project, or some initial investigation needs to be carried out to scope the project. If this is the case, the Champion should work closely with the Project Leader to pick from the activities listed in stage 1 of the planning methodology and stages 1 and 2 of the quality improvement team methodology. This will help clarify the project and next steps will become clearer.

STAGE 4 – SELECT A CHAMPION

Each project should be championed by a member of the steering group. Where there is a project team, the Champion is not a team member but maintains regular contact with the Project Leader. The Champion is the link between the steering group and the project. Being a Champion is not a delegable task.

RESPONSIBILITIES OF THE CHAMPION

The Champion's responsibilities have already been covered in Chapter 3 but are summarized here for ease of reference:

- explains and agrees the remit with the Project Leader
- talks regularly with the Project Leader
- provides strategic direction and guidance
- ensures the necessary resources are provided for the project
- provides help if difficulties are encountered
- reports project progress to the steering group at regular intervals.

WHO IS THE MOST APPROPRIATE PERSON?

Choosing the right Champion from the steering group is often a matter of intuition rather than an exact science. Some considerations are:

- Is technical knowledge about the subject being studied desirable?
- Does a large part of the area under study fall within the responsibility of one particular individual?
- How interested is the individual in the project?

It can actually be quite useful for the Champion to know little about the detail of a project. This will ensure that the Champion sticks to strategic issues rather than low-level detail. Similarly, it can be a useful experience for a Project Leader to be championed by someone other than their line manager.

COMMON PITFALLS FOR CHAMPIONS

Experience has shown that there are some common pitfalls for Champions. These are listed in order of most frequent occurrence:

1. *Does not maintain regular contact with the Project Leader.* This is the most frequent cause of complaint from Project Leaders about their Champions. It is very important that Champions do get in touch regularly. This does not need to be a long formal meeting – a brief telephone call will suffice.
2. *Not really interested in the project.* This is closely linked to pitfall (1). It is far better to have a Champion who is interested in the project rather than the 'logical choice'. This pitfall also reflects on project selection and personal commitment. If the project is important enough to the organization, the Champion should be interested.
3. *Gets too involved.* This is the opposite of pitfalls (1) and (2) and is typified by the Champion attending many meetings, carrying out work on the project, becoming involved in every decision and generally treading on the Project Leader's toes. There are two causes of this. The first is that the Champion simply does not understand their role and needs to step back. The second is that the project has been delegated to an inappropriate level of the organization. In this case the Champion should really be the Project Leader and the Project Leader should perhaps be a team member.
4. *Doesn't really understand the methodology being used in the project.* This is very common in the early days of the project-by-project approach. Project Leaders, Quality Advisers and team members will have normally received some quite detailed training in the methodology they are using and during the project will become very familiar with the intricacies. The Champion, on the other hand, will only be familiar with the steering group methodology and know the project methodologies only in overview. It is quite important that Champions begin to familiarize themselves with the project methodologies and it is not unusual for senior managers to ask for top up training some way into an initiative.
5. *Doesn't give the Project Leader clear guidance about timescales.* It is a difficult position to be in not to know by when a piece of work is to be completed. Even if timescales are not critical, it is useful for a Champion to give an indication about when they expect a piece of work to be completed. There is some more detail about timescales under stage 5.
6. *Puts unrealistic pressure on the Project Leader.* This is the opposite of pitfall (5). Timescales are sometimes very tough. However, some Champions make

them tougher than necessary. One over-enthusiastic Champion linked the conclusion (not the results) of a project to the Project Leader's performance related pay. Needless to say, the Project Leader was far more interested in finishing on time than using a methodology, applying tools and techniques or looking for an optimum result. He finished on time but the project was not a success. I don't know whether he received a pay rise!

STAGE 5 – PREPARE THE PROJECT REMIT

The Champion should prepare a remit to set the scene and define what is expected from the project. The content of the remit will vary according to the nature of the project and the methodology adopted. These are the key ingredients for all project remits and further details specific to each of the project methodologies will be found in the appropriate chapter in Part III:

1. The project title.
2. The subject, process, service, product or problem to be worked upon.
3. The scope.
    ● What departments, sites and locations are involved.
    ● Where the process begins and ends.
    ● Any exclusions.
4. The objectives of the project.
    ● Key characteristics that are to change and can be measured. For example, 'reduce time taken to...', 'eliminate problems in...', 'increase the number of...'.
    ● Benefits the project should realize.
    ● Any benchmarks from other organizations or industries that should be aimed for.
5. Timescales and interdependencies.
    This includes interfaces with other projects.

Tips

✔ Avoid the temptation to write long-winded remits. Keep it short and concise.

✔ Avoid arbitrary targets.
  Targets can not be realistically set until there is a full understanding of the processes involved.

✔ Avoid bland quality language such as excellence, delight and world class.

✔ Experience has shown that individuals and teams often wish to refine their remit once the area under study is better understood. Be prepared to do this but beware of increasing the size or altering the nature of the project.

✔ Ensure that an initial timescale is included. If it is not possible to estimate a timescale for the whole project at the outset, then give a timescale for the first stages and review on completion of these.

STAGE 6 – SELECT PROJECT LEADER

The Project Leader should be selected by the Champion, seeking guidance from their colleagues if necessary. The Project Leader is usually a manager or supervisor in the project area and will either lead a team or be an individual working alone. Careful selection is important and below are some characteristics to take into account broken down into those that are essential and those that are desirable.

ESSENTIAL CHARACTERISTICS

- Knowledge of the project area.
- Availability and workload.
  Part of the job of the Champion is to ensure that the Project Leader has enough time to devote to the project. If the project truly is important to the organization, then it may be necessary to second a Project Leader to it on a full- or part-time basis.
- People skills including the ability to chair meetings.
  Although this is an essential characteristic, the Quality Adviser can help with this.

DESIRABLE CHARACTERISTICS

- Willingness.
  This is a desirable characteristic rather than essential on the basis that it is always better to use someone willing rather than someone who would rather not be involved. However, occasionally there will only be one individual who is capable or qualified to do the job and, in this case, they will have to do it willing or not. This situation would require careful championing.
- Knowledge of methodologies and tools.
  Desirable on the basis that the Quality Adviser can help with these.

Avoid where possible

✖ The same person leading many projects.

✖ Someone who thinks the project or methodology is a waste of time and knows all the answers already.

✖ An active resister.

✖ A poor leader.

Tip

✔ Sometimes there is little choice involved and an individual who you might prefer to avoid is the only person with the necessary knowledge. In this case, the Champion must be particularly active and an experienced Quality Adviser chosen.

STAGE 7 – PROVIDE TRAINING AND A QUALITY ADVISER

TRAINING

Any training necessary will be determined by two factors:

● The nature of the project – complexity and the methodology adopted.
● The individuals involved, both Project Leader and team.

Training might be required in the methodology, tools or how to work as a team. Training is particularly important for quality improvement teams as this can kill two birds with one stone: training in the methodology, tools and techniques combined with real work on the project. If in doubt, the Champion should check with the Project Leader at the pre-project meeting.

WHEN A QUALITY ADVISER IS NECESSARY

A Quality Adviser is essential for all team-based projects. They attend each meeting and work with the Project Leader to help with the methodology, tools, techniques, group dynamics and the effectiveness of meetings. These responsibilities have already been explained in Chapter 3 and there is more detail in Part V.

CONSIDERATIONS WHEN CHOOSING A QUALITY ADVISER

- *Knowledge of the subject area.* The Quality Adviser is interested in the methodology and tools being used, not the content of the project, and therefore does not need any knowledge of the subject being addressed.
- It is sometimes useful to have a Quality Adviser from a completely different part of the organization so that they work from a neutral point of view.
- *Experience.* Don't allocate inexperienced Quality Advisers to vital and complex projects with a tough Project Leader.
- *Consider seniority, particularly in the early days of this approach.* No matter how much we like to pretend that we have a non-hierarchical organization, a very junior Quality Adviser is not always the best person to send to a senior management meeting. Hopefully this will change as time goes on and experience of working with a Quality Adviser grows.
- *Workload.* How many projects has the Quality Adviser already got and what is the workload of their full-time job?

STAGE 8 – HOLD A PRE-PROJECT MEETING AND SELECT THE TEAM

The Champion should now arrange a pre-project meeting with the Project Leader and Quality Adviser (if there is one) to get the project rolling. It is best to have approached the Project Leader in advance of the pre-project meeting so that there are no surprises for either party! The pre-project meeting takes place in two parts, items one to five involving all three people, item six only involving the Project Leader and Quality Adviser. There is more detail for the pre-project meeting under each of the individual project methodologies in Part III. Use the model agenda below as a framework and the additional detail to stimulate your thinking.

MODEL AGENDA FOR A PRE-PROJECT MEETING

1. *Background.* Champion to explain the background to the project, how and why it was selected.
2. *Remit.* Champion to brief Project Leader and Quality Adviser on the project remit. Opportunity for clarification of any issues.
3. *Select team members and others to be involved.* Select team members for team-based projects (see below).
   - If not a team-based project, identify key players who need to be consulted or involved in the project.
   - Plan how these people will be approached and briefed and whether by the Project Leader or Champion.

4. *Logistics*. Set up reporting links between the Champion and Project Leader.
   - Who is going to contact who and at what intervals?
   - Identify potential dates for the first project meeting.
   - Diary next meeting between Champion and Project Leader if possible.
5. *Resources*. Check resources required: training, staff release, budget, administrative support, 'kit' such as computers, meeting facilities and office accommodation.
6. *Project Leader and Quality Adviser*. Quality Adviser to outline role and responsibilities and agree how they will work with the Project Leader.
   - Review the methodology and plan first steps.
   - Where a meeting is to be held, define the purpose and content, prepare an agenda and arrange to have it circulated.

SELECTION OF TEAM MEMBERS

- Team members should be selected by the Project Leader with help from the Champion and Quality Adviser.
- The aim is to ensure that all parts of the subject under study are represented.
- Team members should usually be people who work closely with some aspect of the area under study or who will be affected by changes to its inputs or outputs.
- Only take into account the contribution that each individual can make to the project. Position, seniority or department do not count.
- Consider any processes that are going to be studied. Construction of a basic flowchart will help identify the major stages and who is involved.
- Do not duplicate members from the same work area with the same knowledge.
- Remember that if the same activity takes place at a number of different locations, it is unlikely that the processes will work in the same way at each.
- Don't let the team grow too big. Between five and eight, including the Project Leader and excluding the Quality Adviser, is best.
- If it is not possible to include all individuals who might have a contribution to make, ensure they are involved at the appropriate stage of the project. Visitors may be invited to meetings and specialist advice sought when necessary.
- As the project develops, team membership may need to change. Team members who were only involved in the early stages should be allowed to leave and people who can now contribute join.
- Support departments such as information technology, personnel and finance have an involvement in most projects. Make sure they are called in at the appropriate time.

STAGE 9 – PROVIDE DIRECTION AND SUPPORT, MONITOR PROGRESS

The responsibility for direction, support and monitoring progress of a project rests with the Champion. They need to maintain regular contact with the Project Leader, report progress to the steering group, give strategic direction and arrange for presentations to the steering group when necessary.

HOW TO JUDGE YOUR LEVEL OF INVOLVEMENT

This is something of a balancing act. Here are some factors to take into consideration:

- experience of the Project Leader in leading projects
- complexity of the project
- competence of the Project Leader in the subject under study
- any strong characters amongst the team members.

If you don't know the Project Leader very well or are not sure how complex the project might be, it is probably wise to keep a close eye on things in the early days and back off once you are sure things are going well. Finally, it may well be worth attending for the start of the first meeting and dropping in by prior arrangement on a few others. Beware, however, of outstaying your welcome – teams tend to be polite to Champions even when they would like them to leave so that they can get on with their work!

Tips for working with the Project Leader

✔ Have a brief meeting with the Project Leader after every or every other project team meeting. If the Project Leader is an individual working alone, diary regular review meetings.

✔ Questions to ask about progress:
- Where are you up to in the methodology?
- How's it working?
- What tools have you used?
- How did they work?

✔ Questions to ask about the team:
- How did the last meeting go?
- Did all the team members attend?
- Is the team composition still correct?
- How's it going with the Quality Adviser?

✔ Consider the methodology and ask specific questions about that stage, e.g.
  ● How's the data collection going?
  ● What does the data show?

✔ Give guidance about the direction the project should take.

MAINTAIN A LIST OF PROJECTS AND THEIR STATUS

The steering group must maintain a list of existing projects and their status. This should be reviewed at regular intervals to ensure that progress is being made. Updates about individual projects should be made through Champions reports.

CHAMPIONS REPORTS

● Champions reports should be made about each individual project. A report about every project at every meeting will soon become tedious so try every other meeting or as necessary.
● Reports are particularly important when the results of data collection have been obtained, when options are being evaluated and when there are problems.
● A short oral report is most effective, picking up key points from the last review meeting. This may be supported by written notes if necessary.

PRESENTATIONS TO THE STEERING GROUP

Each methodology specifies stages at which presentations should be made to the steering group by Project Leaders and teams. Presentations should be the first agenda items at all meetings of the steering group. It is also wise for the steering group to ask for presentations at other stages as an update, particularly for strategically important projects. Project Leaders may also wish to make progress reports when they require input and guidance from the steering group as a whole.

TIPS FOR RECEIVING PRESENTATIONS

The prospect of making a formal presentation to a senior management team is one that is not relished by many Project Leaders or team members. Projects selected using the project-by-project approach invariably involve a wide variety of staff. These are often junior members of the organization with little experience of making presentations. All management meetings evolve a set of behaviours among the attendees. Generally, these are fine at an ordinary meeting but, for example, cracking an 'in joke' can disconcert a nervous presenter. Steering group members therefore need to be on their best behaviour when receiving presentations.

✔ Ensure that steering group members introduce themselves to the presenters.

✔ Display supportive behaviour – pay attention, maintain eye contact, nod if you agree, frown if you don't, smile, don't shuffle papers, don't whisper to colleagues, ask constructive questions.

✔ Don't argue about data although you might want to ask questions of clarification.

✔ Don't say yes or no to any proposals there and then. Debate afterwards and let the Champion communicate the result. Make sure the presenters know this will happen in advance.

✔ If you have any doubts, save them for the Champion after the presentation.

✔ Thank the presenters at the end and say what you liked about the presentation.

STAGE 10 – EVALUATE RECOMMENDATIONS, ENSURE IMPLEMENTATION

Recommendations will be made and implementation plans proposed through presentations by Project Leaders and teams. The steering group must evaluate these and agree or reject them. Rejection is a failure not of the project, but of the steering group. If good contact has been maintained between the Champion and Project Leader, there should be no nasty surprises at this stage.

The steering group must identify what support it needs to provide during implementation and use their positions of authority to ensure that proposals are implemented. The most obvious way to achieve this is to brief managers under their control about the changes and what they need to do to implement them.

STAGE 11 – PROVIDE RECOGNITION AND PUBLICITY

A policy needs to be developed for recognition and publicity of completed projects. This works best when developed by the Champions talking to Project Leaders and teams to identify what they themselves would like. This can range from saying 'thank you' formally, through to presentations and taking those involved out for a meal or on a visit.

STAGE 12 – REVIEW

Finally, it is useful to review the methodology by which the project was carried out to identify lessons learned for future projects. A useful way to review a project is to ask what went well, what went badly, what was easy and what was difficult under each of the following headings:

- the methodology
- training
- the remit
- use of tools and techniques
- use of data and measurement
- team composition
- teamwork
- support and guidance
- working with a Quality Adviser
- results.

7 Logistical issues for steering groups

Before a steering group starts to operate, there are a number of logistical issues that need sorting out. These vary slightly depending on whether this is a high-level or departmental steering group. Logistical issues for project steering groups are different, as you will see, and you should use the logistics check-list in Chapter 22 for these.

MEMBERSHIP, LEADING AND CHAIRING

MEMBERSHIP

The aim of a steering group at a high level in an organization is to ensure that interdepartmental projects are possible. It follows, therefore, that all departments need to be represented and this should be by the departmental heads. The easiest way to look at this is to say that the leader and top tier of the organization should make up the high-level steering group. The same principle of leader and direct reports also applies to departmental steering groups.

LEADING AND CHAIRING

High-level steering groups should be led and chaired by the head of the organization, the Director or Chief Executive. Departmental steering groups should be led and chaired by the head of department.

SUBSTITUTIONS

Attendance should usually be top priority for the members. The question is whether or not deputies should be allowed to attend when the departmental head is not available. Both approaches can work, but it is best to debate it, decide one way or the other, try it and review it. The important thing is to make time to consider this and actually have a policy rather than leave it to chance.

Watch out for persistent non-attenders. Not everyone will welcome the approach and attendance is a good measure of commitment and enthusiasm.

QUORUM RULES

Similarly, a steering group needs to have a policy about a quorum. No matter how committed and enthusiastic people are about the meeting, they are allowed to take an occasional holiday. The two questions are:

1. Are there any key individuals who, if they do not attend, the meeting should not go ahead?
2. How many people can be missing for the meeting to still go ahead?

ADMINISTRATION AND COORDINATION

ADMINISTRATIVE SUPPORT

Some form of administrative support may be needed to:

- take the notes at the meeting
- book the venue
- circulate papers and the agenda in advance of meetings.

It usually works well to have the secretary to the leader or equivalent undertake this role.

THE COORDINATOR

The coordinator role is often necessary for a high-level steering group. If the organization is engaged in a quality initiative and has a project manager or quality manager responsible for this, then they are the likely choice for this role. The role of project manager or quality manager for your quality initiative is vital. This is the sort of work that Dave Power and Sue Ormrod are carrying out in the examples in the 'in action' chapters. The roles of the coordinator are:

- to project manage the quality initiative
- to produce and keep up to date a list of projects and their status
- to administer the allocation of Quality Advisers to projects
- to maintain the pool of Quality Advisers, making sure there are sufficient numbers for the needs of the organization and replacing people who may move on

- to arrange training for individuals and project teams
- to lead the Quality Adviser network (see Chapter 25).

LINKS TO OTHER MEETINGS, FREQUENCY AND VENUE

The final decisions to be made are links to other meetings, frequency and venue. These three issues are grouped together as they are heavily interdependent.

LINKS TO OTHER MEETINGS

Most management teams will already have a regular meeting of one kind or another. It is a good idea for the steering group meeting to take place at the same time as this. There are two reasons for this:

1. *Diary commitments*. Few managers have empty diaries. It makes sense therefore to keep the number of occasions when the whole management team is committed to meetings as low as possible.
2. *Institutionalization*. This is a clumsy word but an important one. If the project-by-project approach is to become the way the organization is run, then steering group meetings are often the first manifestation of this intent. There is a danger, however, that two meetings are held – the regular meeting to do the 'real work' and separately the quality meeting, this still being seen as largely optional.

The approach of tying the steering group meeting to an existing regular meeting has a number of advantages and disadvantages. The main disadvantage is that, initially at least, the steering group meeting is still a 'bolt on' to the usual way the organization is run. The advantages are that at least everyone is likely to turn up, plus, as the steering group and associated projects gain momentum, more and more of the daily running of the organization takes place in this manner. The agenda for the regular meeting will therefore begin to diminish and that for the steering group meeting grow.

One final decision needs to be made. This is whether the steering group meeting takes place before or after the regular meeting. Again, it can be done either way, although it may be preferable for the steering group meeting to come first for a number of reasons:

- Regular meetings have a nasty habit of over-running.
- If the steering group meeting is first, it is easier to time presentations by project teams.
- People will be fresher for the first part of the meeting.

Finally, the organizational meeting cycle needs to be considered. It is particularly useful to time departmental steering group meetings so that they follow the high-level steering group, perhaps a week later. The meetings structure of the organization is a good topic for the steering group to consider separately. Tidying this up to form a regular pattern of meetings is an excellent way to free diary time. It is poor practice to diarize what should be regular meetings on an *ad hoc* basis.

FREQUENCY

Monthly meetings are best as far as high-level and departmental steering groups are concerned.

VENUE

The venue will depend very much on the nature of the organization. If you are a single-site organization, then find a suitable room. If you are a multi-site organization, there is an option to vary the location of steering group meetings and provide an opportunity to combine meetings with a visit to another location. However, don't opt for the world tour option where more time is spent travelling than working. In both cases it is useful to occasionally get off the premises for a whole or half day to tackle a broader agenda.

SETTING UP THE FIRST STEERING GROUP MEETING

There are a number of issues that need to be considered before the first meeting. Experience has shown that it is an enthusiastic member of the management team who usually drives this. Sometimes it is the Director or Chief Executive, sometimes not. However, the boss must be involved at this stage. You'll proceed much further at a quicker pace with their support and understanding.

MAKE SURE PEOPLE KNOW WHAT IS GOING ON

Remember to keep other members of the management team involved and informed about what is going on. An early presentation by the individual driving this is recommended. This should cover what the plans are, with plenty of opportunity for questions and debate.

INDIVIDUAL BRIEFING

The final task prior to the first steering group meeting is an individual briefing for all members. This provides a last opportunity to communicate the purpose and identify any concerns. As part of this briefing each individual should be asked to think about existing and possible future projects in preparation for the first meeting.

THE FIRST STEERING GROUP MEETING

Use Figure 7.1 to make sure you have done all the preparation and then follow the model agenda in Figure 7.2, allowing a whole day. It would also be useful to apply the just-in-time training principle and combine training in the methodology with this meeting. The assumption has been made that the management team have some prior knowledge about quality in general and this approach in particular. If not, some early work needs to take place before the first meeting. This should include an introduction to the basics of quality and a presentation about the project-by-project approach and the role of the steering group.

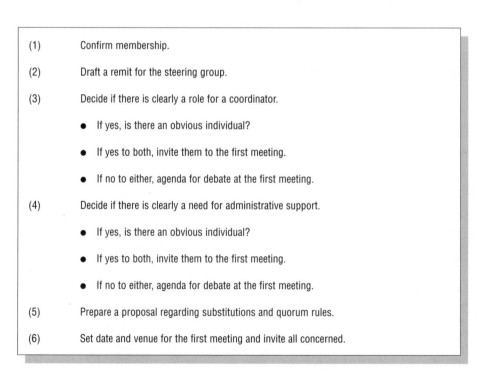

(1)	Confirm membership.
(2)	Draft a remit for the steering group.
(3)	Decide if there is clearly a role for a coordinator.

- If yes, is there an obvious individual?

- If yes to both, invite them to the first meeting.

- If no to either, agenda for debate at the first meeting.

| (4) | Decide if there is clearly a need for administrative support. |

- If yes, is there an obvious individual?

- If yes to both, invite them to the first meeting.

- If no to either, agenda for debate at the first meeting.

| (5) | Prepare a proposal regarding substitutions and quorum rules. |
| (6) | Set date and venue for the first meeting and invite all concerned. |

Figure 7.1 Check-list of tasks prior to the first steering group meeting

(1)   Welcome, purpose of the meeting, run through agenda.

(2)   Introduce, clarify, debate and approve the remit for the steering group.

(3)   Carry out stage 1 of the steering group methodology.

(3a)   List existing projects.

- Clarify remit.

- State who is in the lead.

- Determine status – in progress, stalled, not started.

- Progress and results to date.

(3b)   List possible new projects.

(4)   Carry out stage 2 of the steering group methodology.

- Debate and decide criteria for prioritization.

- Prioritize.

- Select projects to do more work on today.

- Decide what happens to those projects that won't be worked on today.

(5)   Carry out stage 3 of the steering group methodology.

- Determine the appropriate methodology.

(For each project selected for more work today.)

(6)   Carry out stage 4 of the steering group methodology.

Allocate Champion.

(For each project selected for more work today.)

(7)   Identify actions for the Champions.

(For each project selected for more work today.)

This will include:

- Speaking to an existing Project Leader.

- Writing remits for new projects.

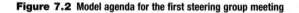

Figure 7.2 Model agenda for the first steering group meeting

- Selecting new Project Leaders.

- Holding pre-project meetings.

(*See stages 5, 6, 7 and 8 of the steering group methodology.*)

(8) Administrative support and the coordinator.

- Introduce proposals, debate and decision.

(9) Substitutions and quorum rules.

- Introduce proposals, debate and decision.

(10) Future meetings.

- Introduce proposals regarding frequency, links to other meetings and venue. Debate and decision.

(11) Communications.

- Consider what and how outcomes of today will be communicated to the rest of the organization.

(12) Review of the day.

Figure 7.2 Model agenda for the first steering group meeting (continued)

ROUTINE OPERATION

Once established, steering group meetings will vary considerably with some standing agenda items but others that will be 'as required' (see Figure 7.3).

(1)   Welcome, introduce guests, run through agenda.

(2)   Presentations from Project Leaders and teams.

            Introductions, presentation, questions, debate and decisions.

(3)   Monitor existing projects – Champions reports.

            (*See stage 9 of the steering group methodology.*)

(4)   Performance indicators. This should not be a tedious run through lots of tables of figures but presentation of high-level performance indicators graphically displayed so that changes, performance and trends can be identified. It might be useful to receive an in-depth presentation about each performance indicator at something like six-monthly intervals.

            (*There is more about performance indicators in Chapter 13.*)

(5)   Departmental reports. Again this should not be a tedious trawl through lots of detail but brief reports on key departmental projects and any important developments.

(6)   Strategic development. This falls under the 'as required' heading. Use the list of strategic issues in Chapter 5 as the source of ideas for this agenda heading.

(7)   New projects. If any potential new projects have arisen as a result of the above agenda items, carry out stages 1 to 4 of the steering group methodology.

(8)   Meeting review.

Figure 7.3 Model agenda for a routine steering group meeting

8 ■ Steering groups in action

The purpose of a steering group, as discussed earlier, is to set up and pull together many disparate strands into a coherent and aligned series of projects. In this chapter we will cover how steering groups have worked in practice. We will be following the stories of Liverpool Housing Trust and Greater Manchester Waste, begun in Chapter 4, to see how steering groups work at an organizational level to steer a quality initiative.

QUALITY STEERING GROUP IN LIVERPOOL HOUSING TRUST

After one or two false starts described earlier, the senior management team at Liverpool Housing Trust were eager to set up something that would be successful and have visible results. When they were introduced to the idea of the project-by-project approach and the steering group methodology they quickly recognized the practicality of these and were keen to proceed. The quality steering group was formed from the top tier of the organization. I asked Dave Power how it went.

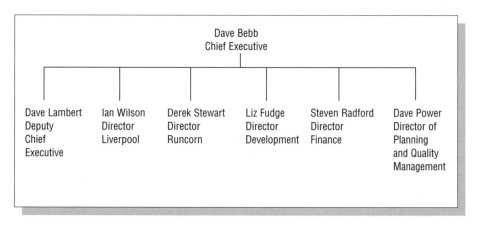

Figure 8.1 Organization and Quality Steering Group in Liverpool Housing Trust

How have you organized your steering group?

DAVE:

We already had Senior Management Group, our regular meeting which we decided to split into two parts. Half of the meeting became Quality Steering Group where we focused on quality education, the quality programme, project sponsors reports (we went for the word sponsor – we didn't really like champion) and communications. The other half stayed as 'traditional' Senior Management Group. After about nine months we undertook a diagnostic review. This fell into two parts. First, we did a review of how we actually worked together as a senior management team both inside and outside the meeting. Second, we carried out a traffic light assessment on the mechanics of the steering group methodology. We wrote up the overview of the methodology on flipchart and then initialled each box: green ink if we were confident with that stage and happy that it was working well; yellow if we were fairly happy; and red if we weren't happy. The pattern was obvious. A great deal of green in the early stages, turning to yellow around 'provide direction and support' with more red around 'implementation'. This was predictable with the benefit of hindsight, given where we were with the whole initiative at the time, but it helped us focus our efforts on where they were really needed.

Now we have reintegrated the two halves of the meeting so that we apply project-by-project principles to the whole meeting. We now have a carefully timed agenda split into three sections. First, we cover strategy and planning. So, for example, recently we spent time considering the remit for our information technology review. Second, we review quality projects so it's here we get the Sponsors reports and other quality programme issues, such as follow up to the leadership development work we've been doing. Finally, we have directors reports which is the day-to-day stuff about running the business.

We've also had another four steering groups working on specific projects. We had a North–Central Move steering group which had five sub-projects to manage a recent office relocation. At a far more strategic level, we've currently got an Asset Management steering group, a Core Services Review steering group and an Information Technology steering group. These are reviewing fundamental aspects of the business and are each led by a director with help from a Quality Adviser and sponsored by the Chief Executive. Each steering group has an overall project plan with sub-teams reporting into it each with an individual project plan.

What's worked, what hasn't?

DAVE:

The key achievement of the Quality Steering Group is that we now have a holistic improvement process rather than odd bits of tinkering, so the project-by-project approach has worked. This has also led to less departmentalism. People now see the process or system as opposed to the department. Incidentally, a major side-effect has been quite a few changes of the senior management structure. We now have two fewer members of Senior Management Group and the housing services part has been reorganized. The diagnostic work I mentioned a moment ago has also led to significant change. It's improved the way we work together as a team but also led to a major leadership development programme for ourselves and other managers in the organization which has been incredibly well received after an initial 'I don't need this.' Senior Management Group meetings themselves have been improved. We've moved away from a tedious minutes-based structure to a mix of presentations and discussion. Presentations from the project teams in particular has meant we know what's going on and that we've got capable, competent people working for us. In fact the demonstration of skills and techniques has been quite embarrassing for us! At one stage we had quite a bit of catching up to do as a senior management team.

On the other hand, sponsoring has been variable and I think Senior Management Group as a whole had an over-reliance on me as Quality Manager to drive things forward. I'm not sure if that's a bad thing but the lesson is to have a dedicated resource. If we hadn't resourced it, I don't think it would have worked.

How has the Champion concept worked?

DAVE:

As I said, it's been variable. Some of our Sponsors have been very assiduous but not everybody. I think initially this was a result of how we chose our first projects and Sponsors. If it wasn't important to them personally, then there was a lack of support. They didn't sit down with the Project Leader and Quality Adviser regularly enough and they didn't get the idea of championing – influencing, following through and simply talking about it. The reporting arrangements were also a bit shaky although we've become better now. We weren't sure of the level of detail to go into. We tended to wait for the project team to finalize their recommendations rather than monitoring where they were going during the project and we didn't provide enough linkages between the projects. As the projects have become more strategically important this has changed. Not only have we improved the structure but Sponsors and Project Leaders have got their necks on the line because the projects are crucial to the business. People are continually asking them questions.

How did you choose your first projects?

DAVE:

I mentioned this earlier when we were talking about project-by-project. Basically we wanted a wide range of departments and people involved. We wanted something about customer contact, something about our basic services and something focusing on an area where we knew things were going wrong.

What lessons did you learn from early projects?

DAVE:

Quite a few. As far as team selection is concerned we picked people who knew their jobs and got it pretty much right. We found though that although they had commitment, they still needed good leadership. The Project Leaders were generally very good but we had one who didn't stick to the methodology. With hindsight I should have shut this project down and started again with a new remit, leader and team but at the time I was probably too anxious for success. The projects that were the most effective were where the Project Leader and Quality Adviser worked well together. In the one case where this didn't happen, the project suffered. I think we got the selection of Quality Advisers right. If it wasn't for their work, the Project Leaders would have struggled and the projects just wouldn't have worked. As far as the use of the project methodologies goes, they were a great help but initially were taking quite a long time because the people weren't confident enough in their use. People are getting through the methodologies much quicker now. Some of the teams got bogged down in analysis. They collected too much data. That's not to say that the data collection wasn't important – generally they did an excellent job. Again, people are much more adept at this now. Finally, we didn't have enough emphasis on communication about what the teams were doing to the rest of the organization.

What differences are there now because of this experience?

DAVE:

First, our coordination of projects is much better. All projects must now be linked to the corporate plan or a departmental quality plan. My own department has a quality plan, as does development, as does housing services, and finance will soon have one. Second, the Project Leaders and Quality Advisers have become much more effective and adept at adapting the methodologies, tools and techniques. They no longer follow a methodology quite so slavishly and can get through them quicker, meaning we can set faster delivery dates. The original Quality Advisers have moved on and are now quite often Project Leaders working with a new generation of Quality Advisers. We've also sorted out resourcing and we're not slow to take people off their regular jobs on either a full- or part-time basis so they can concentrate on important projects.

How has implementation worked?

DAVE:

We didn't concentrate sufficiently on detailed implementation plans and found that recommendations aren't enough. We didn't set a high enough standard for implementation plans and Quality Steering Group weren't hard enough on following through the recommendations. Implementation needs sponsoring through as much as any other part of a project. Also the teams didn't do enough on costing. We needed to know what the saving or cost would be for a recommendation and we should have involved more finance people as and when necessary. More communication might have helped with implementation. Some of the teams went out and did briefings and this worked well. Generally though, recommendations have been implemented and many ideas have been fed into major corporate reviews. Our repairs quality improvement team has fed recommendations into the Asset Management steering group, the reception team into the Core Services steering group and so on. Other strategic issues have gone into the corporate plan.

What have you done about recognition and publicity for project teams?

DAVE:

At the end of the first phase we produced a questionnaire for team members. What came back was not a desire for more money or flexi-time off work but for an involvement in more projects. We've used this experience and information as a feed into individual performance and development reviews. We've also had some one-offs.

The reception team had a meal and the repairs team expressed a wish never to be put together in the same room ever again which I was happy to arrange.

As far as publicity goes, the staff conference last year was based largely around the projects. We've also set up a communications project which, among other things, ensures the work of project teams is publicized. Our next steps will be towards the European Business Excellence Model and self-assessment against this.

MANAGEMENT EXECUTIVE IN GREATER MANCHESTER WASTE

Although the high-level steering group in Greater Manchester Waste is composed of the Managing Director and reports, most of the quality activity in the organization has been driven by three key individuals: Managing Director Stephen Jenkinson, Finance Director Graham Johnson and Human Resources Manager Sue Ormrod. Progress has generally been good but hindered slightly pending the appointment of a new Operations Director. Sue Ormrod answered my questions.

How have you organized your steering group?

SUE:

We took the top tier of the organization. However, if I was to do this again I think I wouldn't have had the same team. I wouldn't have gone by strict hierarchy but would have had a mixed steering group with maybe a trade union representative. This is mainly due to the group dynamics. Some of management executive have not been completely behind the initiative and I guess that every senior management team have people like this. As far as the logistics are concerned, we have a steering group meeting monthly following our regular management executive.

What's worked, what hasn't?

SUE:

The key success has been support and commitment from the very top of the organization. Also championing of the projects and regular reporting to management executive has worked well. The group dynamics of the steering group haven't been so good. We're in a transitional period as far as this group is concerned. Change has already taken place and there's more to come with the appointment of our new director of operations. Linked to this, I don't think management executive has had enough support in terms of consultancy and training that it needs. This has been a conscious decision pending appointment of the new Operations Director and once this post has been filled we'll be consolidating and having a full review.

How has the Champion concept worked?

SUE:

Graham and myself champion nearly all the projects and this is an onerous workload.

We've had to do it though to make sure the projects are successful. I wonder if Champions couldn't come from elsewhere in the organization.

How did you choose your first projects?

SUE:

By priority to the organization. We didn't choose a simple one first. We wanted people at all levels to buy into the project-by-project approach so we chose an area that was important and highly visible. First, we set up a transport steering group which in turn established two quality improvement teams. One of these looked at load optimization – making sure each vehicle trip carries the best load possible in terms of composition and weight. The second looked at fleet composition. We've seen tangible results from both projects. These two teams were composed mainly of people who had been on Quality Adviser training, although there was a broad range from senior manager through to shovel drivers. This was a conscious decision to weight it so that the Project Leader, Quality Adviser and team members would be prepared to have a go, not be frightened to contribute and not be afraid of making mistakes. Additionally, quite a few of the managers who had been on Quality Adviser training went away and set up their own project teams using the methodologies, tools and techniques. These, too, have been much more successful than if they had been tackled using our traditional ways.

What lessons did you learn from the early projects?

SUE:

They take longer than expected. So you really need someone to get the group to meet on a regular basis and define who is responsible for this. We also had a bit of a mix up of roles. I decided that the potential Project Leaders would attend Quality Adviser training so on each project we had a Quality Adviser plus a Project Leader who had been through the same training. This worked really well – when one dried up the other would kick in and they kept each other going. It's not easy to stand up in front of a group for the first time. We also learned that projects must be seen to be as important as the operational needs of the organization. Overtime costs need to be seen to be worth it. Luckily Graham the Finance Director was right behind the teams.

What differences are there now because of this experience?

SUE:

I don't think there are any changes in team selection. This has been really successful. I think the key difference is that we now iron out the problem of staff release early on. We sell the benefits of the project to people who might be too busy to participate.

Have you any advice about selection of the early projects?

SUE:

Yes. Pick projects with impact which will get the message across in the company. Mix Quality Advisers into the teams. For a good start, over 50 per cent of the team should be Quality Adviser trained.

How has implementation worked?

SUE:

Implementation has been very visible and there have been a lot of positive outcomes. The fleet composition team made early recommendations which fed into our capital expenditure programme. It's nice to see a recommendation transform into a large piece of equipment rolling around outside. There's also been measurable improvement in the loads carried. Both teams joined up to come up with an integrated set of recommendations. The projects are still ongoing and have spurred us to work on other things. Incidentally no major resistance was encountered.

What have you done about recognition and publicity for project teams?

SUE:

Something that's been very noticeable is that no-one has asked for any extra money for taking part in a project. That's very unusual in our culture where there's an allowance for just about everything. Recognition has much more taken the form of praise and acknowledgement at various opportunities. The three main ways in which we've approached publicity so far have been through our core brief, the newsletter and at management teams update.

Part III
Project Methodologies

9 Planning methodology

Planning methodology is the blank sheet of paper methodology. It is applicable when you are starting something new as opposed to improving something that already exists. Planning projects vary enormously in their size and complexity. The methodology has been applied in many situations from a relatively simple personal objective through to large-scale reorganizations. What is being planned might be a new service, a new process or a new product. This chapter has been mainly written from the point of view of a team-based project but the stages apply equally well to projects undertaken by individuals.

Some examples of where planning methodology has been used are:

- planning a conference
- reorganizing a company
- installing new equipment
- producing the design for a new house.

You will find examples in Chapter 16.

USING THE METHODOLOGY

The most important aspect of the planning methodology is the involvement of all the people who have a contribution to make. These are people in addition to the project team members. Key players are involved at a project planning meeting early in the methodology (see Figure 9.1).

Remember that the methodology is structured as a linear check-list, intended to be used as a guide to best practice (see Figure 9.2). If you follow the methodology, it will make sure all aspects of your project are covered. However, you can omit any stages that appear unnecessary for your specific project but make sure you give careful consideration to this decision. You may also be able to speed up your project by starting a new stage before the previous one has been fully completed. You will notice that this and other methodologies commence with stage 0. This is work which needs to be carried out before the project actually starts.

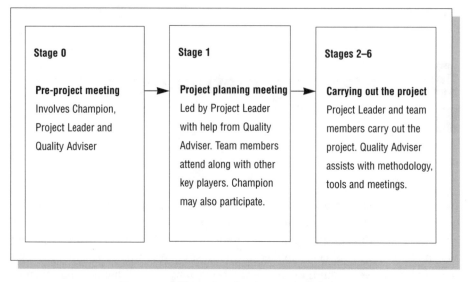

Figure 9.1 The project planning meeting in context

STAGE 0 – HOLD THE PRE-PROJECT MEETING

Before the project starts, the Champion should arrange a pre-project meeting with the Project Leader and Quality Adviser. A model agenda for a pre-project meeting can be found in stage 8 of the steering group methodology and the format for a project remit in stage 5 (both in Chapter 6). Use these as an agenda for your meeting and use the extra information below to stimulate your thoughts.

BACKGROUND

The Champion should explain the background to the project, how and why it was selected.

REMIT

The Champion should brief the Project Leader and Quality Adviser on the project remit. All the headings outlined in stage 5 of the steering group methodology should be covered. However, the headings which you must be absolutely clear about are the scope, any exclusions, benefits the project should realize, and timescales.

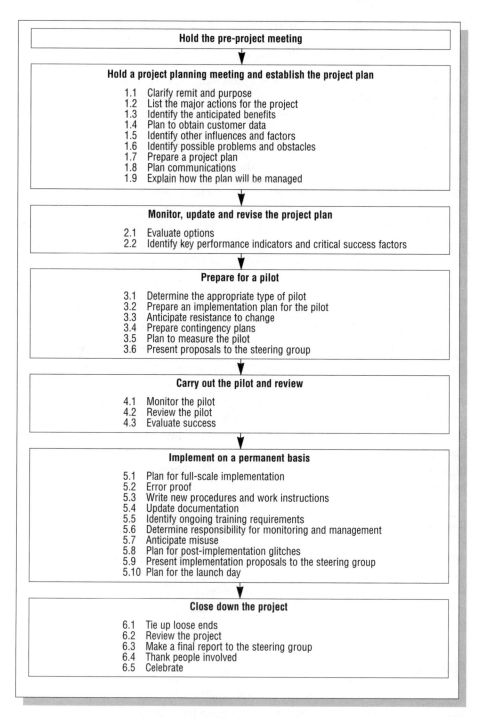

Figure 9.2 Overview of the planning methodology

SELECT TEAM MEMBERS AND IDENTIFY OTHERS TO BE INVOLVED

In planning projects there are three groups to consider:

1. Anyone with specialist knowledge in the subject being planned.
2. Those who will have to implement the new service, process or product – these might be, for example, the people responsible for the installation of a new piece of equipment.
3. Those who will have to operate the process or deliver the product or service in the workplace – these might be the operators of the new equipment.

Use the tips in stage 8 of the steering group methodology (see Chapter 6) to help identify team members. Probably the most important element of the planning methodology is to involve these people at an early stage, gathering them together at a project planning meeting. This will often involve people from different departments and levels in an organization. Planning projects fall into two categories as far as this issue is concerned.

First, there are larger projects where a project team is involved. As far as the pre-project meeting is concerned, select the people who will be permanent members of the project team and consider if there are others who need to be involved, maybe through an invitation to the project planning meeting. Plan how these people will be approached and briefed and whether by the Project Leader or Champion.

Second, there are small-scale projects carried out by an individual working alone. Even in this case, the Project Leader should consult people likely to have knowledge of or who will be affected by the project. The Project Leader has two choices: meet individually with the people concerned or hold a one-off project planning meeting where everyone is invited. Except for the very smallest of projects, the latter is better. At the pre-project meeting, identify the people to be involved in the project planning meeting.

LOGISTICS

Agree reporting arrangements between the Champion and Project Leader. Decide who is going to contact who and at what intervals. Identify potential dates for the project planning meeting and consider whether the Champion needs to attend for all or part of this. Diary the next meeting between the Champion and Project Leader if possible.

RESOURCES

Training might be required in the planning methodology for the project team. For large-scale projects in particular it is important to consider staff release, administrative support, computers and office accommodation especially when people are working full time on a project. Consider the budgetary implications of these for the project.

PROJECT LEADER AND QUALITY ADVISER

Once the Champion, Project Leader and Quality Adviser have covered the above agenda items, then the Project Leader and Quality Adviser need to consider how they will work together. The Quality Adviser will have two main tasks. The first of these will be to help plan and run the project planning meeting. The second is to provide ongoing support to the project team. Stage 1 of the planning methodology should be reviewed and detailed consideration should be given to arrangements for the project planning meeting.

STAGE 1 – HOLD A PROJECT PLANNING MEETING AND ESTABLISH THE PROJECT PLAN

OVERVIEW OF STAGE 1

All of stage 1 takes place at the project planning meeting. The project planning meeting should involve all the key players and plan how the project will be taken forward. This meeting is led by the Project Leader with help from the Quality Adviser. This is a one-off meeting to kick-start the project, and because of its importance the Champion may also wish to attend. A typical project planning meeting might take half a day, although very large-scale projects might need a day or two. All the key players must attend and this might be quite a large number. Key players are not the same as project team members. Project team members are those people who are core to the project and will see it through to the end. Key players are all those who need to have an input because of their expertise or involvement in either implementation or operation of the finished project. Each of the stages 1.1 to 1.9 should form the agenda for the project planning meeting.

For much smaller projects, the Project Leader may wish to undertake the majority of stage 1 working alone. However, the most important principle of the planning methodology is to involve the key players and meetings should be held with all of these to secure their input. One meeting with all people present is still much better.

STAGE 1.1 – CLARIFY REMIT AND PURPOSE

When holding the project planning meeting, all the elements of the project remit should be explained by the Champion or Project Leader. It is important that the key players have a common understanding about the project. If necessary, the project remit can be revised to reflect any new information provided by the key players.

STAGE 1.2 – LIST THE MAJOR ACTIONS FOR THE PROJECT

Based on the remit, the group should now brainstorm (see Chapter 17) the major actions required to achieve the project. It is important to get the level of detail right for this stage. We are looking for significant component parts. As an example, if you were planning a conference you might have 'identify possible venues', 'select venue', 'invite speakers' and so on. Having done this, use chronological clustering (see Chapter 17) to put them in sequence.

STAGE 1.3 – IDENTIFY THE ANTICIPATED BENEFITS

A list of the anticipated benefits of the project should now be produced. The main benefits will usually be stated in the project remit. However, there are often more. What we want to achieve here is a concise list of measurable outcomes. This is important as the plan will make sure that each benefit is planned for and measured. The resulting list will be used in stage 2.1 to identify the optimum options for the project. Produce the list using brainstorming (see Chapter 17). Where there are many people involved, break them up into syndicate groups (see Chapter 21) formed around areas of specialist knowledge, for example technical or marketing. Once the brainstorm has been completed, consider using clustering (see Chapter 17) to sort out the list or prioritize the benefits using must-should-could (see Chapter 17).

Participants should not rely solely on memory. The agenda circulated in advance should show that this exercise will take place and people should be asked to give this some thought and bring along any relevant information.

Once this has been done, check that the list of actions produced in stage 1.2 will achieve each benefit. If not, add the actions necessary to do this. This and the subsequent stages should begin to add much more detail to the chronological cluster.

STAGE 1.4 – PLAN TO OBTAIN CUSTOMER DATA

Identify what data is required in order to understand customer needs and expectations. Use of the Kano model (see Chapter 18) is helpful at this stage.

Consider the following:

1. What is the basic customer need? (Use the Kano model here.)
2. What else do customers want? (Use the Kano model here.)
3. How and when do they want it?
4. How do customers use your service or product?
5. What are the key quality characteristics?
   For example, on time, clean, accurate.
6. What are your competitors doing?

Undertake this stage by brainstorming (see Chapter 17) and then debating each heading. As an alternative or before the brainstorm, consider putting people into pairs or small groups to discuss the headings. Remember that the resulting list may well only be the opinion of the participants. Make sure that the appropriate experts have been invited and they bring along any research information with them. List any information you need to collect. Add any further items necessary to the chronological cluster of action items.

The definition of a 'customer' in this stage includes people outside the organization and 'internal customers', people within the organization at the next stage of the process.

STAGE 1.5 – IDENTIFY OTHER INFLUENCES AND FACTORS

Half way through a project it may sometimes be discovered that someone else is working on something similar elsewhere in the organization. There are also a number of other factors that need to be taken into account:

1. Consider who else might be working on similar projects and what needs to be found out from them.
2. List any policy decisions that need to be made that are outside the authority of the Project Leader or key players. TPN analysis (see Chapter 17) is useful here. Identify who needs to make these decisions and refer the matter to the Champion.
3. Is there any important information that is not available?
4. Will the new service, process or product replace any existing equivalents?
   If so, will this become obsolete and what needs to be done about it?

Again, list any actions arising as a result of this stage.

STAGE 1.6 – IDENTIFY POSSIBLE PROBLEMS AND OBSTACLES

Identification of possible problems and obstacles is an area where the key players are particularly useful. Many projects fail due to unforeseen problems either in implementation or operation. Front-line workers will say what will work and what will go wrong. Possible problems and obstacles can be anticipated and planned out, or contingency plans prepared to combat them. Listing possible problems and obstacles is best achieved through brainstorming in syndicates grouped around areas of expertise. If the list is large, clustering might again be useful or classification by whether there is a high, medium or low chance of suggested problems occurring. Once the list of possible problems and obstacles has been produced, identify actions that will remove as many as possible or make a note of them for contingency planning in stage 3.4.

STAGE 1.7 – PREPARE A PROJECT PLAN

Tidy up the resulting chronological cluster, make sure it is in a logical order, eliminate duplication and look for any gaps. Place someone's name or initials against each action. Even if they won't personally carry this out, they will be responsible for making sure it happens. A planning grid (see Chapter 17) can now be produced by putting timescales to the chronological cluster. You might do this by day, week or month. Finally, the Project Leader should talk through the plan to make sure it makes sense and ensure that everybody is happy with the actions they have been given.

STAGE 1.8 – PLAN COMMUNICATIONS

Plan communications fall into three categories:

1. There may be a few people whose support is vital to the success of the project. These people need to be listed along with what help, if any, is needed from them and who will approach them.
2. The second category is internal communications. Who in the organization needs to be kept informed of the work of the project and how will this be achieved?
3. Finally, external communications needs to be considered. Is there anyone outside the organization who needs to be kept informed?

Add any action items to the project plan.

STAGE 1.9 – EXPLAIN HOW THE PLAN WILL BE MANAGED

How the plan will be managed will have been decided at the pre-project meeting. Although the final responsibility for the project, and hence the management of the project plan, rests with the Project Leader, there are a number of ways this might happen:

1. The project can be taken forward by a team. If this is the case they need to decide when they will next meet and how they will monitor actions between now and then. It is also wise to check with the key players that they agree with the choice of team members. It is possible that new information has come to light during the project planning meeting that might alter the original choice. If so, the Project Leader should consult the Champion. Additionally, the Project Leader might choose to call together some or all of the key players from the project planning meeting as and when necessary.
2. If the project turns out to be very large, a steering group can be formed to break the overall project down into smaller sub-projects. Follow the same considerations as in (1) above.
3. The Project Leader can work alone and take it forward from here.

STAGE 2 – MONITOR, UPDATE AND REVISE THE PROJECT PLAN

Stage 2 is the 'doing' part of the project. Actions are being carried out and the Project Leader and team are meeting on a regular basis to monitor what is happening. Actions and deadlines are being reviewed and amendments made to the plan as necessary. Additionally, there are a number of specific tasks that need doing.

STAGE 2.1 – EVALUATE OPTIONS

If there are a number of options, these should be evaluated. It is important to determine suitable criteria for evaluation. The project remit may well give some clues or the Project Leader might want to seek guidance from the Champion. The list of anticipated benefits produced in stage 1.3 comes in useful here. Each option can be evaluated against how well it achieves these benefits. Typical considerations might be:

- level of improvement or performance obtainable
- cost
- additional or reduced workload as a consequence
- ease of implementation
- training required.

The evaluation matrix and other tools for evaluation and decision making (see Chapter 19) should be used to help.

STAGE 2.2 – IDENTIFY KEY PERFORMANCE INDICATORS AND CRITICAL SUCCESS FACTORS

The results of the project must be able to be measured. Key performance indicators are measures such as 'how much', 'how many' and 'how often'. They are measures of the results of the project at work. Critical success factors are milestones related to the plan – implementation of a particular aspect by a certain date. Consider key areas and anticipated benefits of the project and how the achievement of these could be measured.

STAGES 3 TO 6 – PILOT, IMPLEMENT AND CLOSE DOWN

The next stages of the planning methodology are:

- *Stage 3* – Prepare for a pilot
- *Stage 4* – Carry out the pilot and review
- *Stage 5* – Implement on a permanent basis
- *Stage 6* – Close down the project.

These final stages are identical for the planning, quality improvement team and problem-solving methodologies and are detailed separately in Chapters 14 and 15.

10 Quality improvement team methodology

The quality improvement team methodology is appropriate where the purpose of the project is to improve an existing process or area of work. It is rare for one person to fully understand how something works from beginning to end and a quality improvement team brings together the knowledge of a number of individuals who can together produce a complete picture. These are usually from different departments and levels of the organization.

This is the longest of the project methodologies because of the requirement to understand things as they are at present before making proposals for improvement (see Figure 10.1). The early stages of the methodology focus on understanding the current situation. Next data is collected about customer requirements and how current performance compares. Once this has been done, the team can start to think about how to change things for the better. Much emphasis is placed in this methodology on understanding customers and measuring their requirements and satisfaction against current performance. The usual principles underlying the project-by-project approach apply, but it is particularly important to define the project parameters for quality improvement teams. What might seem small differences in the area to be examined can mean a great deal in terms of the size and focus of the project.

USING THE METHODOLOGY AND TOOLS

As with the other methodologies this chapter is structured as a linear check-list. If you follow the methodology, it will make sure all aspects of the project are covered. However, you can omit any stages that appear unnecessary for your specific project but make sure you give careful consideration to this decision. It is possible to speed up the project by starting a new stage before the last one has been fully completed. This is particularly true of stages 2, 3 and 4.

The tools for planning and organizing – brainstorming, clustering, planning grid, TPN analysis and must-should-could (see Chapter 17) – are useful throughout the project. Deployment flowcharting and Ishikawa diagrams (see

Chapter 18) are vital tools in the quality improvement team methodology as these are used to analyse the existing situation.

Figure 10.1 Overview of the quality improvement team methodology

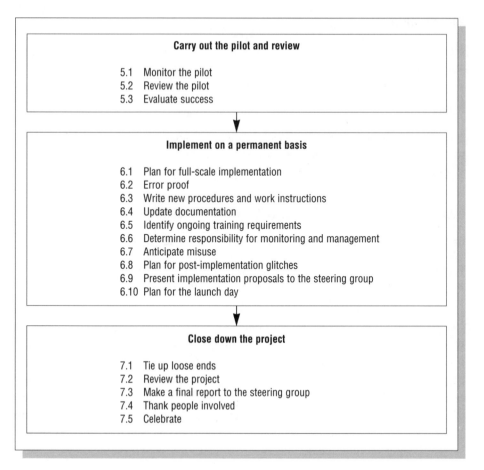

Carry out the pilot and review

5.1 Monitor the pilot
5.2 Review the pilot
5.3 Evaluate success

Implement on a permanent basis

6.1 Plan for full-scale implementation
6.2 Error proof
6.3 Write new procedures and work instructions
6.4 Update documentation
6.5 Identify ongoing training requirements
6.6 Determine responsibility for monitoring and management
6.7 Anticipate misuse
6.8 Plan for post-implementation glitches
6.9 Present implementation proposals to the steering group
6.10 Plan for the launch day

Close down the project

7.1 Tie up loose ends
7.2 Review the project
7.3 Make a final report to the steering group
7.4 Thank people involved
7.5 Celebrate

Figure 10.1 Overview of the quality improvement team methodology (continued)

STAGE 0 – HOLD THE PRE-PROJECT MEETING

The Champion should arrange a pre-project meeting with the Project Leader and Quality Adviser to start the project. The pre-project meeting takes place in two parts, the first involving all three people, the second only involving the Project Leader and Quality Adviser. You will find a model agenda for the pre-project meeting in stage 8 of the steering group methodology (see Chapter 6). There is also the format for a project remit in stage 5 in the same chapter. Use these as an agenda for your meeting and use the extra information below to stimulate your thoughts.

BACKGROUND

The Champion should explain the background to the project – how and why it was selected.

REMIT

The Champion should brief Project Leader and Quality Adviser on the project remit. All the headings outlined in stage 5 of the steering group methodology should be covered. Be particularly careful about the scope of the project.

SELECT TEAM MEMBERS AND IDENTIFY OTHERS TO BE INVOLVED

In quality improvement teams there are two groups to consider:

- People who do the job. Make sure that all are represented.
- People who will be affected by changes to the inputs or outputs of any processes under study.

Consider any processes that are going to be studied. Construction of a basic flowchart (see Chapter 18) will help identify the main stages and who is involved. If you end up with a long list of potential members use must-should-could (see Chapter 17) to keep the team to a sensible size. Those not involved as a full team member may be brought in when required and it is not unusual for membership of a quality improvement team to alter as the project progresses and the focus shifts. Plan how these people will be approached and briefed and whether by the Project Leader or Champion.

LOGISTICS

Agree reporting arrangements between the Champion and Project Leader. Decide who is going to contact who and at what intervals. Identify potential dates for the first quality improvement team meeting and consider whether the Champion needs to say a few words at either the start or close. Diary the next meeting between the Champion and Project Leader to follow this.

RESOURCES

Training is especially important for quality improvement teams. This training should combine an opportunity for the individuals to get to know each other, making sure everyone is clear and happy about the remit, an overview of the methodology, an introduction to the tools and techniques and work on the project itself. Releasing staff from their normal work is sometimes a problem in quality improvement teams because members often have operational jobs. Consider also meeting facilities, administrative support, computers, office accommodation and budget for these project resources.

PROJECT LEADER AND QUALITY ADVISER

The Project Leader and Quality Adviser now need to consider how they will work together. The Quality Adviser has an ongoing and developmental role with a quality improvement team. First, they will help the Project Leader to plan and follow the methodology. Second, they will help with tools and techniques of which a whole host will be used in the project. Finally, they have a responsibility to help develop the team itself as the project progresses.

Stages 1, 2 and 3 of the quality improvement team methodology should now be reviewed and detailed consideration be given to getting the project rolling. If training is to be provided, then many of these stages will be undertaken during the training itself. You may wish to consider bringing the team together for a short preliminary meeting and briefing prior to attending the training course. If training is not going to be provided, then plan for the first project meeting. Prepare an agenda and arrange to issue it to team members (see Figure 10.2).

STAGE 1 – SCOPE THE PROJECT

There are two dimensions to stage 1 – the people and the project. A quality improvement team will bring together a group of people with different backgrounds, experience and attitudes who will usually never have met together before. If this diverse group of people is to work effectively as a team, they must put some conscious effort into team development during the course of the project. The first element of stage 1 is to provide an opportunity for the team to get to know each other and define how they will work together. The second element is scoping the project. This involves defining key facts about the subject under study such as boundaries, departments and people involved. The lists produced during stage 1 will be frequently referred to and refined as the project develops. The lists can be used to identify and prioritize areas for study, select pilot sites, and are particularly important for breaking down the whole project into more manageable component parts. It is also at this stage that the project remit is studied by the team to ensure a common understanding and help with these decisions.

Training should always be provided for quality improvement teams. Bear in mind that this refers to just-in-time training so input on the methodologies and

(1) Welcome, agenda and purpose of the day.	15 mins
(2) Introductions exercise (stage 1.1).	45 mins
(3) Introduce project remit (stage 1.2).	15 mins
(4) Explanation of roles:	
Project Leader, Champion, team members, Quality Adviser.	15 mins
(5) Principles behind and overview of the quality improvement team methodology.	30 mins
(6) Define the project boundaries (stage 1.4).	30 mins
(7) List who is involved (stage 1.5).	30 mins
(8) List the objectives of the project (stage 1.6).	30 mins
(9) Review the project remit (stage 1.7).	30 mins
(10) Plan communications (stage 1.8).	30 mins
(11) Determine project logistics and arrangements for next meeting (stage 1.9).	30 mins
(12) Brief overview of what happens next.	10 mins
(13) Summary of actions.	10 mins
(14) Meeting review.	10 mins

Figure 10.2 Model agenda for the first quality improvement team meeting

tools is combined with real work on the project in hand. Training also provides a jump start for teamwork. If training is being provided for the team, then all of stage 1 should be covered during the course. You will find a suggested format for quality improvement team training at the end of the chapter. If not provided, then stage 1 should form the agenda for the first meeting.

Allow a whole day for the first quality improvement team meeting. The model agenda shows times but these are very much guesswork as the real times will be very much dependent upon the complexity of the project. Breaks and lunch also need to be added in. The Project Leader and Quality Adviser should decide who will lead which session. Items (2), (5), (12) and (14) are obvious candidates for the Quality Adviser who should also lead in the use of the tools.

STAGE 1.1 – GET TO KNOW EACH OTHER

The team should spend some time at the outset getting to know each other. Useful areas to find out about are:

- work background
  current job, how long with the organization, previous jobs
- previous experience of project work
  any involvement with other quality improvement teams
- personal background.

A good way to do this is for the Quality Adviser to set a structured remit for pairwork. Each pair spends some time covering the remit in turn and then the report back to the main group takes the form of 'introduce your partner'.

STAGE 1.2 – INTRODUCE THE REMIT

The next task is to introduce the remit to make sure that everyone understands and is happy with it. The Project Leader should do this. It is a good idea to have the remit on a handout which can be issued in advance. Stages 1.3 to 1.7 are concerned with making sure the team clearly understand the remit and producing thorough lists of areas for further study.

STAGE 1.3 – LIST ANY ISSUES AND OBVIOUS PROBLEMS AS YOU GO ALONG

Listing problems as you progress is necessary because of human nature. People can't wait to get into the thick of the project. Even during the personal introductions quality improvement team members are saying 'have you thought about doing this?' or 'do you know that at our plant we've always had a problem with that' and 'if only we did the other, this wouldn't cause complaints'. I used to be a purist about the methodology and say 'just hang on to that for a moment – we'll be covering issues like that in stage 3'. Five minutes later we would be talking about it again and, sure enough, when stage 3 came along they were right a lot of the time.

Because of this, now is a good time to start keeping an issue park (see Chapter 21). This is a list of any issues or obvious problems that occur in debate and are noted on a sheet of flipchart paper as they arise. The issue park ensures that nothing is lost without diverting the course of a meeting. It is good practice to review the issue park at the end of each major stage in the project and at the end of each meeting. This ensures all angles have been covered and allows those issues that have been dealt with to be deleted.

Not all the issues noted will be within the remit of the project. The Project

Leader should refer these to the Champion if appropriate and then consider them closed.

STAGE 1.4 – DEFINE THE PROJECT BOUNDARIES

The importance of defining the project boundaries varies greatly depending upon the nature of the organization and project. In some cases there will be a one-word definition. In large projects at multi-site organizations the resulting list may be long. The purpose of this stage is to have a comprehensive and definitive list of the areas under study. This will be useful throughout the project since at each stage the team will need to revisit this list. Processes rarely work identically at different sites. Data may need to be collected individually by department. Problems may exist at one location that don't at others. This is also an important stage because it clarifies any locations, departments or other areas that are outside of the remit. Use brainstorming and then maybe clustering (see Chapter 17) to produce lists of the following using the project remit for guidance:

1. *Sites or locations involved.* Sometimes it can be equally useful to list sites or locations definitely not involved.
2. *Departments involved* (and not involved).
3. *Processes in the subject area.* For each of these define where the study area begins and ends, inputs and outputs.

If clarification is needed, consult the Champion. Some teams find this stage too simple and look for hidden detail and meaning. If this only takes you two minutes then good – move on.

STAGE 1.5 – LIST WHO IS INVOLVED

Listing those who are involved is concerned with making sure all angles are covered. The view of a driver might be completely different from that of a fitter. The terms and conditions of a manager might be different from those of a secretary. Depending on the size and nature of the project, you may wish to list people by name, job title or groups of staff. Again use brainstorming to generate the following lists:

1. list the people involved at each stage of the processes at each location
2. list customers – people who use or receive outputs
3. list suppliers – people who provide inputs
4. list anyone else who needs to be kept informed.

These lists are the people who may need to be involved in the project in some way. It is likely their opinions will be needed or you may need to collect data from them. If key people are not represented, the Project Leader may have to re-assess membership of the team. If the lists are long you might wish to go through and use clustering to sort them. Alternatively you might want to classify them in some way. Must-should-could (see Chapter 17) is an option for prioritization.

STAGE 1.6 – BE CLEAR ABOUT THE OBJECTIVES OF THE PROJECT

The project remit should list the objectives. List what is to be improved and be specific. Examples might be:

- cleanliness – improve
- turn round time – reduce
- errors in invoices – eliminate.

This list should be quite short. If you end up with a long list, go through it and use the Pareto principle (see Chapter 20) to classify each objective as either vital few or useful many. As the project progresses, focus on the vital few.

STAGE 1.7 – REVIEW THE PROJECT REMIT

Having completed the above stages review the project remit to ensure that there is common understanding and agreement within the team. The Project Leader should again read through the remit and the Quality Adviser list any questions or comments on the flipchart. It is not uncommon for the team to want to seek clarification or amendment at this stage and the Project Leader should do this through the Champion.

STAGE 1.8 – PLAN COMMUNICATIONS

Despite good intentions, one of the most common criticisms of quality improvement teams by those people not directly involved is that they don't communicate enough. Refer to the lists produced during stage 1.5 and consider what you might want to communicate at this stage. This might be the existence and purpose of the project and the names of people directly involved. Next consider how you will achieve this. For the vital few people this might be by one-to-one briefing. At a minimum, write something for the core brief or staff newsletter. Wherever possible stick to existing methods of communication. It is always tempting to do something special when you are enthusiastic about a new project. The danger here is that everyone does something special and people become inundated with all sorts of bulletins.

Communications needs to become a standing agenda item at the end of each meeting. Bear in mind, however, that it is not necessary to communicate something every time. Restrict it to the important issues.

STAGE 1.9 – DETERMINE PROJECT LOGISTICS

How often?

The most important logistical issue is how often the team will meet. In the early stages of a quality improvement team it is probably best to meet as often as possible. If training is being provided, all of stage 1 and the first two parts of stage 2 should be achievable during this. If training is not being provided, then the first project meeting should see all of stage 1 and stage 2.1 completed. The second meeting should take place as soon as possible after this – within a week ideally. Frequency after this will depend upon the nature of the project and progress being made. You might have to wait until some actions are carried out or data is collected but the rule is have a meeting as soon as you have got something to do. Here are a few common pitfalls to watch out for:

✖ Beware meeting once a month because that tends to be the frequency of most meetings.

✖ Beware the busy diary scenario – project meetings are hard to fit into the diary because of existing less important commitments – dump or delegate these.

✖ Beware 'everybody must attend every meeting' syndrome – you'll never get everyone there all the time so go with the best option.

✖ Beware persistent non-attenders – seek advice from the Champion.

Note taking

The best option for this varies greatly depending upon the individual circumstances of the project. There are a number of considerations to bear in mind:

- The Project Leader and Quality Adviser should not do the note taking – they are busy enough already.
- A volunteer from the team is the best option.
- If no-one is keen, rotation of the task is an option but this sometimes causes problems through a lack of consistency.
- Don't choose someone to take the notes who does not have access to equipment such as a word processor and photocopier.

Keep the notes as simple as possible. The Project Leader should ask the note taker to record action items and decisions as each meeting progresses. These should be typed up afterwards along with any important flipcharts. For typing up, consider any secretarial support that may be available to the Project Leader or any individual team members. If this is a problem, seek assistance from the Champion. The most common pitfall here is that note taking is a bit of a drag and nobody really wants to do it. If necessary the Project Leader needs to bite the bullet and tell someone to do it. Pitfall two is that note taking automatically goes to the woman in the team.

Summary and other considerations

These points have been stressed because they are simple but vital and can cause a lot of trouble if not dealt with properly. Other points to consider include venue, equipment, day of the week, length of meeting, start and finish times and so on. Use the logistics check-list in Chapter 22 to ensure that you have covered all aspects. You will also find some more thoughts about note taking there.

STAGE 2 – ASSESS AND ANALYSE THE CURRENT SITUATION

Before proposals can be formulated to improve something that already exists, it is first necessary to properly understand how it works at present. The tools for analysis are used during stage 2. First an Ishikawa diagram is constructed (see Chapter 18), then one or more deployment flowcharts. Experience suggests that project teams usually find one or the other more useful. Projects that are focused around a clear process will find the deployment flowchart invaluable and the Ishikawa diagram helpful. Projects with a more general remit will find the opposite.

Once all the elements have been identified, the processes defined and the sequence of tasks and relationships understood, the next task is to determine how well matters are working at present – the performance. This is done by identifying what is important to the customer, that is quality characteristics, and then measures of performance or key performance indicators. Data collection is a core element of stage 2 and this is often the most important and time consuming part of the entire project.

STAGE 2.1 – PRODUCE AN ISHIKAWA DIAGRAM

The team should now produce an Ishikawa diagram of the area under study. The purpose of this is to produce a comprehensive picture of all the factors affecting the project area. The alternative is to select areas for further study and improvement based upon experience and judgement. Using an Ishikawa diagram removes the danger of preconception and pet theories. It makes sure that all angles are covered. The headings strongly recommended are methods, equipment, people, environment and materials. Follow the guidelines given in Chapter 18. However, also consider whether to construct a positive or negative Ishikawa diagram. Keep adding to the issue park as you are constructing your Ishikawa diagram.

To illustrate how this has worked in practice, the Reception Quality Improvement Team at Liverpool Housing Trust constructed a negative Ishikawa diagram at this stage in their project. The head was 'reception service from hell'. This highlighted some key processes for further study. In Greater Manchester Waste the Load Optimization Quality Improvement Team constructed an Ishikawa diagram with 'an optimized load' as the head. Discussion up to that point had been pretty heated with friction between the different types of staff. The general feeling was that 'if only you drivers would do your jobs right', followed by 'if only you loaders loaded properly'. The Ishikawa diagram was a turning point for the team. Until then the focus had been on getting people to do their jobs better. The Ishikawa diagram had very little of substance along the people arrow, the most significant factors there being related to training. The vast concentration of factors was along the equipment bone.

Once the Ishikawa diagram has been completed there are a number of options regarding next steps. The most appropriate should be apparent and will depend upon the nature of the project. Possible next steps are:

- Study individual factors from the Ishikawa diagram in more detail.
- Produce deployment flowcharts of any processes identified (stage 2.2).
- Collect data about the relative importance of each factor (stage 2.5).
- Feed the factors identified into suggestions for improvement (stage 3).
- Look for ideas to remove problems (stage 3).

STAGE 2.2 – PRODUCE AND ANALYSE DEPLOYMENT FLOWCHARTS OF EXISTING PROCESSES

Some projects are based on one clear process. An example of this is the 'ordering a day-to-day repair' project in Liverpool Housing Trust. This is one clear process which has an identifiable starting place, a tenant reports a repair, and a definable finishing point, the repair is carried out. Other projects concentrate more on areas of work rather than specific processes, for example the fleet composition project at Greater Manchester Waste. Fleet composition is not a process. There are, however, some distinct processes which fall under this heading such as the process by which a vehicle is allocated to a particular job. Stage 2.2 takes the main process or processes and produces deployment flowcharts for these so it is well understood how these work. Producing a deployment flowchart helps you to understand:

- How the process actually works.
- Customer–supplier relationships.
- Stages at which measurements of performance might be taken.

Follow the guidelines for deployment flowcharting in Chapter 18. Quality improvement teams should also bear in mind the following tips:

✔ Construct deployment flowcharts of processes as they actually work, not as they should work according to the procedures manual or how we would like them to work.

✔ Different individuals, departments or locations may operate the same process in different ways. Don't generalize. The options are to produce one flowchart as an example and make notes of the key differences or to produce an individual flowchart for each.

✔ The people involved in a process should be present on the team. If everybody is not actually represented, you may need to invite additional people along for this stage. Start off by identifying the people or departments involved and check that the necessary expertise is present. If it isn't, don't guess – invite them along.

✔ Once again issues and ideas are likely to arise while the deployment flowchart is being constructed. Make sure these are recorded in an issue park.

✔ Flowcharting is a complex task and can be quite difficult to achieve. The Quality Adviser should lead in the use of this tool so all team members and the Project Leader can participate. If there is disagreement about how specific stages work, the person who does the job normally has the final say. If people are still not happy, note it on the issue park and investigate further later.

Once a deployment flowchart has been completed it should be analysed. This identifies areas for improvement. Use the 'Analysing your deployment flowchart' checklist in Chapter 18 to help with this.

STAGE 2.3 – IDENTIFY HISTORICAL INFLUENCES

Processes in the workplace tend to evolve over time due to many different factors. These factors may be important background information for the team who need to establish whether these are still valid. Never assume that the background to a situation is obvious or that everyone knows it. History, private or public ownership and reorganization have led to some quite unusual circumstances in many organizations. The stories behind the facts can be very illuminating and point to things that might trip you up at a later stage.

Some project teams find this stage fascinating and important. Others produce blank looks. If this stage does not seem relevant to your project, consult the team and then omit it.

STAGE 2.4 – IDENTIFY SOURCES OF INFORMATION

The team should now be in a position to identify existing sources of information which may be of use during the project. Team members should be allocated the task of obtaining these and reporting back their findings at the next meeting. The type of information which might be of use includes:

- performance statistics
- training materials
- policies, procedures, manuals.

There might also be work going on elsewhere in the organization which may be important. Consider how information will be obtained about this.

STAGE 2.5 – COLLECT AND ANALYSE DATA ABOUT THE CURRENT SITUATION

It is now time to collect detailed information about the existing situation. Data will need to be collected about:

- *Customers*. Factual, such as age profile or where they live, needs and expectations, how important specific aspects of your service are, and satisfaction data, how happy they are with specific aspects of your service.
- *Employees*. What they think about the current situation, what ideas they have for improvement.
- *Process performance*. How well you are doing at the moment. Process performance data answers questions such as 'how many' and 'how quickly'.
- *Errors*. This is data such as how many errors, where they are occurring and what is causing them.

Follow the data collection, display and analysis methodology as detailed in Chapter 13. Once data has been collected, displayed and analysed, the team can actually quantify the current situation and will have hard facts to prove the existing state of affairs. This is the base to which any improvements made from now on can be compared.

STAGE 3 – CONSTRUCT AN IMPROVEMENT PLAN

Stage 3 converts your findings about the current situation into ideas for improvement and firm proposals. Alternatives are evaluated, potential benefits estimated and an improvement plan produced.

STAGE 3.1 – FIX OBVIOUS PROBLEMS

Where possible, obvious problems should be fixed immediately. Obvious problems are those where an obvious discrepancy has been identified, the solution can be quickly and easily implemented and is within authority of the members of the team to alter (both organizationally and financially). A record should be kept of any changes made which fall under this heading. Resulting improvements should also be measured and these included in any presentation to the steering group.

STAGE 3.2 – IDENTIFY MAJOR CHANGES AND ALTERNATIVE OPTIONS

Draw a distinction at this stage between major changes and changes in detail. A major change is one which substantially alters a method of working or the way things are done currently. Examples include changes of location, changes of equipment, significant alteration to the way in which processes work, redeployment of staff, alteration to shift patterns. A major change is one of the vital few which on its own will result in a step change in some aspect of performance. Detail changes are of an important but relatively minor nature. These are the useful many that when combined will result in worthwhile improvement in performance but in isolation are fairly small. Examples include changes in the way a specific task is carried out, alteration to a job description, small changes in working hours.

The team should by now have a good idea of the major changes they would like to see. These should be listed together with the various options available. For example, if a team has found that a particular process is in a dire state and requires major overhaul the options might be:

- *Option 1: Minimum change* – improve the efficiency of the existing process through detail change only.
- *Option 2: Redesign* – major changes in the way the process works involving relocation of staff.
- *Option 3: Computerization* – new computer system needed. Existing staff will be made redundant.

STAGE 3.3 – EVALUATE AND COST THE OPTIONS

Choosing an option

If there are a number of options these should be evaluated. It is important to be clear about the criteria you use for evaluation. This is normally quite complex because there will be balancing factors. Use brainstorming to list the criteria you wish to use for evaluation. The project remit and your list from stage 1.6 should be the primary source of ideas. Others might be:

- anticipated effect on performance
- additional or reduced workload as a consequence
- ease of implementation
- training required.

Use of an evaluation matrix (see Chapter 19) is a good way to pull all these strands together. Carrying out a helps and hinders (also Chapter 19) on each option is another.

Choosing a supplier

If you need to choose a supplier, compile a short list and get written and guaranteed quotes from these. Don't make your decision on price alone. Consider after sales service, long-term relationships, any possible follow on work, and any other relevant factors. Consider visiting the supplier to see their operation at first hand or visiting another customer of theirs to see what they think.

Costing your options

Costing of options and proposals is an area which frightens many project teams. Don't worry – you don't need detailed knowledge about accountancy and finance for this, just a bit of common sense. You also need to cost routine operation as it is at present. Use an Ishikawa diagram to cost each option. The head should be something like 'all costs for option 1'. Stick to methods, equipment, people, environment and materials for your main arrows although you won't always have something on each arrow. Have two branch arrows coming off each of the five main arrows. The first of these should be headed 'one-off costs' and should include things such as investment, redundancy, and retraining. The second should be 'costs of routine operation' and should include things such as payroll costs, maintenance and any materials necessary.

Now is a good time to invite in someone from the finance department and run your proposals past them. In addition to any specific questions you might have try the following:

- Can you see any flaws in our thinking?
- Can you think of anything we've missed?
- Are our costings accurate enough?
- Are there any policies or procedures we need to comply with such as compulsory competitive tendering or investment regulations?

This is also a good time to have a detailed meeting with the Champion. This is particularly important where expenditure decisions need to be made.

STAGE 3.4 – IDENTIFY DETAIL CHANGES

Finally, lists of detail changes need to be produced. There may be several of these, one list of detail changes as a sub-set of the major changes.

STAGES 4 TO 7 – PILOT, IMPLEMENT AND CLOSE DOWN

The next stages of the quality improvement team methodology are:

- *Stage 4* – Prepare for a pilot.
- *Stage 5* – Carry out the pilot and review.
- *Stage 6* – Implement on a permanent basis.
- *Stage 7* – Close down the project.

These are dealt with in Chapters 14 and 15.

QUALITY IMPROVEMENT TEAM TRAINING

WHO ATTENDS?

The whole team including Project Leader and Quality Adviser. The Champion might attend to open and/or close the event and take any questions. More than one team can attend. I have run quality improvement team training with three teams without any problems. This is especially valuable where there are related projects as coordination can be achieved from the outset. For example, Greater Manchester Waste had two teams looking at different aspects of transport who attended the same training. However, it does not matter if the teams have nothing to do with each other. For example, one course had a team of civil engineers attend alongside a team looking at customer service. Although the projects were completely different, the teams got a lot out of seeing how each other were using the same methodology to tackle their individual projects. It can easily be done with one team but my experience is that it's always better with more. There seems to be a big advantage gained from cross-fertilization.

HOW DOES IT WORK?

You need someone to run the event, do the formal input and manage the timetable. This needs to be an experienced consultant or trainer who knows the various methodologies inside out and is experienced in working with groups. The course leaders also need to have a short briefing session with the Project Leader and Quality Adviser in advance and work closely with them during the course.

The Project Leader leads all the syndicate sessions which include work on the project. The final say about project issues rests here. The Quality Adviser leads in the use of the tools during the syndicate sessions and works closely with the Project Leader. It can be very daunting especially for new Quality Advisers to have to lead a group through a complicated deployment flowchart but with quality improvement team training they have the knowledge and support of the course leader to fall back on if they need advice.

DURATION AND VENUE

Two days will see you well into stage 2 of the methodology. To come this far would probably take a team at least a month of traditional meetings, probably longer if they were not using a structured approach, so the investment in terms of time and money is well worth while. These courses have been run on business premises and on a residential basis and both work equally well. The main requirement is for a large room and a syndicate room for each team.

CONTENTS

A number of elements need incorporating into the timetable. These will vary slightly depending upon the organization, the nature of the projects and any previous experience the participants may have:

- introductions
- some basics about quality
- background to the project-by-project approach
- explanation of the four roles: Project Leader, Champion, team members, Quality Adviser
- overview of the quality improvement team methodology
- input and practice of the tools for planning and organizing: brainstorming, clustering, must-should-could, TPN analysis, planning grid
- carry out stages 1.3 to 1.8 using these tools
- input on effective meetings
- carry out stage 1.9
- input and exercises on effective teamwork

- input on tools for analysis: Ishikawa, deployment flowcharting, measles, Kano model
- carry out stages 2.1 and 2.2: produce an Ishikawa diagram and deployment flowcharts for the project area
- input on any other tools or carry out other specific tasks relevant to the particular projects
- plan to continue the projects back in the workplace.

11 Problem-solving methodology

Problem-solving methodology is concerned with sorting things out when they are going wrong. A common question is 'What's the difference between this and quality improvement team methodology?' The main difference is that problem-solving methodology does not actually improve things, it gets them back to how they were and no better. Quality improvement team methodology is applicable when you have a relatively stable state of affairs that you would like to see improved – there may be some problems present and these will be ironed out as part of the improvement process. At the end of the project there will be noticeable improvement. Problem-solving methodology is appropriate when you know you're in a mess. Something is going wrong and needs correcting. Performance might have dipped below acceptable levels, customer complaints might be high or the number of defective products being produced rising. Something needs to be done to redress the situation (see Figure 11.1).

Problem-solving methodology is quite simple in its structure. Gather together the people directly involved in the situation, clearly define what is going wrong, identify possible causes, confirm your theories with data and then remove them.

STAGE 0 – HOLD THE PRE-PROJECT MEETING

Before the project starts the Champion should arrange a pre-project meeting with the Project Leader and Quality Adviser. The agenda outlined below follows the format detailed in stage 8 of the steering group methodology (see Chapter 6) with some additional tips for problem-solving projects.

BACKGROUND

The Champion should explain the background to the problem and resulting project, how and why it was selected, what is going wrong and what effect this is having on the organization and customers.

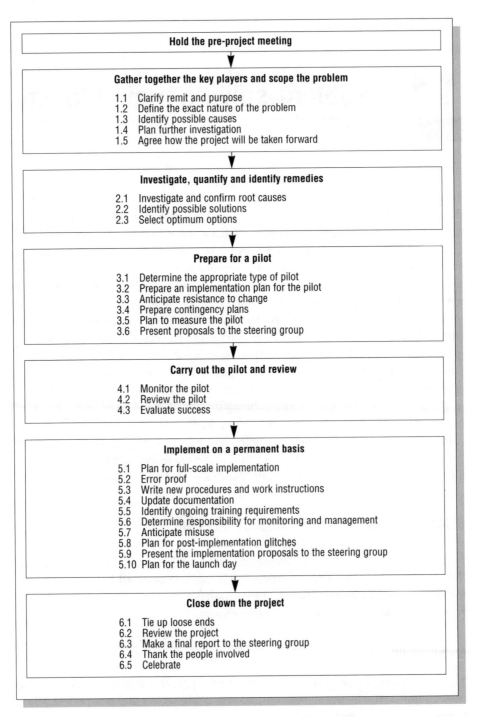

Hold the pre-project meeting

Gather together the key players and scope the problem

1.1 Clarify remit and purpose
1.2 Define the exact nature of the problem
1.3 Identify possible causes
1.4 Plan further investigation
1.5 Agree how the project will be taken forward

Investigate, quantify and identify remedies

2.1 Investigate and confirm root causes
2.2 Identify possible solutions
2.3 Select optimum options

Prepare for a pilot

3.1 Determine the appropriate type of pilot
3.2 Prepare an implementation plan for the pilot
3.3 Anticipate resistance to change
3.4 Prepare contingency plans
3.5 Plan to measure the pilot
3.6 Present proposals to the steering group

Carry out the pilot and review

4.1 Monitor the pilot
4.2 Review the pilot
4.3 Evaluate success

Implement on a permanent basis

5.1 Plan for full-scale implementation
5.2 Error proof
5.3 Write new procedures and work instructions
5.4 Update documentation
5.5 Identify ongoing training requirements
5.6 Determine responsibility for monitoring and management
5.7 Anticipate misuse
5.8 Plan for post-implementation glitches
5.9 Present the implementation proposals to the steering group
5.10 Plan for the launch day

Close down the project

6.1 Tie up loose ends
6.2 Review the project
6.3 Make a final report to the steering group
6.4 Thank the people involved
6.5 Celebrate

Figure 11.1 Overview of the problem-solving methodology

REMIT

The Champion should brief the Project Leader and Quality Adviser on the project remit. All the headings outlined in stage 5 of the steering group methodology should be covered. An important element in problem-solving methodology is how quickly the problem needs to be sorted out. If, for example, the problem is leading to high levels of waste or customer dissatisfaction, time may well make the difference.

SELECT TEAM MEMBERS AND IDENTIFY OTHERS TO BE INVOLVED

In problem-solving projects there are three groups to consider:

- The people who do the job in the area affected.
- Any people with specialist knowledge in the problem area.
- Any complainants – people for whom the problem is causing a headache, maybe internal customers of a process.

Use the tips in stage 8 of the steering group methodology to help identify people. The most important element of the problem-solving methodology is to involve these people at an early stage, gathering them together at a problem-solving meeting. This will often involve people from different departments and levels in an organization. A problem-solving project may be handled in two ways:

1. The first option is for the Project Leader to lead a team which meets regularly. Other people may also be invited along to the problem-solving meeting or as required but there is a clearly defined core team involved.
2. The second option is for the Project Leader to mainly work alone but gather the key players together at appropriate intervals.

As far as the pre-project meeting is concerned, a decision needs to be made as to whether or not there will be a project team and, if so, who these people will be. People to be invited to the problem-solving meeting need to be identified. This might be a larger number of people than just the project team. Plan how these people will be approached and briefed and whether by the Project Leader or Champion.

LOGISTICS

Agree reporting arrangements between the Champion and Project Leader. Decide who is going to contact who and at what intervals. Identify potential dates for the problem-solving meeting and consider whether the Champion needs to attend for all or part of this. Diary the next meeting between the Champion and Project Leader if possible.

RESOURCES

Training might be required in the problem-solving methodology and tools. Problem-solving projects often involve front-line staff so ensure that release from their normal duties is considered.

PROJECT LEADER AND QUALITY ADVISER

Once the Champion, Project Leader and Quality Adviser have covered the above agenda items, then the Project Leader and Quality Adviser need to consider how they will work together. The Quality Adviser will have two main tasks. The first of these will be to help plan and run the problem-solving meeting. The second is to provide ongoing support to the project team at subsequent meetings.

It is now that stage 1 of the problem-solving methodology should be reviewed and detailed consideration should be given to arrangements for the problem-solving meeting.

STAGE 1 – GATHER TOGETHER THE KEY PLAYERS AND SCOPE THE PROBLEM

All of stage 1 should take place at the problem-solving meeting. This involves all of the key players and is led by the Project Leader with help from the Quality Adviser. Typically, the Project Leader will lead when there is input to be made about the problem itself and the Quality Adviser will set remits for syndicate work and lead in the use of tools. The Champion may wish to attend to start the event. This is a one-off meeting to break the back of the problem and might take half a day depending upon the scale and complexity of the problem. All the key players identified at the pre-project meeting should attend. Key players are not the same as project team members. Project team members are those individuals who are core to the project and will meet regularly between now and the end of the project. Key players are those who have an important input because of their knowledge about some aspect of the problem but they will not attend the regular project team meetings. Stages 1.1 to 1.5 should form the agenda for the problem-solving meeting.

STAGE 1.1 – CLARIFY REMIT AND PURPOSE

The first agenda item at the problem-solving meeting should be to clarify the remit and purpose. All the elements of the project remit should be explained by the Champion or Project Leader. The key players need a common understanding about the project. If necessary, the project remit can be revised to reflect any new information provided by the key players.

STAGE 1.2 – DEFINE THE EXACT NATURE OF THE PROBLEM

This stage clearly defines the exact nature of the problem and ensures a common understanding among the key players. The questions in the check-list for problem definition should be answered by the group (Figure 11.2). It is important to be as specific as possible and, if necessary, list any exclusions as well. As with all check-lists, omit any questions that do not apply to your specific situation.

It is usual for people to start speculating about possible causes and ideas to put things right while this is going on. Have an issue park (see Chapter 21) to make sure these are not lost.

(1)	What is the problem?
(2)	Where is the problem occurring?
(3)	When is it occurring?
(4)	When did it start happening?
(5)	Who is involved?
(6)	What are the effects?
(7)	Who is affected?
(8)	How much of a problem is it? (Have you any data about the problem?)

Figure 11.2 Check-list for problem definition

STAGE 1.3 – IDENTIFY POSSIBLE CAUSES

The exact nature of the problem has been defined, so it should now be possible to suggest possible causes. Note the use of the words 'suggest' and 'possible causes'. An important feature of problem-solving methodology is that first, theories regarding causes of the problem are generated. These are then confirmed through investigation, experiment and/or data collection. To identify possible causes an Ishikawa diagram should be constructed. Follow the guidelines in Chapter 18, but note especially the tips in Figure 11.3.

> ✔   The head of the Ishikawa diagram should show the problem, not the solution, so for example 'rent arrears' as opposed to 'no rent arrears' or 'major breakdowns' as opposed to 'trouble free fleet'.
>
> ✔   Use the MEPEM headings – methods, equipment, people, environment and materials – as a starting place. Think about changing these if you really struggle.

Figure 11.3 Tips for using Ishikawa diagrams when problem solving

STAGE 1.4 – PLAN FURTHER INVESTIGATION

Once possible causes have been identified, the next stage is to carry out further investigation and see how important each possible cause is. Exactly what you do at this stage will depend upon the nature of your project and how easy the previous stages have been. Allocate actions to the appropriate people as you go along. Some suggestions are:

- If you want to know more about where your problem is occurring, gather data and display this as a measles diagram (see Chapter 18).
- If you have many possible causes and want to determine which are the most important, try applying the Pareto principle. There are two ways of doing this. The rough and ready way is to go through each possible cause and get the group to say whether they think it is 'vital few' or 'useful many'. The more correct way is to go away and collect data about each and display this as a Pareto chart (see Chapter 20).
- You may have some possible causes which are more or less guesswork. Get someone to go away and find out whether or not this is the case.
- Involve the suppliers of any highlighted areas.
- Allocate parts of the Ishikawa diagram to sub-groups to go away and look at it in more detail.

STAGE 1.5 – AGREE HOW THE PROJECT WILL BE TAKEN FORWARD

How the project is to proceed will already have been considered at the pre-project meeting and it should be clear as to whether there will be a project team taking the project forward. However, it is wise to revisit this now especially in the light of any actions identified in stage 1.4. Consider especially how the results of any data gathering or investigation will be reported and whether any of the key players who are not part of the project team will need to be involved again.

STAGE 2 – INVESTIGATE, QUANTIFY AND IDENTIFY REMEDIES

Investigation, quantification and identifying of remedies comprises the real work in problem solving. Individuals and perhaps small groups collect data, investigate theories and generally do the detective work to identify the root causes and importance of each. These are then reported to the Project Leader and team. Based on this information, possible solutions are identified from which the optimum solution will be chosen.

STAGE 2.1 – INVESTIGATE AND CONFIRM ROOT CAUSES

Investigating and confirming root causes is a difficult stage to write guidelines for as the exact nature of the work will vary immensely depending upon the specific project. People might be out collecting defects and investigating exactly what is wrong with them. They might be comparing the outputs of two offices. They might be testing theories about what is causing something to go wrong. People might be collecting data about different causes so they can identify which are the most important. Once done the findings should be reported back to the Project Leader and team at the next meeting.

STAGE 2.2 – IDENTIFY POSSIBLE SOLUTIONS

Possible solutions should be identified in the following manner. Revisit the Ishikawa diagram of possible causes and for each hear the result of the investigation carried out. If the cause has been confirmed as valid, brainstorm possible solutions for this particular cause. Do this in turn for each possible cause. As you go on, you may well find that a solution will eliminate more than one cause.

There are a couple of additional points you might want to consider at this stage. First, is there a possibility of blitzing the problem? This might take a number of forms such as focusing all efforts on removing it for a short period of time. Electrical appliance manufacturers are unfortunately quite well known for recalling all products of a certain model to do this. Second, consider the effect that the problem has had on your customers. Do you need to carry out a special exercise to show that the problem is over or offer them some form of recompense as a means of apology?

STAGE 2.3 – SELECT OPTIMUM OPTIONS

Once the brainstorm against each possible cause has been completed, list all the possible solutions on a separate sheet of flipchart paper if you have not already done so. Clustering (see Chapter 17) may be helpful here if the list is long. Against each make an estimate of what effect the implementation would have on the problem. Then identify criteria against which you wish to evaluate each solution. These might be cost, workload, ease of implementation or others as appropriate. Finally, go through the list again and use an evaluation matrix (see Chapter 19) to identify the optimum solution. The basic equation you are looking to solve is how much of the problem can you eliminate with lowest cost and effort. You may need to seek guidance from the Champion at this stage. Sometimes problems are so serious that they must be solved no matter what. For others a slightly lower rate of solution might be traded off against the cost of putting everything right.

STAGES 3 TO 6 – PILOT, IMPLEMENT AND CLOSE DOWN

The next stages of the problem-solving methodology are:

- *Stage 3* – Prepare for a pilot
- *Stage 4* – Carry out the pilot and review
- *Stage 5* – Implement on a permanent basis
- *Stage 6* – Close down the project.

These stages are detailed separately in Chapters 14 and 15 so follow the guidelines there. What you are looking for in your pilot is the eradication of the problem either completely or by the amount predicted when choosing your solution. If this is achieved, go ahead and implement. If not, you need to find out why it hasn't worked and identify alternative solutions.

12 Network methodology

Nearly every organization has a number of people doing similar jobs in different departments or locations who do not fall under the same line manager. It makes good sense for these people to meet now and again to make sure they are approaching their jobs in a consistent manner. This principle also applies between different organizations. Sometimes where there is a specialist in one organization, they might meet with their equivalents in other organizations to share experience and for mutual support. The success of these meetings is variable. Some are invaluable, others become coffee clubs or talking shops and attendance begins to dwindle. The purpose of network methodology is to secure a grip on these meetings and to provide a structure which will optimize their effectiveness. Using the methodology should enable the individuals to approach the job in a common manner, not duplicating effort, eliminating problems and prioritizing their efforts from an organizational rather than from their own point of view (see Figure 12.1).

The network methodology differs from the others in that it is not a step-by-step linear structure. There are, however, distinct stages. Stage 0 concerns what happens before the network is set up. Stage 1 relates to defining the purpose of the network and setting it up. Stage 2 is about running it. Another difference is that a network will have a much longer life-span than a project team. A project team will complete their specific remit and then wind up. A network is ongoing. Membership and the specific tasks being undertaken change but a network will continue as long as there is a need. Despite this there will still be a need to review progress and this is stage 3.

Networks have considerable potential, but it is often unfulfilled. Note also that although this chapter is written from the point of view of a network within an organization, the methodology applies closely to those between organizations.

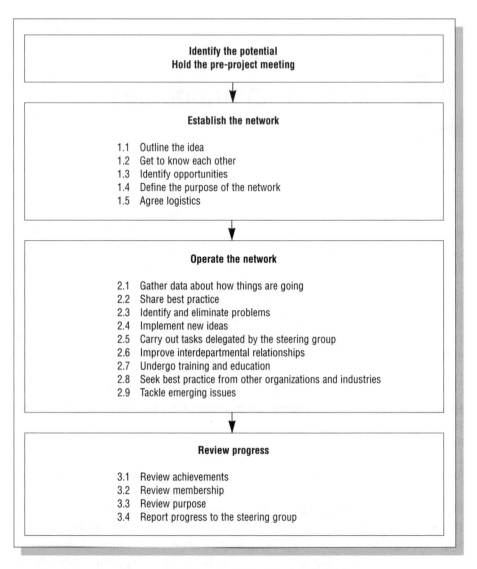

Figure 12.1 Overview of the network methodology

STAGE 0 – IDENTIFY THE POTENTIAL

HOW MOST NETWORKS ARE STARTED

While the theory says that it should be the steering group that identifies the potential for a network, in practice this is rarely the case. Nearly all the successful networks have been formalized by an individual learning about the methodology and saying 'that's just what I need to sort out such and such'. If you are that individual you have a number of options. If there is an existing meeting of which you are the chairperson or leader then start to use the methodology. If there is a steering group in your organization, go and see one of its members, get yourself a Champion and tie your network into the project-by-project infrastructure. If there is an existing meeting which you attend but you are not the leader, firm up a few ideas about what might be done differently if the methodology were to be adopted and then go and see the leader with these suggestions. Finally, if there is no existing meeting but you can see the potential for a network, put together some ideas about the scope and purpose of the network, who might be in it and some of the things that it might do. Then put your proposal to the steering group.

NETWORKS ESTABLISHED BY STEERING GROUPS

A steering group will often identify the potential for a network in two situations. First, there may be a number of quite small but important tasks which need to be carried out, often the implementation of something new. Taken alone they do not warrant the setting up of a project team but they are beyond the scope of one individual because they affect a number of sites. This is a good indicator of the potential for a network. The second common starting place for a network is for a steering group to ask itself 'exactly what do the so and so managers do when they get together each month?'. This might be a random thought or may be the result of reviewing the meetings structure in the organization. If this is the case then the steering group needs to allocate a Champion and start to define more clearly what is expected of the meeting, who attends and so on. Formalizing this meeting as a network within the project-by-project infrastructure will ensure that it follows the methodology and as part of this will make regular reports to the steering group so that they actually know what is going on and provide suitable direction. The advantage in establishing some networks for a steering group is that, whereas tagging on odd bits to project teams is a bad idea because it clouds the real purpose of the project, with a network you can keep giving it more and more to do.

STAGE 0 – HOLD THE PRE-PROJECT MEETING

Networks also need a pre-project meeting even if this is not strictly the start of something new. This should be the Champion, Project Leader and Quality Adviser. The agenda follows the standard format for all the project methodologies as detailed in stage 8 of the steering group methodology (see Chapter 6) with some additional tips for networks.

BACKGROUND

The Champion should explain the background to the network and how the potential was identified. If the network is being formed from an established meeting, the Project Leader will normally be the existing chairperson and they should outline some of the history of the meeting and what it has focused on in the past.

REMIT

The Champion should brief the Project Leader and Quality Adviser on the remit for the network. The most important aspect of a project remit for a network is not about a specific task but more importantly about the scope of the network. As far as specific objectives and timescales are concerned, these need to be defined for each individual project delegated by the steering group to the network. Keep the remit loose at this stage and ask the network itself to do some work on this at the first meeting.

SELECT TEAM MEMBERS AND IDENTIFY OTHERS TO BE INVOLVED

For a network, membership will be determined by the nature but basically should be all the people who do that particular job in the various departments or locations. The size of networks can be bigger than that recommended for project teams. Around 12 can work fine as long as you structure the meetings accordingly.

LOGISTICS

The reporting links between Champion and Project Leader depend largely on the nature of the work being carried out by the network. If they are undertaking a specific project, regular meetings may be required. At a minimum, the Project Leader should speak to the Champion following every network meeting. It is also a good idea to set the date for the first network meeting and decide if the Champion should attend to open this.

RESOURCES

A commitment to release all the network members on a regular basis is the most important resource required. Second, networks have benefited from some training in tools and techniques and the methodologies – more on this in stage 2. Consider also where the network is going to meet.

PROJECT LEADER AND QUALITY ADVISER

As far as a network is concerned, the Quality Adviser will have two main tasks. The first of these will be to help plan and run each meeting particularly the application of tools and techniques. Second, the Quality Adviser needs to help in the ongoing development of the individuals into a team.

STAGE 1 – ESTABLISH THE NETWORK

Stage 1 concerns setting up the network. It is best accomplished in one go at an all-day meeting. Use stages 1.1 to 1.5 as the basis for the agenda for this.

STAGE 1.1 – OUTLINE THE IDEA

The idea should be outlined by the Champion or Project Leader and is simply an explanation of the thinking behind the network for the benefit of the members. At this stage provide an overview of the network methodology so people get an idea of the sort of things they will be doing as the network develops.

STAGE 1.2 – GET TO KNOW EACH OTHER

While all project teams should develop good team dynamics and work together effectively, this aspect is particularly important where networks are concerned. A good chunk of time should be devoted to some form of personal introductions exercise. There are two aspects to this. First, concentrate on some personal information about each individual. The CV exercise is a good idea for this. Next focus on some information about their job. The Quality Adviser might want to prepare a remit, for example covering key responsibilities, what they like, dislike, or achievements. This theme should be developed as the network progresses. Details of the CV exercise and further ideas for warm-up exercises are in Chapter 21.

STAGE 1.3 – IDENTIFY OPPORTUNITIES

Next the group should move to developing ideas about what the network might accomplish. You need to get some specific ideas here and could use either pairwork (see Chapter 21) or brainstorming (see Chapter 17) to generate a list. Following this, clustering and classification into high, medium or low priority (see Chapter 17) is a good idea. Any specific projects delegated by the steering group also need to be added to this list. The resulting prioritized list can be used as a feed into the regular network meetings.

STAGE 1.4 – DEFINE THE PURPOSE OF THE NETWORK

Now that people have a good idea of what they can hope to achieve, it is advisable to take a step back and examine the purpose of the network. The best way to do this is to produce a short statement of purpose. Try using a snowball (see Chapter 21) to achieve this. Each individual writes a couple of sentences explaining the purpose of the network, then pairs up with someone else to refine and combine their work, then the groups combine until a single statement is achieved.

STAGE 1.5 – AGREE LOGISTICS

Use the logistics check-list in Chapter 22 as the basis on which to agree logistics. Two points to give extra attention to are where to hold the meeting and how often. If the network brings together people who work at different locations, it may be a good idea to visit some of these as part of the cycle of meetings. The meeting itself would then incorporate a guided tour of the location, perhaps involving some key individuals. This gives people an opportunity to see at first hand what is going on elsewhere in the organization. As to frequency, a monthly meeting linked to the organization's meeting structure would be advisable. Vary this rule if you know better or have more frequent meetings if the network is undertaking an important project.

STAGE 2 – OPERATE THE NETWORK

Stage 2 concerns routine network meetings. There are two aspects to this stage. The first is actual project work, removing problems, implementing new ideas and carrying out tasks delegated by the steering group. The second aspect is more developmental for the individuals, the network and the organization. This includes undergoing training, education, improving relationships and looking outside the organization for new ideas. It is worth emphasizing again that network methodology is not linear so don't work through stages 2.1 to 2.9 in order. Pick those which are most appropriate to the current situation.

STAGE 2.1 – GATHER DATA ABOUT HOW THINGS ARE GOING

Data is a source of lots of ideas for a network. Data can be collected about customers, process performance and errors using the data collection, display and analysis methodology (Chapter 13). It can also be used to compare performance at different locations, the underlying causes and thus identify best practice.

STAGE 2.2 – SHARE BEST PRACTICE

'Share best practice' is a phrase often bandied about. How do you go about it? This is a little more difficult so here are two suggestions. First, include it as an agenda item at an early meeting and ask the network members to brainstorm (see Chapter 17) ideas for sharing best practice between them. Second, identify key areas of work where it would be useful to share best practice. Then ask for a volunteer who thinks that they have got this aspect of work pretty much under control. For the next meeting they should prepare a short presentation about how this works at their location. This can be followed by questions and answers and the generation of ideas for further improvement. Where there are processes involved, it might be useful to construct deployment flowcharts (see Chapter 18) so that they are better understood and can be standardized across the organization.

STAGE 2.3 – IDENTIFY AND ELIMINATE PROBLEMS

Problems should be listed using brainstorming and then categorized into high, medium or low priority (see Chapter 17). Problems will normally fall into one of two categories – those that are being experienced by most or everyone in the network and those that are only being experienced by one or two people. As far as the latter are concerned it may well be the case that another network member has already done some work to eliminate the particular problem and that this solution can simply be adopted elsewhere. For problems common across the network it will be necessary for the group to apply problem-solving methodology (see Chapter 11).

STAGE 2.4 – IMPLEMENT NEW IDEAS

Part of the role of the network should be to come up with new ideas. These ideas might be the result of data collected, might be generated by means of a special session or might just emerge from the routine operation of the network. The network may need to use planning methodology (see Chapter 9) or the piloting methodology (see Chapter 14) to introduce these.

STAGE 2.5 – CARRY OUT TASKS DELEGATED BY THE STEERING GROUP

The tasks delegated by a steering group may be many and varied. Examples might be to gather some data, implement a new idea, remove a problem, help another project team implement its recommendations or a major project in its own right. The network should use the appropriate methodologies, tools and techniques to carry these tasks out. Sometimes it is appropriate to form sub-groups of the network to tackle these. Additional contact with the Champion will be necessary to ensure the success of these and it may also be necessary to make presentations to the steering group.

STAGE 2.6 – IMPROVE INTERDEPARTMENTAL RELATIONSHIPS

Improving interdepartmental relationships is almost an outcome of network methodology rather than a specific activity. However, there are a few specific actions that can be taken. First, the network can ensure it works cooperatively between departments and, as mentioned earlier, might want to visit different locations. Second, the network can act as a catalyst to remove problems between departments, offering to investigate and eliminate these.

STAGE 2.7 – UNDERGO TRAINING AND EDUCATION

The network must continue to develop its knowledge and skills. These fall into two categories. First, technical training and education in the specific area of work. Second, training and education in quality, project-by-project methodologies, tools and techniques. Identify potential areas, prioritize these and arrange as necessary, if needed seeking authorization from the Champion. Training and education need not always be an expensive business – there are often trainers or experts within the organization who can provide this.

STAGE 2.8 – SEEK BEST PRACTICE FROM OTHER ORGANIZATIONS AND INDUSTRIES

Stage 2.8 concerns looking outside rather than inside the organization all the time. There are a number of ways in which this can be achieved. Members of the network might attend conferences and then report back highlights, key learning points and ideas to the next meeting. Many organizations are also happy to host visits so draw on your contacts both formal and informal. The key to this is for these not to be day trips but to have a formal session afterwards maybe using brainstorming (see Chapter 17) with headings like 'what they do better than us'.

STAGE 2.9 – TACKLE EMERGING ISSUES

Tackling emerging issues is the 'catch all' stage. One of the key purposes of a network is to provide mutual support among the members and to be flexible in how it operates. Thus any member should be free to agenda any issue which is worrying them or with which they need help. Establish a routine that makes certain these issues are placed on the agenda in advance otherwise there is a danger of there being an unruly odds and sods session at the end of each meeting.

STAGE 3 – REVIEW PROGRESS

Stage 3 should be undertaken at roughly six- to nine-monthly intervals. This is the review stage where the network sees how it's doing.

STAGE 3.1 – REVIEW ACHIEVEMENTS

Achievements should simply be listed, perhaps using the notes from earlier meetings. Be sure to include both 'hard' and 'soft' improvements so that you might have an example of improved performance alongside something more anecdotal such as improvement in working relationships. However, be as specific as possible and where you have data to prove your point make sure you use it. It may also be worth listing and totalling any cost savings the network has made. Finally, review what the network originally set out to do and identify any objectives that have not been achieved and the reasons for this.

STAGE 3.2 – REVIEW MEMBERSHIP

Make sure that the current membership is correct. Is there any obvious imbalance between the contribution from each individual? If yes, why? Are there one or two individuals who are not members of the network who keep being drawn into its work and should these be invited to join on a full-time basis?

STAGE 3.3 – REVIEW PURPOSE

Next, review the statement of purpose produced at the outset. Has this been adhered to? Does it need revising in the light of experience?

STAGE 3.4 – REPORT PROGRESS TO THE STEERING GROUP

The final part of the review process is for the network to make a presentation to the steering group. A suggested format is shown in Figure 12.2.

(1)   Introduction – the presenters.

(2)   The network, membership and purpose.

(3)   Achievements to date including personal development and key
       learning points.

(4)   Work in progress and next steps.

(5)   Any specific support required from the steering group.

(6)   Summary.

(7)   Questions and answers.

Figure 12.2 Suggested format for a presentation to the steering group by a network

13 Data collection, display and analysis

We asked one hundred managers about how they use data.

We asked:	Our survey said:
Do you collect or use data?	Yes.
How much use is it to you?	Not much.
Do you know what it is telling you?	Not very often.
What do you do as a result?	Not a lot.

Most organizations are overflowing with data. Senior managers receive monthly performance statistics and nod knowingly when someone refers to these at a meeting. For example, income is 2 per cent up on last month and the number of complaints has gone down by 30. There has been an improvement so we can relax for another month. Unfortunately, most data available in organizations suffers from one or more of the following:

- The wrong thing is being measured in the first place.
- The data collected is inconsistent or inaccurate.
- Once collected, the data is displayed in an inappropriate manner, often thick reports consisting of lots of tables or single figures with no context.
- The meaning of the data is poorly understood.
- Few, if any, actions are taken as a result.

The move towards a project-by-project approach results in the use of data becoming more prominent in an organization. This happens for a number of reasons. Quality Adviser and quality skills training raise awareness about the importance of a systematic approach to work and the use of data. Project teams begin to collect data about customers, process performance and errors. This data is then presented to senior managers at steering group meetings. Additional training may be provided specifically in data collection, display and analysis. As a result people begin to see the weaknesses in existing data and start to overhaul this.

DATA AND THE PROJECT METHODOLOGIES

- Steering groups may wish to collect and use customer satisfaction data to identify possible projects. They should also use 'questions to ask when presented with data' later in this chapter to help evaluate recommendations from projects.
- Planning methodology requires collection of customer data to understand needs and expectations, the use of key performance indicators to measure the achievement of anticipated benefits, data collection during the pilot stage and review of achievements.
- Quality improvement team methodology requires collecting data about customer requirements plus before and after data about customer satisfaction, process performance and errors.
- Problem-solving methodology requires data to be collected to identify the magnitude and causes of things going wrong.
- Network methodology suggests that data is collected in areas that are within the responsibility of network members as a means of monitoring progress and identifying areas for improvement.

DATA IN YOUR EVERYDAY WORK

Perhaps the biggest area of opportunity for an individual as far as data is concerned is to apply these ideas to your everyday work.

- Do you know how you spend your time?
- Do you know if you were busier this week than last week? If you think you were, by how much? Are you busier than you were this time last month or last year?
- Are your customers happy with the service you're giving?
- Who spends the most money with you?
- How many telephone calls do you get each week? What about?
- How are you doing against budget?
- How much have you spent on stationery this year?

These are all questions you can answer with specific data rather than vague answers and it only requires a little effort. Collecting data in your everyday work will help you do a better job, identify areas for improvement, help you see patterns in your work and, as a result, increase your efficiency and hopefully satisfaction. There is nothing worse than not knowing how you're doing.

DAUNTED BY DATA?

Many people have been put off using data by experience at school. This methodology, however, is intended to be commonsensical and practical. The gathering and use of data can initially seem very daunting. It is also fair to make the assumption that most people who need to do this will not have a degree in statistics but they will be able to differentiate between information that is useful and that which isn't. Almost everybody will have produced a few simple graphs at school. If you can do this, then you can understand and apply the basic concepts needed for successful data collection, display and analysis.

SOME NOTES ABOUT USING THE METHODOLOGY

Of all the methodologies this is the one where you need to be most selective. If you follow every stage this will become a job for life. Be clear and specific about what you want to collect and why. As usual, the methodology adopts a comprehensive check-list structure (see Figure 13.1). Omit the stages that do not apply to your particular piece of work.

STAGE 1 – DETERMINE THE STRATEGY

Determining the strategy is the 'why are you doing this?' stage. It involves being clear about why data is being collected and what you are going to do with it. It is here that you decide whether you are collecting data about your customers, your processes, problems or more than one of these.

STAGE 1.1 – ESTABLISH WHY DATA IS NEEDED

Be sure that you are clear why you are going to collect data. The most common reasons are:

- to understand the customer better
- to understand how a process is performing
- to investigate errors
- to help make a decision
- to prioritize
- to make forecasts or predictions.

Other reasons include:

- to prove a point
- to convince

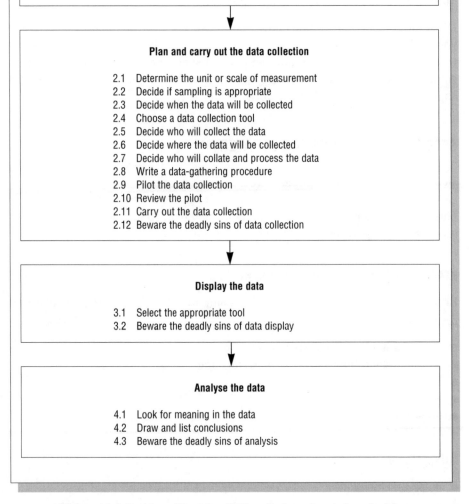

Determine the strategy

1.1 Establish why data is needed
1.2 Determine what customer data is needed
1.3 Determine what employee data is needed
1.4 Determine what process performance data is needed
1.5 Determine what error data is needed
1.6 Establish the data type
1.7 Think how the data will be used
1.8 Consider existing sources of data
1.9 Beware the deadly sins of strategy

Plan and carry out the data collection

2.1 Determine the unit or scale of measurement
2.2 Decide if sampling is appropriate
2.3 Decide when the data will be collected
2.4 Choose a data collection tool
2.5 Decide who will collect the data
2.6 Decide where the data will be collected
2.7 Decide who will collate and process the data
2.8 Write a data-gathering procedure
2.9 Pilot the data collection
2.10 Review the pilot
2.11 Carry out the data collection
2.12 Beware the deadly sins of data collection

Display the data

3.1 Select the appropriate tool
3.2 Beware the deadly sins of data display

Analyse the data

4.1 Look for meaning in the data
4.2 Draw and list conclusions
4.3 Beware the deadly sins of analysis

Figure 13.1 Overview of the data collection, display and analysis methodology

- to impress
- to eliminate debate.

STAGE 1.2 – DETERMINE WHAT CUSTOMER DATA IS NEEDED

To understand the customer better either factual, needs and expectation or satisfaction data can be collected.

Factual data is information about your customers themselves such as:

- age profile
- male or female
- where they live
- ethnic origin.

Customer needs and expectation research asks questions like 'what do you want?' and 'what don't you like?'. Useful questions to consider when deciding what you need to know from customers are:

- What do customers want?
- How customers use your product or service.
- The key quality characteristics, for example clean, on time, accurate.
- What don't your customers like?
- Problems they encounter.
- What improvements would they like to see?
- How important are specific aspects of your product or service?

Customer satisfaction data measures how happy people are with specific aspects of your product or service. Everybody will have seen some sort of questionnaire asking for satisfaction information. Even your local fish and chip shop has one.

Please tick appropriate box:	Excellent	Good	Fair	Poor
Quality of Fish	☐	☐	☐	☐
Quality of Chips	☐	☐	☐	☐
and so on.				

Use brainstorming, clustering and then must-should-could (see Chapter 17) to determine what you need to find out under each of the three categories of customer data.

STAGE 1.3 – DETERMINE WHAT EMPLOYEE DATA IS NEEDED

Data about the workforce and what they think is another important part of project work. This can be broken down into the same categories as customer data. Factual data is about the workers themselves, needs and expectation research asks them their opinions and satisfaction data asks how happy they are with specific aspects of the job. Factual and satisfaction research is really the responsibility of senior managers. However, you may well wish to collect data about what people think about proposals you might have. Use the same tips as for customer data if this is the case.

STAGE 1.4 – DETERMINE WHAT PROCESS PERFORMANCE DATA IS NEEDED

Key performance indicators provide data about a specific aspect of the process under study. This might be, for example, how long a particular stage of the process has taken, how long the whole process has taken or how many items have been processed. Key performance indicators can also provide information about how the process is performing over time – are things getting better, getting worse or staying the same? It is also useful to know what variation is present – for instance, what are the highest and lowest values. If you have a deployment flowchart of how a particular process works, use this to look for measurement points.

The following are suggested as places where measurements might be taken:

- at the beginning of a process
- at the end of a process
- at decision points
- at customer–supplier interactions (wherever there is an interaction between different people or departments).

Consider also if the following or any other possible sources of variation in a process might be important:

- time to time
- machine to machine
- person to person
- day to day
- shift to shift
- location to location.

Some examples of process performance data:

- Number of days taken to complete a repair to a property.
- Amount of money owed in rent arrears.
- Tonnage of waste transported each day.
- Tonnage of waste transported on each lorry.
- Income per month.
- Number of transactions per day.

- Number of patients treated.
- Waiting time from arrival to treatment at a casualty department.
- Number of televisions produced each shift.

Use brainstorming, clustering and must-should-could (see Chapter 17) to determine what process performance data you would like to collect.

STAGE 1.5 – DETERMINE WHAT ERROR DATA IS NEEDED

Error data is in many ways similar to performance data. The main difference is that error is not only about quantification (how many) but also about analysis (where, why and what sort). Some ideas about what you might want to collect are:

- How many errors?
- Where are they occurring?
- What is wrong?

Use the same clues as for key performance indicators in stage 1.4 when determining where to measure.
   Some examples of error data:

- causes of delays to trains
- reasons for non-payment of rent
- reasons for emergency repairs
- reasons for lorries arriving with underweight loads.

Collection of error data is particularly important in the problem-solving methodology and I strongly recommend this context rather than a one-off data collection. If you are using problem-solving methodology you will have already constructed an Ishikawa diagram to identify possible causes. These are the factors about which you need to collect data.

STAGE 1.6 – ESTABLISH THE DATA TYPE

This needs to be established to help select the most appropriate collection and display tools in stage 2. There are three data types:

- variable
- attribute
- qualitative.

Variable data occurs on a continuous scale. Although this scale can be broken down into infinite graduations, a precise numerical value can be given. Examples are temperature, length or time. Attribute data (sometimes called count data) either satisfies or does not satisfy a simple criterion and can be counted in single units. Examples are on or off, right or wrong, red, blue or green. Qualitative data occurs on a sliding scale but can not be given a numerical value and requires an opinion. Examples are taste, helpfulness or comfort. To illustrate the three data types, these are key quality characteristics that might be important to a shopper:

- waiting time at the checkout (variable)
- availability of goods (attribute)
- cleanliness of the shop (qualitative).

Qualitative data is the most difficult to measure but is often most important to the customer:

- friendliness
- service
- ease of use
- sense of security
- comfort.

Go through the lists of customer, process performance and error data you have drawn up and classify each as to whether it is variable, attribute or qualitative. Once you have done this review those that are classified as qualitative. You may wish to break some of these down to make them more easily measurable. This is done by identifying the variable and attribute components. An Ishikawa diagram

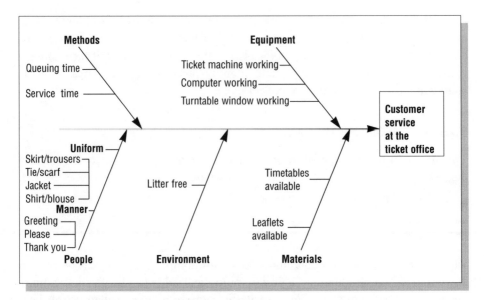

Figure 13.2 Ishikawa diagram breaking down a qualitative attribute

(see Chapter 18) showing the qualitative attribute you wish to measure in the head is a useful tool to help with this. Figure 13.2 shows an example of this. Here the qualitative attribute of customer service has been made more specific by narrowing it down to customer service at the ticket office. The wearing of the correct uniform has been identified as one element and this has been broken down into attribute components. Over on the methods arrow queuing and service time have been identified as variable components.

STAGE 1.7 – THINK HOW THE DATA WILL BE USED

Now is a good time to check that the data you propose to collect will be useful. The following check-list should help eliminate any wasted effort.

- Is the data relevant?
  For example, if the aim of a project is to speed up a process, timings will need to be taken.
- Who is the data intended for?
  Is it for your own use? If it is not only going to be seen and used by you, who are you going to show the data to, what are they interested in and what would you like them to do as a result?
- Imagine the data laid out in front of you.
  What might it tell you and how would you use this information?

Bear in mind that you will sometimes be asked to collect data for statutory reporting purposes. A good example of this is data collected for the Patient's Charter in hospitals. This data is required in a particular format and has many rules about what is included or not in the 'charter figures'. The result is that charter figures bear little resemblance to what has happened in real life. This is also true of school league tables, and many others. If you have to produce data that is suspect for statutory reporting purposes, make sure that you are clear in your own mind about the difference between this and reality.

STAGE 1.8 – CONSIDER EXISTING SOURCES OF INFORMATION

Data which you collect at first hand especially for the purpose you have in mind is known as primary data. However, most organizations already collect vast amounts of information. Secondary data is that which has already been collected for another purpose but you believe it may be useful to you. Possible sources of secondary data are:

- Any information already being collected.
  The reliability and format of this data must first be validated.

- Comparable processes elsewhere in the organization or in other organizations. However, ensure that the comparison is valid and that the nature of the measurements are also comparable.
- Customer research.
- Customer complaints.
  This data is often heavily biased towards a particular aspect of a product or service.

STAGE 1.9 – BEWARE THE DEADLY SINS OF STRATEGY

✖   Collecting comparative data about apples and oranges.
     Can you compare an inner city school with a country school? One office with another? On some things probably, on others definitely not.

✖   Information overload – if it's collectable, collect it.

✖   No customer for the data. Who is the data meant for and what are they expected to do with it?

✖   Duplication of data production. A good example is finance departments and personnel departments producing figures about staff numbers and payroll costs – of course the two sets of data are never the same!

✖   Collecting data to embarrass or punish people.
     League tables are a good example of this.

✖   Selective collection of data. This involves using only part of the whole picture to prove a point.

STAGE 2 – PLAN AND CARRY OUT THE DATA COLLECTION

OVERVIEW OF STAGE 2

Before you start this stage, find the nearest car park. Count the number of cars in it. Say how many are red. Say how many are large. Say how many are old. If there is no car park handy, go around your home or office and count the number of pieces of electrical equipment. Say how many are modern. Say how many are clean and how many are dirty. Make a note of any difficulties you encounter. Once you have completed stage 2, revisit your list and see if there are any parallels with the data collection you are about to do. Stage 2 consists of careful planning for the data collection including selection of the appropriate tool. A data collection procedure is developed and then piloted before the exercise is carried out for real.

STAGE 2.1 – DETERMINE THE UNIT OR SCALE OF MEASUREMENT

Go through the list of data you wish to collect and write against each the unit or scale of measurement you wish to use. For variable data you might need to choose between centimetres, metres, feet or inches, seconds, minutes, hours or days. For attribute data this is likely to be by a unit of that attribute, number of people, number of households, number of red cars, number of boxes. For qualitative data, you may have to define the unit you are going to use. This is often done by creating your own scale – poor, fair, good, excellent.

STAGE 2.2 – DECIDE IF SAMPLING IS APPROPRIATE

It is often too great a task to collect 100 per cent of the data, particularly where customer data is concerned. In this case, a sample should be taken. The purpose of sampling is to get as much information as possible with the minimum of effort. Sampling is an area where, if in doubt, you should seek expert help. It is important that a representative sample is chosen. This will need to be of at least a certain size depending on the nature of the whole group under investigation, known as the 'population'. The sample must be selected so that there is an equal chance of any of the whole population being chosen. This is called random sampling. Sometimes stratified sampling is required. For example, if a population consists of a mixture of age groups or ethnic backgrounds, you would need to determine what percentages apply and select a sample which reflects this. Other examples of this might be staff from different offices, finished articles from different assembly lines and so on. Once again go through your list of data to be collected and say whether or not it will be possible to collect data from the whole population or whether a sample will be taken.

STAGE 2.3 – DECIDE WHEN THE DATA WILL BE COLLECTED

Questions to consider at this stage are:

- Over how long a period will data be collected?
- How often should data be collected?
- Starting when? (date/time)
- Finishing when? (date/time)

Another decision for performance and error data is whether it is possible to collect it 'real time' – as the process operates – or in arrears from any records that might be kept. As a general rule, real time collection is preferable.

STAGE 2.4 – CHOOSE A DATA COLLECTION TOOL

There are many and varied data collection tools, techniques and instruments and it would be possible to write a great deal about each. There are, however, a few simple tips that should be adequate in most situations. The level of detail shown here is largely related to the complexity of the tool. Run through the list of data you wish to collect and write the appropriate tool against each. Once again, if in doubt, seek expert help.

Data collection form

A data collection form is used for all three data types, variable, attribute and qualitative. For process performance and error data, this is the tool used most often. As the name suggests, this is a form specially designed for the occasion by those involved in the data collection. In addition to the specific data required, record the date, the name of the data collector and any other relevant information. The most important tip here is 'keep it simple' both for the purposes of collection and collation.

Tally sheets

Tally sheets are particularly useful for collecting attribute data and are basically a simpler version of the data collection form. The attributes are listed on the sheet and the number of occasions denoted by ticks or 'five bar gates' (卌 II).

Computer generation

Computer generation can be used for all three data types but is most often used for variable and attribute data. Secondary data is pulled out of an appropriate database. Early involvement of the computer people in the organization is essential to the success of this method.

Photography

Photography can be useful for collecting qualitative data such as tidiness. A master photograph can be used to show how things should look and subsequent photographs taken for comparison.

Technical instruments

There are a whole host of technical instruments, mainly used for collecting variable data. Suitable for collecting data such as weight (scales), length (ruler), temperature (thermometer), porosity (?!), tensile strength (?!) and the anatomy of aliens (tri-corder).

Questionnaire

The questionnaire is the tool most often applied when collecting customer data. A written questionnaire is produced which is usually completed by the respondents themselves. The design of questionnaires is a complex subject but some simple guidelines will stand you in good stead. Use brainstorming, must-should-could and chronological clustering (see Chapter 17) to generate a list of specific questions. Then apply these tips when designing the questionnaire itself.

✔ Have a brief introduction. Explain the purpose of the questionnaire to the respondent including what the results will be used for.

✔ Consider confidentiality and if this needs to be mentioned in the introduction.

✔ Keep the number of questions as low as possible.

✔ Be careful about the language used. Avoid leading questions and jargon.

✔ The more 'open questions' used, for example 'What do you think about ...', the more analysis will be required. If possible aim for questions with a 'yes', 'no', 'poor', 'fair', 'good', 'excellent' answer. Alternatively, try multiple-choice answers – 'Choose the answer which most closely corresponds with your opinion.'

✔ Make sure that the questionnaire looks attractive and follows a logical sequence. Chronological clustering should help with the second of these.

✔ Don't ask a customer questions that you should know the answer to. For example, 'Does our office open on time?' Focus on things that only the customer knows something about. For example, 'Are our opening hours convenient?'

✔ Make sure that the answers to questions are going to be useful. Following the example above, if everyone answers 'no' to the opening hours question you're not much further forward. You won't have any information about when you should be opening.

✔ Beware of questions that focus on the negative aspects of your product or service, for example 'Do you think our toilets are dirty?'

✔ For customer satisfaction data, construct a rating scale as shown in the example in Figure 13.3.

✔ Consider how the questionnaire will be distributed – in person or by post.

✔ Consider an incentive to encourage people to respond. A response rate of 20

Please rate the following aspects of our service:

Tick appropriate box:	Unacceptable	Poor	Satisfactory	Good	Excellent
Speed of response	☐	☐	☐	☐	☐
Courtesy of agent	☐	☐	☐	☐	☐

Figure 13.3 Customer satisfaction rating scale

per cent is considered quite good for a questionnaire so this may be worthwhile. Beware having an incentive that will appeal only to a specific part of your sample and invalidate it or encourage replying twice.

✔ Consider how completed questionnaires will be collected or returned.

Some common pitfalls:

✖ Over-ambitious questionnaire resulting in too much raw data.

✖ Inappropriate sample – too small, too large or unrepresentative.

✖ Questions worded so that the answers given are not useful.

✖ Use of too many open questions resulting in too much analysis.

✖ Use of arbitrary numerical ratings – 'our customers think we are seven out of ten' – so what?

A useful alternative to questionnaires is to seek the views of or involve front-line customer contact staff, maybe in a focus group.

Interviews

Like questionnaires, interviews are mainly used to obtain customer data. They are particularly useful where a vital few respondents such as key customers have been identified. The chief disadvantage of this tool is the high cost in terms of time and therefore money. Additionally, the interviewer can be the cause of much bias in a survey so a certain skill level is required. Interviews should also be well structured. Use brainstorming, must-should-could and chronological clustering (see Chapter 17) to originate the questions and the same tips as for questionnaires for the detailed design work.

Focus group

A sample of respondents are brought together and asked questions in a group setting. A skilled group worker such as a Quality Adviser is needed to lead such a session. Make sure that the session is well structured and questions are carefully worded. If you are running a series of focus groups, make sure that the same structure and questions are used. Beware these common pitfalls:

✖ Unrepresentative sample.

✖ Contagion – the discussion focuses on a specific aspect which the whole group catches.

Mystery shopper

The mystery shopper is someone unknown to the front-line staff at a particular location who goes and acts as a customer to test a specific aspect of service. This is not designed to catch people out but to collect data. The use of this tool also needs to be well structured and the mystery shopper well trained and briefed in what they are looking for.

STAGE 2.5 – DECIDE WHO WILL COLLECT THE DATA

For customer data a special exercise will have to be carried out. This is also possible for process performance and error data. Often when data is being collected as part of a project, the team members will carry out collection. However, sometimes it is possible to ask the people operating the process to collect the data as they work. In this case consideration needs to be given to whether the data collection will interfere with the running of the process. The person making the measurement should understand what is required, have been trained to do the task, and perform this task in the same manner as colleagues making the same measurement.

STAGE 2.6 – DECIDE WHERE THE DATA WILL BE COLLECTED

Where the data will be collected might be obvious or it might not. Often the data can only be collected where the work is carried out. If you wish to examine a faulty product, you may want to take it away from the production line. If you are conducting an interview or running a focus group you need to find a suitable room.

STAGE 2.7 – DECIDE WHO WILL COLLATE AND PROCESS THE DATA

If the data is being collected as part of a project, this is often done by members of the project team. If not, consideration needs to be given as to who will do this, particularly if this is likely to be a big job. It can be useful sometimes to have the data processed by computer rather than manually. A simple spreadsheet will normally suffice.

STAGE 2.8 – WRITE A DATA-GATHERING PROCEDURE

A data-gathering procedure now needs to be produced. This is a clear set of instructions as to how the data will be collected, incorporating all the elements of stages 2.1 to 2.7. This is also a useful check to make certain that all the preceding stages have been completed and that all decisions are clear.

Operational definitions are particularly useful at this stage. An operational definition specifies how something should be observed, and in what manner it should be judged or measured, in order to remove any variation caused by different interpretations between individuals. It must be made clear exactly what is being measured and how the measurement is being made. The aim is to obtain a definition all agree with and that will give the same result no matter who does the measuring. As an example, the 'arrival time of a ship' might be defined as when the ship passes the harbour entrance. If so, is this the time when the bow or the stern passes the entrance? Does this matter? Alternatively, it might be measured as when the ship first touches the dock. A third measurement might be when all mooring lines are secured to the dock. Are any of these important to the customer? Perhaps a better measure might be the time when the doors are opened to allow disembarkation. Even this measure might not be appropriate to the last person in the queue to disembark. Another example is a rust-free component. Does it matter if 1 per cent of the surface area is covered by rust? What has to be rust free – surface, sides, base, all or some?

STAGE 2.9 – PILOT THE DATA COLLECTION

No matter how meticulous the planning of data collection is, there is always a chance that some factor 'in the real world' has been missed or underestimated which could invalidate the data collection procedure or any data collected. A pilot run must be conducted so that it can be confirmed that the data collection procedure works. A pilot needs to strike a balance – big enough to show up any problems but not so big that it produces masses of work. Use the principles shown in Chapter 14, 'Piloting your proposals'. It's not necessary to use the complete methodology but make sure you cover all the angles.

Try to anticipate what resistance there might be to your data collection. A spanner in the works for many enthusiastic data collectors is that their attempts at data collection are rarely greeted with glee from those involved. Doubt and suspicion are more common reactions.

- Consider potential areas of resistance.
- Consider what people in the area under study might want you to find out and might not want you to find out. (In my days working in a ticket office it was standard practice to hold some cash back and account for it on the less busy days – particularly Sundays when you were paid at an enhanced rate. That particular scam is no longer possible because of computerization. New methods are no doubt used nowadays.)
- Make certain that the purpose of the data collection and how the information will be used is understood. Provide an opportunity for questions to be answered.

STAGE 2.10 – REVIEW THE PILOT

There are four main tasks at this stage:

1. Review the data collection procedure with those involved.
2. Review collation and processing with those involved.
3. Review the usefulness of the data generated.
4. Amend the data-gathering procedure as a result.

STAGE 2.11 – CARRY OUT THE DATA COLLECTION

Carrying out data collection is where many people start when they are thinking about using data. Hopefully your efforts will now be successful. Monitor progress regularly to ensure that there are no unforeseen problems and that consistency is maintained throughout the data collection period.

STAGE 2.12 – BEWARE THE DEADLY SINS OF DATA COLLECTION

✖ Collecting data in different ways and then comparing it.

✖ Asking people to collect data without telling them why or how it will be used.

STAGE 3 – DISPLAY THE DATA

OVERVIEW OF STAGE 3

The choice of data display tool will result in the success or otherwise of your analysis. The secret of stage 3 is simply to select the right visual tool. If you do this it will mean that the tool does your analysis for you and you need only glance at the data to draw your conclusions. As with the data collection tools, the data display tools are many and various and some are more complex than others. The rule is 'keep it simple'. You will need to refer to Part IV for further details on most of these tools.

STAGE 3.1 – SELECT THE APPROPRIATE TOOL

To use this section, refer back to your original lists of the data you have collected which state whether it is customer, process performance or error and variable, attribute or qualitative. Use the following which suggests tools for the various data types. See which best fits your application.

1. *Attribute data* – how often something is happening. Try a bar chart. A Pareto chart is better when you are interested in prioritization. (See Chapter 20.)
2. *Attribute data* – where something is happening. Try a measles diagram combined with a Pareto chart. (See Chapters 18 and 20.)
3. *Variable data.* Try a run chart. This is particularly useful for displaying time-related variable data such as the performance of a process. Even more powerful when used in conjunction with a histogram of the same data. This displays time-related data as a frequency distribution allowing you to see the spread, location and shape of a population of variable data. A control chart (a run chart with arithmetic mean, upper and lower control limits added) allows for easy identification of special and common causes of variation. (See Chapter 20.)
4. *Qualitative data.* Try the Kano model. This is used to break down customer information into basic, performance and distinctive elements. (See Chapter 18.)

STAGE 3.2 – BEWARE THE DEADLY SINS OF DATA DISPLAY

✖ Overuse of averages.
 Averages hide an awful lot of information such as highest and lowest values, variation and patterns over time.

✖ Use of aggregate data.

Lots of different sets of data added up to produce totals.

✖   Use of percentages instead of actual figures.

✖   Using different scales on graphs and then comparing them.

✖   Too much data on one graph.

✖   Over-presented graphs – three-dimensional or multi-coloured. The presentation actually detracts from the information being shown.

✖   Displaying time-related data in tables or as a bar chart – always use a run chart.

STAGE 4 – ANALYSE THE DATA

OVERVIEW OF STAGE 4

If you have chosen a good data display tool, analysis will be quite simple. Stage 4 is the culmination of the methodology. You should now be in a better position to predict, understand, make decisions and manage.

STAGE 4.1 – LOOK FOR MEANING IN THE DATA

Here is a check-list to run through either by yourself or with a team. Read through the list and ask yourself do you see any of these in your data?

- Surprises.
- Trends – upwards, downwards, cyclical (related to another variable), seasonal.
- Variation – the difference between the highest and lowest values, whether measurements are quite closely spread or vary a lot.
- Outliers or special causes – odd measurements here or there which don't really fit with the rest of the data.
- Similarities.
- Differences.
- Correlation between different factors.
- Confirmation of what you thought was going on.
- Pareto principle – vital few, useful many (see Chapter 20).
- Gaps – what the customer wants versus what they are actually getting, desired performance versus actual performance.
- Stratification – the population splitting into component parts with different characteristics.

STAGE 4.2 – DRAW AND LIST CONCLUSIONS

Finally, when everyone involved has seen the data, it is useful to have some time dedicated to discussing 'why', 'what', 'how', 'when', 'where' and 'who' type questions. Key learning points and theories should be noted as a session of this type unfolds.

STAGE 4.3 – BEWARE THE DEADLY SINS OF ANALYSIS

✖ Jumping to conclusions.

✖ Comparing two sets of figures out of context.

✖ Confusing specifications or targets with process capability – how something should work with how it is actually working.

✖ Mistaking or treating special causes of variation as common causes. Something unusual has happened but it is treated as a common occurrence.

✖ Mistaking or treating common causes of variation as special causes. Something is happening all the time but it is treated as unusual or a one-off. In fact, the process may well need to be redesigned to remove this cause.

✖ Comparing apples and oranges – making invalid comparisons.

✖ Ranking or producing league tables without meaning. In any group of data, there will always be a highest value and there will always be a lowest value. The rest will always be in between. The question is what do these differences mean? Best and worst are not useful labels.

✖ Looking at an unrepresentative sample or over too small a period of time.

✖ Looking at a run chart and setting a target because 'it's been done once, it can be done again'. You first need to understand the underlying factors.

✖ Looking back and saying 'we were doing better or worse then' without an understanding of the underlying factors.

QUESTIONS TO ASK WHEN PRESENTED WITH DATA

Using the data collection, display and analysis methodology should make you much more aware of the validity of data which you encounter every day. If you want to consider whether or not data you see can be relied upon, try the following check-lists.

QUESTIONS TO ASK YOURSELF

- Do I believe what I'm seeing?
- Does it feel right?
- What conclusions can I draw?
- Is this presented in the best way?
- What is this data actually showing?

QUESTIONS TO ASK THE PRESENTER

- Why are you showing me this?
- What was the sample size?
- How was the data collected?
- Who collected the data?
- Did you encounter any problems gathering the data?
- Over what period was the data collected?
- Is this all of the data?
- Is this data aggregated?
- If yes, have you got the real data anywhere?
- If a target is shown, how was it established?
- What conclusions have you drawn? How?
- What would you like me to do now?

If you are presenting data, then these are questions you should be prepared to answer.

14 Piloting your proposals

Each of the project methodologies suggests that a pilot should be conducted before full-scale implementation of any change (see Figure 14.1). To pilot means to try it out on a small scale first. This means that:

- Any unforeseen problems can be resolved before full-scale implementation.
- The risk of large-scale failure is reduced.
- Proposals can be further improved and fine tuned before implementation.
- Feedback can be obtained from people outside the project team.
- Data can be collected whether or not the proposals meet their objectives.

PREPARE FOR A PILOT

STEP 1 – DETERMINE THE APPROPRIATE TYPE OF PILOT

Pilots can be conducted in one or more of the following ways. The choice will normally be determined by the nature of the project.

1. *In a limited area.* This is appropriate when the proposals will affect more than one site or area. One is chosen to pilot the proposals while the remainder retain the old method of working. For example, new ticket machines are usually tried out at a small number of stations before full-scale introduction. If there are a number of options for a pilot area, choose open-minded people rather than force the trial on an unwilling group.
2. *Over a trial period.* This is appropriate when it is possible to try out the proposals and then revert to the old method of working once the pilot is over. For example, a new product might be made available for a limited period of a month or so to test customer reaction and demand.
3. *Through parallel running.* This is particularly appropriate when you wish to minimize risk. Both the old and new methods are operated in parallel for a time. If the new system does not work, it is possible to revert quickly to the

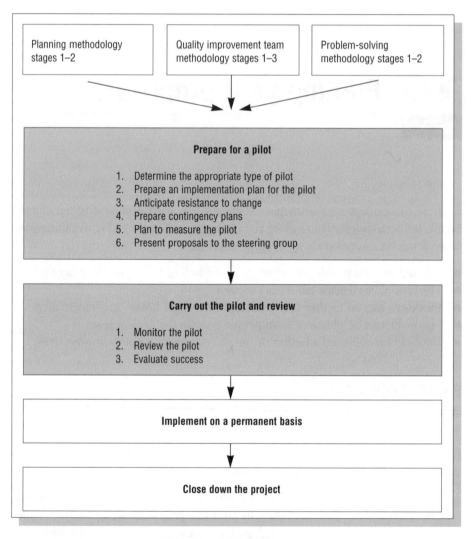

Figure 14.1 Piloting in context

old. For example, if you are swapping from a manual to a computerized payroll system, you might want to operate both systems for a week as a trial.

4. *Have a trial run or practice.* This one is self-explanatory. For example, if you are organizing a conference you might want to hear each of the speakers practise their presentation.

5. *Build a prototype or a pre-production model.* This applies particularly in engineering projects. When new designs or technology are being introduced, a prototype may be built to test these. The purpose of a prototype is to test design and concepts – it is not ultimately intended to enter service and there

may be significant change between a prototype and any subsequent production build. A pre-production model is slightly different in that this is the first of the production run and subsequent models of the production series will be built to the same design. However, a gap is usually built in the production schedule between the pre-production model and subsequent build to give both the production line and finished product a 'shake down'. This allows detail changes to the production process and finished article. Although this sounds very engineering based, a slightly softer example is the production of new uniforms for members of staff. It is usual to produce some prototypes and ask staff for their views plus test them in day-to-day work situations. An administrative example might be the production of a sample of a new form.

6. *Build a model or mock-up.* This is a cheaper and quicker way of producing a prototype and again this is a concept most often used in engineering. However, there are many service industry applications. Designers use mock-ups and drawings to test reactions to publicity material for example. Staff uniforms and office refurbishment are areas where drawings are an important first stage. Architects might produce a model showing changes to a housing estate.

7. *There are some situations where a pilot is not possible.* If implementation has to be a 'big bang', then the focus should be on contingency planning and early review. However, you should still view the early days of implementation as your pilot and plan as below.

STEP 2 – PREPARE AN IMPLEMENTATION PLAN FOR THE PILOT

1. *Produce deployment flowcharts* (see Chapter 18) of any new processes. These will identify precisely what and who will need to change and how the new processes will operate. They will also be useful for briefing and training.

(1)	What changes are to be made?
(2)	What are the component parts of each change?
(3)	Who will be involved?
(4)	In what sequence must the changes be made?
(5)	By when must each change be made?
(6)	Who will be responsible for each change?

Figure 14.2 Implementation check-list

2. *Consider the changes in detail.* Use the implementation check-list (Figure 14.2) to be as specific as possible about any changes. If you have produced deployment flowcharts of new processes these will help you to answer these questions.
3. *Consider training requirements.* Use the training requirements check-list (see Figure 14.3) as a prompt. Many of the answers to this will be linked to those above.
4. *Produce the plan.* Use the above information to produce a planning grid for implementation, perhaps by applying chronological clustering (see Chapter 17). Actions, by whom and when need to be identified.

STEP 3 – ANTICIPATE RESISTANCE TO CHANGE

If the project-by-project approach has worked well, then people doing the job should have been involved in the project from the start and anyone affected should have been kept informed. However, change and resistance to it is a large and complex area and it would be unwise to assume that there will be no resistance. Consider the following and any effect they might have. Add any actions that you identify as a result to your implementation plan.

1. Who has been directly involved and who hasn't? Participation is the single most important factor in eliminating resistance to change.
2. If you are following the planning methodology, review your list of possible problems and obstacles produced earlier.
3. Have all existing rules, both written and unwritten, been considered?
4. Are there any current practices that will be difficult to alter?
5. Might anyone be afraid about job security?
6. Consider what the change might do for self-respect and perceived status of the people affected. What might people have to give up?
7. What other worries might people have?
8. How might the proposals affect each individual? Are there any specific personal circumstances that need to be taken into consideration?

(1)	What training will be required?
(2)	Who needs training?
(3)	When will training take place?
(4)	Who will provide the training?

Figure 14.3 Training requirements check-list

The single most important factor in successful management of change is an opportunity for those people affected to be involved and participate in the planning process. The project-by-project approach plans this participation into the methodology. However, difficult decisions still need to be made. Here is a list from personal experience of 'difficult decisions' that cause angst for those affected:

- restructuring of pay and conditions of employment
- relocation
- closure or merger of departments and locations
- reorganization of the staffing structure
- changes to shift patterns
- retraining or learning new skills – 'How will I cope?'

These are areas that are very important to people for all sorts of reasons so tread very carefully. Sometimes a decision will need to be made which makes good sense for the organization but is likely to adversely affect some of the people. Where this is the case, be certain that those affected are identified and dealt with individually and with consideration.

STEP 4 – PREPARE CONTINGENCY PLANS

No matter how carefully you have planned your pilot there will still be banana skins carefully positioning themselves for your benefit. Whether you need to have contingency plans depends very much on the nature of the project. Small-scale, low-key projects can probably skip this step. However, if what you are piloting is vital to the running of the organization or is highly visible either inside or particularly outside the organization, then contingency planning is vital. This step is thinking about what might go wrong, what the effect would be and how to minimize those risks. Here are a few prompts to identify areas where contingency plans might be needed:

1. What is most likely to go wrong?
2. Anything that would have a devastating effect.
3. Critical parts of the implementation plan that would delay the entire pilot.
4. What happens if there are slippages in timescales?
5. Are there any weak links?
6. What would make a good story in the newspapers if it went wrong?

If you identify areas that you particularly want to keep an eye on, then it may well be worth allocating a project team member or manager to monitor this during the crucial stages.

STEP 5 – PLAN TO MEASURE THE PILOT

It is no good having a pilot if you don't know how successful it's been. This step ensures that you have quantifiable data about how things went. You need to obtain:

1. Data about what the customers think – customer data.
2. Data about what the staff think – employee data.
3. Data about how the pilot performs – process performance data.
4. Data about anything that goes wrong – error data.

Use the work you have already done to identify what you wish to measure and use the data collection, display and analysis methodology (see Chapter 13) to help with this. A word of warning – don't collect too much data. Use brainstorming to identify all the things you would like to measure and then apply must-should-could to narrow this down (see Chapter 17). Add the necessary actions to your implementation plan.

STEP 6 – PRESENT PROPOSALS TO THE STEERING GROUP

Proposals should now be presented to the steering group by the Project Leader and team. Findings and work to date will be presented along with the proposals for moving forward. The Champion should have updated the steering group at key stages so they should already have a good idea about the work carried out. However, this is likely to be the first time they will have seen the work and proposals in detail. The steering group needs to provide two things. First, their endorsement and agreement to the proposed option and pilot. Second, their support in managerial terms for the pilot. Use the suggested format shown in Figure 14.4.

The Quality Adviser will help the Project Leader and team plan, structure and practise their presentation. The Quality Adviser might well attend on the day but will not normally participate in the actual presentation except perhaps in any questions and answers about the methodology.

The steering group is unlikely to say 'yes' there and then. They will need to consider and debate the proposals. The result of this should be fed back to the Project Leader and team by the Champion.

CARRY OUT THE PILOT AND REVIEW

STEP 1 – MONITOR THE PILOT

There is little to write on monitoring the pilot as everybody involved should be

> (1)   Introduction – the presenters.
>
> (2)   Project remit.
>
> (3)   Approach taken, people involved, progress to date.
>
> (4)   The current situation: impact on customers, process performance.
>
> (5)   Proposals: options evaluated, criteria used, preferred option.
>
> (6)   Proposed pilot: why chosen, implementation plan, measurements to be taken, expected results.
>
> (7)   Support needed from the steering group. (This includes any decisions they need to make of a strategic nature.)
>
> (8)   Conclusion.
>
> (9)   Questions and answers.

Figure 14.4 Suggested format for presenting recommendations and pilot proposals to a steering group

out and about looking after it. Progress of both the pilot and data gathering should be closely monitored to make certain that it is progressing as planned and providing the information needed. Here are two tips for this step:

✔   Schedule a meeting for early in the pilot for an initial review.

✔   Team members should keep notes of anything interesting they notice or hear during the pilot.

STEP 2 – REVIEW THE PILOT

As soon as possible after the pilot the views of the staff involved should be sought. This can be done through a questionnaire, interview or focus group and there are further tips about this in the data collection, display and analysis methodology. Ask questions specific to the situation but you may also want to try some of the following:

1. What did you think generally?
2. What went well?
3. What went badly?
4. What was easier?
5. What was more difficult?
6. What did your customers think?

The next step is to hold a full review meeting. Consider carefully who needs to attend and use the check-list in Figure 14.5 as the basis for an agenda.

STEP 3 – EVALUATE SUCCESS

If the objectives of the project remit and the anticipated benefits have been achieved in the pilot, implementation on a permanent basis should now be planned. If not, consider what refinements need to be made and if a second pilot is necessary.

(1)   Reminder about objectives.

(2)   Achievement of critical success factors.

(3)   Results of the data collection:

- Customer data

- Process performance data

- Error data

(4)   What the staff thought.

(5)   Problems and resistance encountered, revisions on the day, contingency plans activated.

(6)   Unexpected side-effects, both positive and negative.

(7)   Effectiveness of the implementation plan.

Figure 14.5 Pilot review check-list

15 Implementing your proposals and closing down the project

The final tasks of a project team are to take the results of their pilot, implement them across the organization so that they will be long lasting and then to close down the project (see Figure 15.1). Part of the implementation stage is to error proof the process. This is one of the last pieces of work a project team has to undertake and is necessary to ensure consistency, reliability and that there is no deterioration once the project team has disbanded. Closing down includes the tidying up of loose ends and a formal review of the project.

IMPLEMENT ON A PERMANENT BASIS

STEP 1 – PLAN FOR FULL-SCALE IMPLEMENTATION

The plans developed for the pilot should now be reviewed, improved and adapted for full-scale implementation. In the case of large-scale projects, it is often desirable to consider phased implementation site by site. Use the check-lists from the piloting methodology to ensure your implementation plans are comprehensive.

Consider, too, whether or not all points have been covered. No matter how comprehensive and well thought out your pilot has been, it is unlikely that it has included every eventuality, at every hour of the day, the whole year round. Do the following make a difference?

- Early in the morning or late at night.
- Weekends.
- Bank holidays, Christmas or the new year.
- Spring, summer (when it's hot), autumn or winter (when it's cold).

STEP 2 – ERROR PROOF

Error proofing is necessary to prevent mistakes in the new method of working

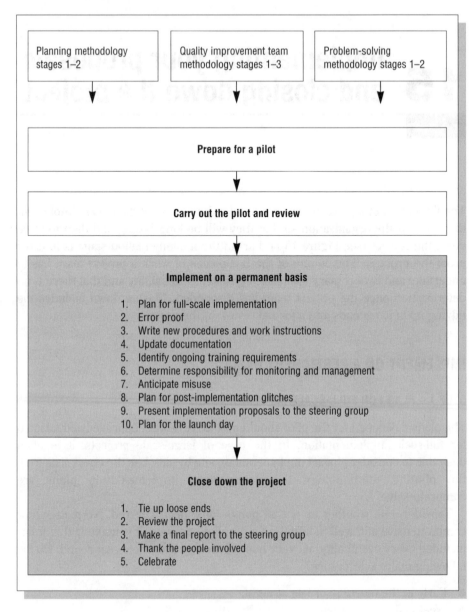

Figure 15.1 Implementation and close down in context

and to ensure there is no slipping back into the old way of working. Error proofing is also important where there is a specific aspect which would cause a lot of trouble if it went wrong. Safety-related issues fall into this category. To give two railway examples, many European railways have a check digit on their locomotive numbers. Fleet number 111.212 indicating class 111, number 212 is painted on the locomotive and recorded as 111.212-7. This final digit is calculated by a mathematical formula from 111.212. On every occasion that locomotive number is entered into a computer, the formula is automatically applied to the first six digits. If the answer is not seven, then the computer tells the person making the input that they have made a mistake. The second example goes back more than 100 years. Signals and points which switch trains from track to track are controlled from signal boxes. An early problem was human error. What happened if the signaller set signals or points that conflicted? So one train might receive a clear signal when the points were set to let another train cross in front of it. The solution was mechanical interlocking. The levers in the signal box were connected to a series of mechanical devices that made it impossible for the signaller to set conflicting moves. Interlocking, both mechanical and electronic, is still in use today because it is still an extremely efficient form of error proofing.

There are many different ways you can error proof something, largely depending on the nature of the project. Use the following approach:

1. Introduce the concept of error proofing to the group.
2. Identify key areas that you wish to error proof.
3. Run through the tips for error proofing below to stimulate thinking.
4. Brainstorm (see Chapter 17) specific ideas for error proofing.

Tips for error proofing

✔ Provision of check-lists or visual instructions at key stages.

✔ Use of pictures, diagrams or flowcharts instead of written instructions.

✔ Revision of the order in which tasks are undertaken.

✔ Altering the layout of a form in an administrative process.

✔ Altering the layout of the workplace.

✔ Mechanical checks in manufacturing processes.

✔ Some form of automatic cross-check in computer systems.

✔ Colour coding.

✔ Audible or visual alarms.

You will notice that inspection is not recommended as a technique for error proofing. This is because inspection does not prevent errors – it merely identifies them or weeds them out once they have been made. If you are tempted by inspection consider audit or random sampling as an alternative. These both work on the same principle. They also will not prevent an error but may highlight where errors are occurring.

STEP 3 – WRITE NEW PROCEDURES AND WORK INSTRUCTIONS

Written procedures and work instructions should be produced for any new processes. Deployment flowcharts (see Chapter 18) are an excellent tool to use as the basis for these as they provide a quick visual reference. If you have already produced these as part of the project, it should be quite easy to convert them into a procedure or work instruction. It is wise once again to consult the people who are expected to use these procedures and involve them in production.

STEP 4 – UPDATE DOCUMENTATION

Consider if alterations will be required to any written policies or job descriptions. You may need to involve the personnel department now. If your organization is accredited in any way, to the ISO 9000 series for example, you may need to revise and update any documentation relevant to this.

STEP 5 – IDENTIFY ONGOING TRAINING REQUIREMENTS

The implementation plan will already incorporate arrangements for training. Three further tasks related to training now need addressing:

1. Any existing courses, training materials or manuals need to be identified and amended.
2. Any induction programme or training for new entrants needs to be considered.
3. Is any follow on or developmental training required?

STEP 6 – DETERMINE RESPONSIBILITY FOR MONITORING AND MANAGEMENT

Step 6 is the hand-over from the project team back to line management. Future results and performance must be monitored continuously to identify emerging trends, making sure there is no deterioration and identifying opportunities for further improvement. Any data collected earlier in the project will provide a good basis for what to monitor but the questions given in Figure 15.2 also need addressing.

STEP 7 – ANTICIPATE MISUSE

Anticipating misuse is the philosophical part. In life regardless of how nice you make things someone will want to spoil it for you either deliberately or

(1)	What measurements are appropriate?
(2)	Who will make these and how will they do so?
(3)	What records need to be kept?
(4)	To whom will the results be reported?
(5)	How will this information be used?
(6)	What needs to happen if performance drops?

Figure 15.2 Check-list for monitoring future results and performance

accidentally. Brainstorm (see Chapter 17) possible areas of misuse. Some areas you might want to think about are:

- Vandalism – what happens if someone wants to break it?
- Theft – what happens if someone wants to steal it?
- Children, babies and animals – what happens if someone or something plays with it or tries to swallow it?
- What might people try to use it for apart from the original purpose?

STEP 8 – PLAN FOR POST-IMPLEMENTATION GLITCHES

No matter how good the planning, there will always be something that arises after implementation that will need sorting out. Have a process in place to deal with this. Don't assume the project is over once the overall deadline has been met.

STEP 9 – PRESENT IMPLEMENTATION PROPOSALS TO THE STEERING GROUP

An initial presentation will already have been made to the steering group prior to the pilot. This second presentation is to report the results of the pilot and make proposals for permanent implementation. Use the format shown in Figure 15.3.

STEP 10 – PLAN FOR THE LAUNCH DAY

Following steering group approval, consideration should be given as to how all those involved will be made aware of implementation. Written advice is an obvious and traditional method but there are many options for reinforcing this, such as altering the appearance of the workplace on launch day. Alternatively, you may want to have some special activities in the lead up to launch day. Brainstorm some ideas (see Chapter 17). These might vary from road shows to ceremonial ribbon cutting.

(1)   Introduction: the presenters.

(2)   Project remit.

(3)   Summary of previous presentation.

(4)   The pilot – results, revisions made as a consequence.

(5)   Proposals.

(6)   Implementation plan, planned measurements and expected results.

(7)   Support needed from the steering group.

(8)   Conclusion, questions and answers.

Figure 15.3 Suggested format for presenting implementation proposals to the steering group

CLOSE DOWN THE PROJECT

STEP 1 – TIE UP LOOSE ENDS

Check the project remit one last time to ensure that all the objectives have been met. Loose ends should be identified and sorted out.

STEP 2 – REVIEW THE PROJECT

The approach taken to the project, tools used, team composition and contribution should be reviewed to identify lessons learned for those who follow. Improvements to and tips about using the methodology should be identified (see Figure 15.4). Document the results of the review and perhaps publish findings and experiences both good and bad as well, as this will provide important information for others.

STEP 3 – MAKE A FINAL REPORT TO THE STEERING GROUP

Step 3 might be a written report or a final presentation but should include final results and lessons learned about the methodology.

STEP 4 – THANK PEOPLE INVOLVED

Publish the formal end of the project and thank people who have made a contribution.

Say what went well, was easy, what went badly, was difficult under each of the following headings. Identify lessons learned.

(1)   The remit.

(2)   The approach taken – methodology.

(3)   Tools and techniques.

(4)   Use of data and measurement.

(5)   Team composition.

(6)   Teamwork.

(7)   Support and guidance.

(8)   Results.

Figure 15.4 Project review check-list

STEP 5 – CELEBRATE

The nature of the celebration will depend entirely upon the team. Often this will take the form of a drink or meal. My favourite was a quality improvement team consisting of civil engineers from InterCity West Coast. They had been working on improving their bridge inspection process and had made some remarkable improvements. Their treat to themselves was a visit to the Forth Railway Bridge.

16 The methodologies in action

This chapter focuses on teams using one of the project methodologies. There are three examples from Liverpool Housing Trust, one each of planning, quality improvement team and network, and another from Greater Manchester Waste. If you haven't already done so you should read the background in Chapters 4 and 8. You will see the links from selection of projects and how the Champions work in practice. The last example will show you how it is possible to put together a tailor-made methodology to suit a specific need.

PLANNING DEVELOPMENT STANDARDS

This is an interview with Steve Jones. Steve is Development Manager with Liverpool Housing Trust and was the Project Leader of the first team to use the planning methodology within the organization. The nature of the project is explained below but you might also be interested to know from the start that it took nine months, 25 separate meetings including 10 full group meetings and between 250 and 300 staff hours to complete 17 pieces of work, much of it detailed and technical.

Can you tell me a bit about the project?

STEVE:

The project was an examination of the standard of new houses we produce. There was a bit of history to the project before it started. We knew we had funding problems and we were grappling with how to sustain a decent quality of new homes given that the amount of money available was falling and was likely to continue to do so. Existing tenant satisfaction levels were high and the challenge for us was how we would sustain levels of satisfaction while designing housing which will last well into the twenty-first century. I personally had already done about 18 months' work but I wasn't getting anywhere because there was no structure. It had become a departmental issue within Development and it shouldn't have been. This was a Trust-wide issue and needed tackling as such.

What was your remit?

STEVE:

The objective for the project was 'to plan a house within cost constraints which will comply with criteria defined by the Housing Corporation's scheme development standards, LHT's policies and meet tenant requirements'. The Housing Corporation, by the way, is a government quango who fund and monitor Housing Associations. This was a pretty tall order, the equivalent of solve world hunger in my job, and my first reaction was 'how the hell am I going to do this?'. But when I worked through the remit with the Sponsor and Quality Adviser it needed the four elements of cost, Housing Corporation standards, LHT policies and tenant needs for it to be worthwhile.

What was it like to be asked to be Project Leader?

STEVE:

It didn't come as a surprise. I knew there was a major issue and I was pushing for it to be tackled. I was pleased to be asked and appreciated the challenge of being the first to have a go at a new methodology.

What were your first steps?

STEVE:

We had a sort of preliminary meeting to talk about how the remit was shaping up. Next we had a departmental training session and the training helped us to evolve the remit. Andy Barrett was my Quality Adviser and he also came on the training. Next we talked about key players. First, we put down everyone who could conceivably be involved. This gave us a long list which we sorted and then organized a planning meeting where we invited them all along.

Can you tell me a bit more about the planning meeting?

STEVE:

Andy and I were pretty daunted. We had a list of 20 people including Board members, directors, consultants, and LHT staff. We looked at the methodology and saw that a planning meeting should take place but we didn't know if it would work.

Basically we stage managed the whole thing. We followed the methodology to the letter but prepared scenarios in case it went wrong. We had prompts in case it was going off track. Andy and I planned it meticulously, we sorted out all the timings, practised our presentations, made sure everything was in the room, wrote up remits for everything, prepared handouts and it was this preparation that really made it work. Another problem we had identified was that not everyone had been on a quality course so Andy and I felt we had to do some grounding. Andy did a session on the basics of quality and we did a big section on identifying customers and customer satisfaction before we started work on it. The people who'd been on a quality course complained afterwards that we'd spent too much time on this but I would do the same again. Bearing in mind that I'd already done a lot of work and didn't want to waste it, I also did a session on that.

On the day I think the main reason we were nervous was not only the 20 people, some senior, but our main concern was that it would all go wrong. One of the problems we had was that one or two people wanted to talk about anecdotal problems but we directed them back onto what would be productive. Actually everybody clicked in quite quickly and the day went very well. Out of the planning event we were hoping to identify all the issues and identify a team of people to move them forward. The only thing we didn't do was attempt to produce a project plan. This was simply because there were too many people. The team did this later. Inevitably when you bring together 20 people, the resulting lists were long. We felt we needed to be brave and were strict on editing these to focus on the real issues.

How did you choose the team?

STEVE:

We already knew before we started who we wanted on the team and we suggested this to the key players. We wanted people who were either involved in producing the product or on the receiving end of it. We initially thought that we needed a tenant but who is representative out of 8 000 tenants? What we did instead was do a tenant survey to get a wider view.

Did you get it right?

STEVE:

In the end yes. When we started we were worried about two members. First, who would be the maintenance representative? Maintenance had not so far been terribly cooperative and I took a lot of advice from Andy. He knew people at his office and suggested someone with an open-minded approach. He was proved to be right. The other issue was that I wanted someone from Housing Management and my first choice was refused because the manager wouldn't release her. I got my second choice though and he did a decent job. One member we effectively gave up on. We tried various means of getting him to attend meetings but in the end took the approach of if he came, he came. I'm not sure if this was the right thing to do but it didn't affect the outcome of the project. We did still earmark him for specific work which he did a good job of and I was pleased about that.

How did you work with the Quality Adviser?

STEVE:

I know Andy very well and I think that helped a great deal. What was great was the planning of each meeting. We met before to make sure it was properly organized and he made sure we didn't wander off the agenda. He was great at getting people back to the topic. He also said 'do you want me to be a purist or contribute if necessary?' I wanted an effective team member and it would be daft to have a Housing Manager on the team keeping quiet when he had a useful contribution to make to the discussion. He also helped as well with the problem of getting on with Maintenance. He knew the guy very well and talked to him about the project and the contribution he could make.

How did it go with the Sponsor?

STEVE:

It worked well. I don't think we met as often as we ought to have done. I'm sure I'm worrying unnecessarily because the project was a success and we maybe didn't need to meet any more. There were key stages when we needed further direction and we met then, as necessary rather than regularly. Also we met when we were a bit worried about departing from the methodology and needed her guidance.

How did you use the methodology and tools?

STEVE:

We took the view not to get hung up on following the methodology word for word and to ask is this stage appropriate for this project? Some parts we followed word for word and others we interpreted for our project. Overall though we did follow the structure closely. We used brainstorming and clustering a hell of a lot. It's a useful way of bringing lots of issues together. We found the planning grid extremely helpful for the project plan. It gave us the planned approach to the issues we had to address and where we had to get to. We also used the Kano model. People kept referring to this all the time. We tried to break down what we put into a house into the three categories. We had 'must be there' such as a roof, 'more is better', storage space was a big issue in this category and 'delighters'. One delighter we've tried out is giving people choices of alternative design layouts. They didn't expect this and were pleased to be asked.

What data did you collect?

STEVE:

Probably the biggest chunk was the tenants survey. We designed a questionnaire and commissioned a survey of all new build tenants who had been in occupation between 18 months and two years, about 350 people. We started with a combination of things, knocking on doors and running focus groups with the open question, 'If you could, what would you change about your home or your estate?' This carried on until the answers were becoming repetitive, then we clustered all the answers and designed our survey around these issues. We also included some questions around issues that didn't come up. So, for example, we included some design layout diagrams and asked if you had the option, which would you like? We had a response rate of well over 60 per cent and this gave us a really solid base to decide if we were providing what people wanted.

Just to give an example of how we've followed some of these through, one big issue was heating controls. We filled a desk with heating controls from every manufacturer who'd send us one, which was a lot, and then played with them until we found the one that was easiest to use. One was selected and now we've fitted a sample of the controls in each of our district offices so that our Housing Managers can show tenants how to use them.

Generally, how do you think the project went?

STEVE:

I was delighted with it. As a Development Manager it gave me what I wanted, an opportunity to look at what was going on and make changes. I felt I'd been given the authority to get on with it and the freedom to be more innovative and try things out. I've got to say I thoroughly enjoyed it. When the team started to work as a team I was looking forward to each meeting and felt we were doing something really productive. The project allowed us to be more innovative rather than just be stagnant, continuing to produce the same product as we had done in the past. And the work resulting from the project is carrying on. It doesn't stop when the project finishes.

Not only did we change the product but we've also now got a structured way of agreeing further changes on a regular basis. Each review will lead to the next generation of schemes.

What was the best and worst moment?

STEVE:

The best moment was the reaction to the end of project report by the steering group. The thing in my mind was 'will LHT accept our recommendations?' and it wasn't until that point that I knew we'd get support. My worry was that senior managers would say 'thanks, that was interesting' and do nothing. I didn't find that attitude at all. We did the presentation and it was refreshing. They felt we'd tackled the issues and come up with a report that they could support.

The worst moment was minutes before the planning event started. It had been a bad morning all round. I'd burned my hand making the tea, a flipchart collapsed and a whole series of things went wrong, not for the want of planning. Luckily these didn't turn out to be omens.

What results can you see now?

STEVE:

The product is different, the houses we build now have changed. We know now where there is sensitivity in design and construction of houses because we consult tenants about the things they consider important. As a project it's very identifiable and easy to see the difference. What I'd like to do is continue to find more delighters. At least we are working in an atmosphere that allows us to do that now. Previously, it was easier to produce something that wasn't controversial. Personally, I like to see a bit more innovation. Purely from a job satisfaction point of view I don't want to be building the same little boxes year after year.

IMPROVING THE HAND-OVER PROCESS

Carol Crawford was the Project Leader for one of the first quality improvement teams in Liverpool Housing Trust. This project concentrated on the hand-over process for newly built properties, all the things that happen between work starting on a site and the contractor handing over the keys to LHT.

How did you get involved in the project?

CAROL:

The first thing I knew was when Derek Stewart who was the Sponsor and Dave Power asked me in and explained what was going on. They explained what they wanted and what the various roles were. I hadn't had any training at this stage and they chose the team members not me although I approached them to check if they were available.

How did you feel about being asked to be Project Leader?

CAROL:

Quite proud and excited about something new. I was confident about being able to do it but needed more information about how to do it. I was interested in quality and positive about it. I was a bit anxious about where to find the time from but you do find it.

Was the team selection right?

CAROL:

Yes. Everybody brought something different. The process affected every department in the Trust, the team were all from different backgrounds and brought their own points of view. Tina was a member from the point of view of setting rents, John was from Development where a lot of the process gets carried out, Pauline was from Housing Management and had been involved with work on-site and hand-overs previously. Janet was the Quality Adviser. She didn't get involved in the content but understood the basics of the process. Karen was the most reticent team member because she knew least about the process and Maintenance hadn't been involved in the past. However, she was interested in developing the role.

How did the team work together?

CAROL:

They were brilliant. It was quite unexpected. We'd never all been in the same room together before and no-one really knew how it would go but we had some fun as well as working hard. We gelled together and went from strength to strength. No-one was disinterested or didn't contribute. This really helped me as a leader.

How useful was the training?

CAROL:

Very, because it started us off on the project. I felt it was not just a course but had given us a kick-start. The deployment flowchart really got us going. One of the things that did happen was that we asked the Sponsor to alter the parameters of the project to include properties that are being rehabilitated and to move back where we started examining the process a couple of steps.

How did it go with the Quality Adviser?

CAROL:

Janet was excellent. She always had a tool or technique to suggest and really understood the methodology. It's essential to have a good Quality Adviser and for them to understand the methodology, what happens next and what that means for your particular project. We always had a pre-meeting of ten or fifteen minutes before the main one. Luckily we always seemed to be in agreement about everything. We're both from similar backgrounds and that might have helped. In the meeting itself I chaired, reviewed what we'd done and planned the next steps. Janet would do a warm up and then keep an eye on how things were going and keep us on track. I'd ask for advice when we weren't sure what to do next. It was very useful when she suggested tools and techniques when we got stuck.

How did it go with the Sponsor?

CAROL:

I get the feeling we didn't use him enough. He generally asked me to come in and update him and he kept an eye on us but we didn't ask him for help very often. Normally we worked things out for ourselves and I'd ask him to attend a meeting occasionally just to be seen, not particularly for a decision.

What did you think of the methodology?

CAROL:

It felt really in-depth and it was hard to get to grips with. You start to worry when you're on stage 2 for a long time but I found it best to concentrate on one stage at a time. We followed it to the letter and never skimmed over it and probably followed it too closely. We got a bit tied up in knots at times trying to work out what each stage meant for us. Next time I'll be more inclined to think of it more as a guide.

Which were the most useful of the tools and techniques?

CAROL:

Probably deployment flowcharting and clustering. We used clustering on the data we collected from tenants and staff. We spent a lot of time designing closed questions which gave 'yes' or 'no' answers and then had an 'any other comments' box. The comments turned out to be more interesting and important than the yes/no answers and this was a surprise. No chart could ever show this information so we put all the comments onto 200 post-it notes. These clustered into five groups of issues to be resolved and then we went back to the deployment flowchart to find out where the issues occurred in the process. We put the yes/no answers onto histograms.

Generally, how do you think the project went?

CAROL:

We were all on a high. By the time we made our recommendations to the steering group we were all quite proud. After that we had a more difficult stage. We had to wait for a pilot project. The process does not happen on a day-by-day basis so we needed a development that hadn't started. It also takes a long time from the start to end of the process. The keys have just been handed over in the pilot so I've now got to arrange a meeting to analyse what went on. Although success still needs to be proven one way or another I do feel we've achieved our objective.

What were the best and worst moments?

CAROL:

There was a really bad point, I don't remember exactly when, but somewhere just before data collection. We knew we needed to collect data but we needed to decide how we were going to do it. We had no experience and didn't seem to have anywhere to go for help. Looking back it seems obvious now but it wasn't then. The high point was when we got over this – we'd designed, piloted and completed the survey. This point was probably better than finishing the whole project. I think the most difficult parts wouldn't be the same again. What was difficult then seems silly now and it makes you realize how much the Trust has changed.

What would you do differently next time?

CAROL:

Specifically, if I was leading a group again, I would timetable the project as I now have a better idea of how long each stage takes. I would also split tasks up more among the team members and use the methodology as a guide rather than trying to make each stage fit the project. I would still be careful though, not to miss any stages out.

The whole idea of quality is evolving into something different all the time. Training and experience is building up and building up. Everyone is getting more geared up. I'd never have the same experience again because myself and others will approach it differently. Some people still view quality as something you apply to a project but I see it as a day-to-day thing. We're already working on larger projects like Dymchurch, a large transfer of homes from the council. At first we found ourselves slipping back into the old ways but we've now got a steering group, a clear remit and a project coordinator. It's easier to recognize when projects need better organization nowadays and how to go about improving things.

NETWORKING THE PAs

Networking the PAs is an interesting example of the network methodology in action. The first network I ever worked with was called the Fleet Technical Managers meeting and this was fairly typical. It brought together specialists who were based at different geographical locations and involved a lot of in-depth technical work. The example here is rather different in that it brings together a group of people who often find it hard to find a voice in an organization. Audrey Davidson is the Personal Assistant to Dave Bebb the Chief Executive at Liverpool Housing Trust. Audrey leads a network of PAs and secretaries called the Quality

Image Network. The QIN has been very successful in bringing together a group of people who aren't part of the same work team but who are vital to the functioning of the organization and must closely cooperate to get things done. I asked Audrey how the network came about and how things were going.

REMIT

The Quality Image Network exists to promote a consistent and coherent corporate image by using and developing the skills of LHT's PAs and support staff to:

- identify and coordinate work on a range of day-to-day projects throughout the organization
- develop systematic approaches to all projects
- establish and share best practice among members
- continuously improve standards and systems
- achieve cost savings wherever possible
- promote communications between the QIN members.

Can you tell me how the network came about?

AUDREY:

It came about after a quality skills course I attended. We were discussing a couple of projects that hadn't been successful. John who was running the course suggested network methodology might help. I found out more about it, then spoke to David my boss who wanted a full proposal. I then spoke to the other secretaries and personal assistants, took the proposal to Senior Management Group and went for it.

What were your first steps?

AUDREY:

Once we'd got Senior Management Group approval, the next step was to decide on projects. We had a day with John where we covered some quality training basics for the people who hadn't had any, tools and techniques and then brainstorming of possible projects, which we prioritized and then took back to Senior Management Group for approval.

Who are the members and how have they worked together?

AUDREY:

All the PAs, all the secretaries and a couple of key administrative staff who work with large teams which is just over a dozen people in total. We've worked together very well. We had a couple of sceptics at the beginning but when we started doing something they were fine. We learned a few lessons from the first projects and have altered the membership slightly to reflect changes going on in the organization.

Which of the tools and techniques have been most useful?

AUDREY:

We've done most of our actual work in the network meetings so group work techniques have been very important. Brainstorming and clustering have been important so that everyone gets a say in an organized way. We've also found TPN analysis useful mainly to identify areas requiring authority from above before we could proceed but it has also proved useful in starting to get delegated authority from the managers for those areas that directly affect our work.

How have you worked with your Quality Adviser?

AUDREY:

We've worked very closely and I'm not sure if we've stuck strictly to the Project Leader and Quality Adviser roles. We developed the ideas together, worked out the agenda together beforehand, Ronnie made sure the meetings ran to the agenda. We found we were getting a bit bogged down in the planning methodology and Ronnie encouraged us to be creative. He also made sure we didn't sell ourselves short and pushed us as well.

How have you worked with your Sponsor?

AUDREY:

It's been good. My Sponsor is David who is the Chief Executive and my boss. He's attended a couple of meetings and briefed us about what's going on in the Trust and for questions and answers. It was also useful that he saw at first hand what we were doing, the work that was going into the early stages of one of our projects and got a feel for the enthusiasm in the group.

What have been your best and worst moments?

AUDREY:

The best part has been working together as a group. We've got more understanding of the demands of each other, we're more likely to help each other out and we've raised the profile of PAs and secretaries. There's no worst bits although we've had a few difficult moments when people have slipped on their deadlines.

What has the network achieved?

AUDREY:

As well as greatly improving our working relationships, we've been working on the standardization of documents, the servicing of meetings, paper and stationery supplies and photocopier contracts. Take the paper supply contract, this is the sort of thing that normally floats through budgets. We now control it and have achieved substantial cost savings. People don't have to order it now. We worked out the usage and it gets delivered automatically. We just have to adjust it if there is a sudden fluctuation. We've also taken on the job of social committee – this year we had the best Christmas do for a long time – this was straight after the staff conference and the best kept secret in the

Trust, no-one knew where we were going – and we're organizing other evenings out for the staff.

What are your next steps?

AUDREY:

We've just had a review day and the key thing to emerge was that we'd done too much project work and not enough networking. We've decided to concentrate on one or two projects at any one time, do the research and analysis outside of the meeting and do networking when we're together. We're also tightening up on project monitoring. We also identified areas for our own development, like report writing and assertiveness training. The Sponsor, Quality Adviser and I will sort this out.

Have you got any other advice?

AUDREY:

Yes, two pieces. First, if you do something positive people will take notice but you've got to do it yourself. Second, you need to find the best way for your own particular network. You can't be prescriptive about it.

IMPROVING FLEET COMPOSITION

Ray Tasker has the best job title in this book. He is Pulverizer Manager at Greater Manchester Waste although he is currently seconded to the post of Transport Manager largely because of his involvement in the fleet composition project team of which he is the Project Leader. The company operates a fleet of around 60 heavy goods vehicles of several quite different designs. These operate from and to a number of sites. The purpose of the project was to look mainly at the make up and location of this fleet of vehicles.

Can you tell me something about the project?

RAY:

The project started out as investigation of fleet composition. This was an area where we felt we could improve dramatically in terms of both cost savings and efficiency. We started by looking at the overall picture and we found we were going places but not as quickly as we could have. We'd taken on too much so we focused on a narrower area with the same team.

How was the team chosen?

RAY:

Graham the Champion selected the team. We needed people with experience in the transport side of things, civic amenities (where the public bring their waste) and pulverizers (where waste is pulverized prior to being buried in a landfill site) so that

179

we had all aspects of the operation covered. I was chosen because of my pulverizer experience, we had a transport management consultant for his experience of legislation and Carol was my Quality Adviser.

How did the team work together?

RAY:

I thought we were excellent. As Project Leader the task was made easy for me because of the involvement and commitment of the team. I didn't feel it was my project, it was the team's. We've come in about four days behind schedule thanks to their efforts. We started in early November and finished in January. Our target date was linked to budget cycles.

How useful was the training?

RAY:

I don't think that I'd be able to do it without it. I could probably have muddled through but only as good as that. It certainly speeded things up and I think if we hadn't have done it the proposal wouldn't have been ready on time – we'd really have struggled.

How helpful was the Quality Adviser?

RAY:

Carol was very good indeed. She gave us guidance and kept us on track. As Project Leader I tended to get away from the methodology and into detail of the project. A Quality Adviser will get you back in line. She suggested tools and techniques while I focused on getting things done.

How did it go with the Champion?

RAY:

Fine. We kept meetings to a minimum because I had a very clear remit and deadline. He would enquire how things were going but Carol my Quality Adviser is also his secretary so we had another link there. I knew I could call on him if needed but it goes back to the clarity of the remit. I had no problems.

How closely did you follow the methodology?

RAY:

We tended to start by the book then maybe digress, but we soon drifted back into the procedures. If you were to ask me how useful it was, well, it got the result on time.

Can you take me through some of the key stages?

RAY:

The focus became the closure of a transport depot to base the vehicles where they actually did the work. First, we identified who would be affected and exactly what equipment we were talking about. Next we did site surveys to see if relocation was feasible. We found there would be no personnel problems, we could relocate them and the sites could accommodate what we wanted them to do. Next we calculated the savings from the closure and compared them against the extra costs for all the additional work – extra security, parking, fuelling, welfare facilities for the staff and equipment. We looked at the legal side and got advice from an expert not on the team. Someone else did a separate report about supervision requirements and we also did a matrix of potential mileage savings. After all this work we could see that the idea was feasible and next we set a realistic closure date once we'd listed the interdependencies, identified obstacles, who might object, identified training and considered installation of equipment. We also identified a couple of 'what happens if'; for example, what changes if a landfill site closes?

What were the best and worst moments?

RAY:

The best moment was reading the final draft of the report and being happy with it. The worst was in the middle of the project when I didn't think we'd meet the deadline. It was a very tight timescale to take on a major change but we got through.

Anything else?

RAY:

On a personal note it's the first time I've presented anything to Graham who is the Finance Director. I've nearly finished another project where the Champion is Pat who I've worked with for a long time and I knew how to finish it off in a style that he'd like. Graham is a bit of an unknown quantity and I could be totally off track. Luckily I've had help from Carol and I know that Graham likes things concise. The final report is only four pages long except for all the appendices and data. So I think that your relationship with the Champion is very important although I won't be half as daunted next time.

ADAPTING THE METHODOLOGIES

Tony Finnegan and I worked together in the railway industry and this piece, written by Tony, is interesting for two reasons. First, Tony starts with a look back at how things used to be before we started using methodologies. Second, Tony is a very experienced Facilitator and proficient at adapting the methodologies to suit a particular situation. The examples show how he has done this in two different projects. Tony writes as follows:

A BRIEF HISTORY

My first experience of facilitating projects was guided by what I could remember from an intense programme of training, personal judgement and considerable effort in trying to look like I knew what I was doing. Much of my training had concentrated on problem solving. In due course we realized that we needed to broaden the scope into process improvement and still further into applying an appropriate methodology for each project. When the first attempt was made at creating a clear structure for quality improvement teams to follow it was like manna from heaven. Judging this against my first experiences, it was at least 200 per cent improvement and I followed it religiously. We were becoming aware that if people were having problems of any sort, they wanted to set up a quality improvement team (QIT) to sort it. All manner of quango groups were setting up and calling themselves QITs, largely because it was fashionable to do so. We began to tailor our approach to the different nature of projects.

This work coincided with the onset of privatization of the industry and people moved away from setting up QITs, mainly because they had their eyes on other, more pressing matters. However, there were still quality champions in the organization and there was still plenty of project activity. When working with these champions it was important to be flexible in your approach. Here are some examples of projects I was involved in which used key bits of methodology but did not strictly follow them as written.

CUSTOMER RELATIONS

Our Customer Relations Department handles thousands of letters every month and often had an unacceptable number of days between receipt of letter and response. The organization was well aware of the importance of this service as it was our last chance of redeeming ourselves after delivering a poor service. An exceptional leader, Lucy Evans, had recently been appointed who had, as part of her organization, the Customer Relations Department. I would suggest that with less experience we might have approached the project thus:

Remit:	Reduce customer correspondence response time.
Method:	Set up a QIT.
One year later:	A few recommendations, probably good, but only part of the system improved.

Another approach (practised elsewhere) might have been to concentrate on sending an acknowledgement quickly as first response is what you are measured against. You can then take as long as you like to finalize the matter because you are not measured against that.

The actual method used was broadly based on steering group methodology and was a much more holistic approach which tackled the complete customer relations system. The first step was for the Champion and Facilitator to meet. The project was broken down into six key elements. Remits were then written for six projects including why each project was required, what was needed and how the projects should be approached. Some of these elements were the introduction of more flexible working practices, improving product knowledge and improving the quality of the response. Next, we did it like this:

- Arrange a meeting for the whole Customer Relations team (about 20 people). Explain reasons for the meeting. Request volunteers for Project Leaders and teams.
- Make final team selections.
- Train Facilitators.
- Hold project meetings.
- Have regular project review meetings.

- Propose improvements.
- Implement improvements.

Over the following year measurable improvements were achieved in all project areas. This included dramatic reductions in response times.

REVENUE PROTECTION

This was a project with the aim of implementing 'penalty fares' for people travelling without a ticket. An example of how this was introduced in another company:

Consultant:	'Penalty fares can save you hundreds of thousands of pounds per year.'
Managing Director:	'I want it implemented for the new timetable in four weeks.'
Result:	Shambles.

This time we adopted a combination of steering group and planning methodology. Nine objectives were given to the Project Leader by the Champion. The first stage was to hold meetings between the Project Leader, Facilitator and key operational managers. Each objective was dealt with in turn at the meetings and actions allocated to achieve them. The most sizeable of these was the introduction of penalty fares. A full project plan was developed to include:

- Identify services most vulnerable to abuse.
- Produce a roster of revenue protection for each service.
- Organize training for staff.
- Meet with the Rail Regulator.
- Introduce systems of measurement to gauge impact.
- Arrange publicity.
- Pilot.
- Phased implementation.

After one or two meetings I found that I was no longer required and retired gracefully. Result: success.

Part IV
Tools and Techniques

17 Tools for planning and organizing

The tools for planning and organizing will stand you in good stead in projects and your day-to-day work, whether you are an individual working alone or part of a team. These tools are not intended to be used in isolation. At their most powerful they are used sequentially, so brainstorming might be followed by clustering and then must-should-could. Always consider what you want to achieve, which of the tools will help you achieve this and what order they should be applied in.

WORKING WITH GROUPS OF PEOPLE

All of the tools for planning and organizing can be used by groups of people working together. A few simple guidelines apply to all of these:

- Make certain the people involved in the subject under study are present.
- Ensure everyone knows the purpose of the tool.
- Read through how to use the tool beforehand.
- Make sure the room is appropriately arranged. If using a flipchart, arrange the group around it so that everyone can participate. Consider where completed sheets will be displayed.
- Ensure that there is only one person leading at any one time. This is particularly important when carrying out clustering. If not, the result is likely to be several people moving post-it notes at once. Ideally the person leading should be a trained Quality Adviser.

WORKING ALONE

Although the tools have been written from the point of view of working in a group setting, it is possible to use clustering, must-should-could, the planning grid and TPN analysis when working as an individual. Brainstorming is not a tool designed for an individual but anyone can produce a list!

BRAINSTORMING

DESCRIPTION

Brainstorming is a tool which can be used by any group to produce a list.

WHEN TO USE BRAINSTORMING

- To generate lists such as:
  - problems
  - questions
  - ideas
  - options
  - things to do.

HOW TO USE BRAINSTORMING

1. *Prepare the equipment.* You will need a flipchart stand, pad, pens, blu-tack and post-it notes. Write onto post-its so that you can rearrange the list after the brainstorm.
2. *Choose a scribe.* Use the Quality Adviser if you have one. Failing this, one of the group will have to do the writing. Remember, if this is the case they will find it much harder to contribute – if someone is concentrating on writing, their mind will not be on the subject being brainstormed.
3. *Define the focus.* Detail what the brainstorm will be concerned with, check that everyone is clear about this and write it at the top of the first sheet of flipchart paper.
4. *Start the brainstorm.*
   (a) Go round in strict rotation as this makes sure there is balanced contribution.
   (b) Be concise.
   (c) Record every idea exactly as it is said.
   (d) As soon as the scribe finishes writing down one idea, the following person shouts out the next.
   (e) No comments allowed from other members of the group.
   (f) 'Pass' is allowed.
   (g) Ensure completed sheets are displayed so that people can see them.
5. *Freeform.* Once 'pass' becomes more common, end the strict rotation and invite further contributions at random.
6. *Sort the list.* This is the key to the successful use of brainstorming. Use either clustering, TPN analysis, must-should-could, or a planning grid depending on the nature of the list. During this stage eliminate any duplication, look for gaps and clarify where necessary.

Tips

✔ Brainstorming is taught on many courses every day. Each course will teach a slightly different version. The following are excellent rules but you can choose to disregard any of them, particularly if you know the group well, but first consider the purpose of the rule and what the implication of not using it might be.

✔ Make certain you know the context of your brainstorming session – why you are doing it, what tool you are going to use next and what you will do with the results.

✔ Beware of the common misconception that brainstorming is a creative tool – it just generates lists. If you put a group with average creativity in a room and have them do a brainstorm, they will produce a list of average creativity. If a high degree of creativity and innovation is required, find some techniques specifically designed to promote creative thinking.

✔ Brainstorming is not a good analytical or problem-solving tool when used in isolation. This is because it takes the group in fairly random directions mainly dictated by the whims of and associations made by the human brain. If you wish to analyse a particular situation, use one of the tools for analysis.

✔ It is debatable whether you should use structured brainstorming, going round in strict rotation, or freeform, where anyone can shout out an idea. Structured brainstorming allows everyone to have an equal say and so encourages quieter people to contribute while at the same time limiting the impact a dominant person might have on the group. Always start with structured brainstorming, especially if you do not know the group. If you are working with a group of people you know well who have developed good group behaviours, then freeforming is an option.

✔ Don't opt for quantity over quality. Some versions of brainstorming encourage quantity over quality and 'anything goes'. This does not apply in project work. Projects are difficult enough without having to sort through unnecessarily long and poorly focused lists. Expect therefore that the resulting list may be short or long depending upon the nature of the subject.

✔ Consider the size of the group you are working with. Structured brainstorming in particular can become very tedious with more than six people in the group. When working with a large number of people, split them up into sub-groups of five or six.

CLUSTERING

DESCRIPTION

Clustering is a tool for organizing and managing lists by grouping similar items together.

WHEN TO USE CLUSTERING

- Whenever there is a long list of items such as ideas, things to do, problems or questionnaire results, clustering enables the list to be grouped and hence more easily managed.
- Clustering is an excellent tool to use following brainstorming.

(See Figure 17.1.)

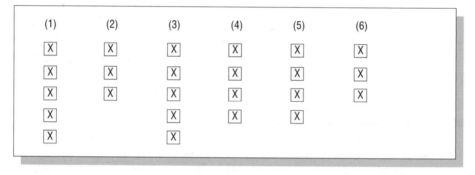

Figure 17.1 A finished cluster with six headings

HOW TO USE CLUSTERING

1. The list to be clustered needs to be written up on post-it notes. Make certain there is sufficient flipchart space – you might need to blu-tack some sheets to the wall.
2. Take a post-it at random, read it out and place it on the flipchart paper.
3. Take another post-it, read it out and ask 'does this goes with the first?' If yes, place it underneath. If no, start a new cluster.
4. Take another post-it, read it out and ask 'does this go with either of the others?' Continue clustering until all the post-its have been grouped.
5. Taking each cluster in turn, ask the group to suggest a heading.
6. Spend a few minutes considering the clusters. Look for any duplication, gaps or inconsistencies.
7. Decide what to do with the finished clusters. This will depend upon the nature of the list. You may, for example, wish to make a person responsible for each cluster.

Tips

✔ In the event of a disagreement about where a particular post-it should be placed, you have a number of options:
(a) Ask the contributor to clarify what they meant.
(b) Place the post-it to one side and return to it at the end.
(c) Duplicate the post-it and place it in both clusters.

✔ Headings for the clusters will often emerge while carrying out the clustering. However, always leave choosing a name until the end and let the clusters determine the headings rather than the headings determine the clusters.

CHRONOLOGICAL CLUSTERING AND HOW TO USE IT

Another way of clustering is in chronological order. This would apply, for example, if dealing with a list of actions (see Figure 17.2).

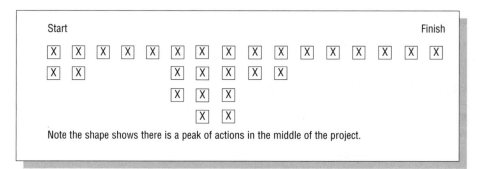

Figure 17.2 Finished chronological cluster

1. The list to be clustered needs to be written up on post-it notes. Make sure there is sufficient flipchart space – you might need to blu-tack some sheets to the wall. Note that you will be clustering from left to right in time order.
2. Take a post-it at random, read it out and place it on the flipchart paper.
3. Take another post-it, read it out and ask 'does this happen before, at the same time as or after the first?' Place as appropriate.
4. Take another post-it, read it out and ask 'where does this go?' Keep asking 'before, at the same time as or after' in relation to other post-its. Place in chronological order as appropriate. Where post-its happen 'at the same time', place these underneath the original post-it. Continue until all the post-its have been placed.
5. Spend a few minutes considering the finished chronological order. Look for any duplication, gaps or inconsistencies.

191

6. Decide what to do with the finished result. You may, for example, wish to allocate actions to individuals or formally present it in the form of a planning grid.

Tips for chronological clustering

✔ The shape of a chronological cluster will tell you a great deal about when the bottlenecks and peak periods in a project will occur. If there are several actions due to take place at the same time, see if any can be rescheduled to less busy periods or use must-should-could to prioritize.

✔ Chronological clustering used in conjunction with must-should-could is also an excellent tool to use when writing reports, preparing an agenda for a meeting or designing a training course.

MUST-SHOULD-COULD

DESCRIPTION

Must-should-could is a tool for prioritization.

WHEN TO USE MUST-SHOULD-COULD

● To prioritize a number of tasks.
● To prioritize agenda items at a meeting.

HOW TO USE MUST-SHOULD-COULD

1. List the items to be prioritized.
2. Categorize:
    ● must be done now
    ● should be done now
    ● could be done now.
3. Carry out.
    Do the 'musts' first, 'shoulds' second and 'coulds' if time permits.

Tips

✔ Alternatives to must-should-could are now-soon-later or high-medium-low priority. When planning a strategy, try short term-medium term-long term.

✔ If working with a group, be clear about the criterion that is being used for evaluation. Follow the majority decision, but ensure any strong dissenters have an opportunity to explain their thinking – it may change the decision.

✔ Must-should-could is an excellent way to manage your in-tray.

PLANNING GRID

DESCRIPTION

The planning grid, sometimes called a PERT or Gantt chart, is a tool for project or implementation planning and contains three elements:

● What has to be done.
● Who will do it.
● When it will be done.

WHEN TO USE THE PLANNING GRID

● During any planning activity.

HOW TO USE THE PLANNING GRID

1. Identify each element of the plan and record it on a post-it note possibly by brainstorming.
2. Use chronological clustering to put them in order.
3. Check for gaps and missing actions.
4. Decide who will be responsible for each action, define exactly what they will do and write their initials on the post-it note.
5. Add timescales above the post-it notes. These might be by month, week or specific dates.
6. Decide whether you want the plan formally presented as shown below or whether to leave it on the flipchart paper to allow for easy revision (see Figure 17.3).
7. Review to mark completed actions or reschedule as necessary as implementation progresses.

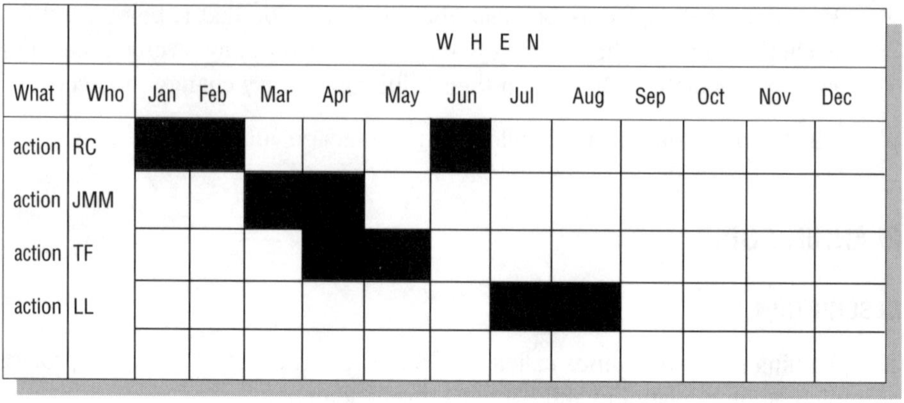

Figure 17.3 Planning grid

TPN ANALYSIS

DESCRIPTION

TPN analysis is a tool for determining who controls an issue.

WHEN TO USE TPN ANALYSIS

● Whenever you have a list of issues to be dealt with and need to determine whether they are within your control.

HOW TO USE TPN ANALYSIS

1. List the issues.
2. For each issue decide if it is:
   ● T = Totally within the control of the group.
   ● P = Partially within the control of the group.
   ● N = Not within the control of the group.
3. Decide how the Ts will be taken forward, possibly using must-should-could to prioritize. Identify who needs to be involved to move the Ps forward. Determine to whom the Ns will be referred.

18 Tools for analysis

The tools for analysis are:

- Ishikawa diagrams to help identify cause-and-effect factors.
- Deployment flowcharting to help understand the way processes work.
- The Kano model to break down customer needs.
- Measles diagrams to help analyse by location.

These tools can be used by an individual working alone or by groups of people working together.

WORKING WITH GROUPS OF PEOPLE

The guidelines for working with groups of people are very similar to those for the tools for planning and organizing:

- Make certain the group is composed of the people involved in the subject to be analysed, either as a supplier, worker or customer.
- Ensure everyone knows the purpose of the tool.
- Read through how to use the tool beforehand. For Ishikawa diagrams and deployment flowcharts which are more complex, you might want to consider preparing a handout.
- Make sure the room is appropriately arranged. If using a flipchart, arrange the group around it so that all can participate. You will need a fair amount of wall space for Ishikawa diagrams and deployment flowcharts.
- Ensure that there is only one person leading at any one time. This is particularly important when carrying out deployment flowcharting or Ishikawa diagrams. Ideally the person leading should be a trained Quality Adviser.

A WORD OF WARNING

The tools for analysis, especially Ishikawa diagrams and deployment flowcharts, are probably the most technically complicated of all the tools although in practice they are actually very simple to use. It is common, however, for a group using these tools to strive to produce a technically perfect Ishikawa diagram or deployment flowchart but forget that the purpose of what they are doing is to analyse something. The reason a tool is being used is to help and not to hinder. If following all the guidelines in this chapter makes something more complicated than necessary and you can think of a better way, then do it your way! Don't worry about what Professor Ishikawa might have said – it would probably be 'well done'.

ISHIKAWA DIAGRAMS

DESCRIPTION

Ishikawa diagrams, often called cause-and-effect or fishbone diagrams, are a tool most commonly used to display causal relationships by stating a quality characteristic or 'effect' at the 'head' of the diagram and then listing possible causes along branch arrows (see Figure 18.1).

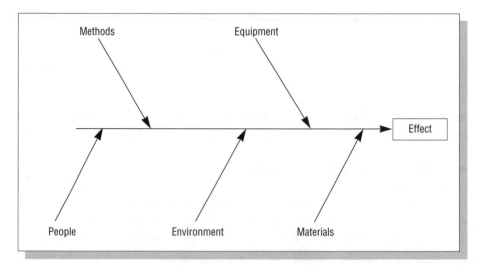

Figure 18.1 Ishikawa diagram

WHEN TO USE ISHIKAWA DIAGRAMS

● When you wish to carry out a thorough analysis of a particular quality characteristic or situation and ensure that all possible contributory factors have been identified, an Ishikawa diagram will force you to think about each of the five MEPEM categories (methods, equipment, people, environment, materials).

- In the early stages of a project. An Ishikawa diagram will identify possible areas for study and highlight processes which need to be flowcharted and analysed.
- To identify possible causes of problems and how they relate to each other.
- When you wish to clearly illustrate how contributory factors are related. An Ishikawa diagram is an excellent presentational tool.

HOW TO USE ISHIKAWA DIAGRAMS

1. You will need flipchart paper, pens, post-it notes, pencil, blu-tack and sellotape. Make sure you have plenty of wall space. A rough guide is one sheet of flipchart paper for each of the MEPEM categories (see (4)).
2. Define the quality characteristic or 'effect' you wish to analyse and write it in the head of the diagram. This might be in the form of a desired state or a problem. Examples of these are 'the ideal reception area' and 'breakdowns of forklift trucks'.
3. Draw a broad arrow from left to right leading to the effect box.
4. Decide upon the headings for the branch arrows. The suggested headings are: methods, equipment, people, environment, materials – although these may not be appropriate in every situation. If in doubt, ask the group.
   Remember that an Ishikawa diagram is an analytical tool. The purpose of using MEPEM is to ensure that all angles are covered.
5. Taking each branch arrow in turn, go around the group in rotation and list possible causes or factors on post-it notes and place them against the appropriate branch arrow. Related post-it notes should be grouped together to form sub-arrows. Use a pencil to draw in the arrows to start off with to allow for later rearrangement.
6. Make sure you exhaust all ideas under each branch arrow before moving on to the next. You might want to pick an 'easy' one to start off with. You may well find that ideas are duplicated under more than one branch arrow. Don't worry about this.
7. Tidy up the diagram, look for any gaps, draw in the arrows using flipchart pen and sellotape down the post-its.
8. The next steps will depend on the nature of the work you are doing. A good starting place is to ask the group what they think should happen next. This might be to identify specific areas for further study if you have a number of theories, to collect data about individual factors or to allocate specific actions to people. You'll find some examples in Chapter 23.

NEGATIVE ISHIKAWA DIAGRAMS

In some situations you can choose to construct either a 'positive' or a 'negative' Ishikawa diagram. For example, 'an ideal reception area' in the head would become 'the worst reception in the world' and factors would change from 'phone answered promptly' to 'phone left ringing'. The idea of this approach is to see how many of the negative factors actually exist and eliminate these. This can be an enjoyable way to analyse a situation. Use the same steps as for a normal Ishikawa diagram.

Tips

✔ Unlike brainstorming you must be very clear what is meant by each item and therefore discussion must take place during the construction of the diagram.

✔ Don't worry if there is an imbalance between branch arrows. Sometimes there will be an equal spread of factors between all branch arrows. Sometimes there is one branch arrow with very few factors. On other occasions, all factors are mainly concentrated on one branch arrow with few on the others. It's often hard to predict where a concentration might be but there is often a pattern dependent upon the nature of the topic under study. Service industries, for example, will often have few factors on 'equipment' and 'materials'.

✔ Use Ishikawa diagrams to focus discussion. Most people will have a pet theory about the causes of a particular situation. Without an alternative, a meeting or project can spend considerable time discussing these pet theories without knowing if they are correct or not. Constructing an Ishikawa diagram will provide a good focus for discussion.

✔ Use the Ishikawa diagram as a starting point for data collection. This applies particularly in problem solving but in all situations, once an Ishikawa diagram has been constructed, it is important to evaluate the relative importance of each. Collect data about how important each factor is and display this as a Pareto chart (see Chapter 20).

✔ A common cause of confusion is the distinction between 'equipment' and 'materials'. It often helps to clarify this at the start. Equipment can be described as fixed or mobile plant – vehicles, machinery or photocopiers. Materials are consumables, fuel, component parts in production or stationery.

WHY ISHIKAWA?

Ishikawa diagrams are named after their inventor, Professor Kaoru Ishikawa. Professor Ishikawa graduated from the Department of Applied Chemistry at the University of Tokyo in 1939. He had a varied industrial and academic career including acting as an instructor for the Quality Control Research Group of the Japanese Union of Scientists and Engineers. He first used his diagram in the summer of 1943 while he was working with a group of engineers at the Kawasaki Steel Works. The root of the Ishikawa diagram in heavy industry and manufacturing is apparent but experience has shown that it is equally valuable in service industries. This is because Ishikawa recognized the importance of both people and their interaction with other factors and this relationship is vital in every situation. The principle behind the tool is universal – organizations are a web of complex interrelationships.

DEPLOYMENT FLOWCHARTING

DESCRIPTION

A deployment flowchart is a diagram of the people, tasks and decisions that make up a particular process (see Figure 18.2). The unique feature of a deployment

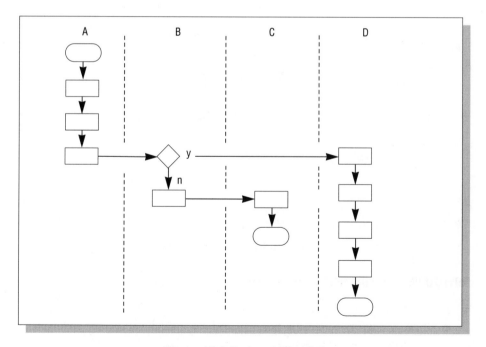

Figure 18.2 Deployment flowchart

199

flowchart is that it shows the people or departments involved across the top of the chart and their relationship with the process and each other. As all organizations are completely dependent upon the processes they use to get work done, this makes deployment flowcharting one of the most important tools.

WHEN TO USE DEPLOYMENT FLOWCHARTING

- To analyse an existing process. The guidelines here have been written from the point of view of analysing an existing process. Deployment flowcharting does have a number of other uses, however.
- To help establish points where measurements can be taken within a process.
- To plan a new process.
- To illustrate work instructions or procedures.

STANDARD SYMBOLS

There are many symbols in flowcharting, some of which have specialist applications such as computer programming (see Figure 18.3). The use of five symbols will suffice in most situations.

⬭	Sausage:	Start and end of the process
▭	Rectangle:	Task or activity
◇	Diamond:	Decision with 'yes' and 'no' exits
▭	Shadow box:	Hides detail
→	Arrow:	Flowline

Figure 18.3 Flowcharting symbols

HOW TO USE DEPLOYMENT FLOWCHARTING

1. Preparation:
   - If analysing or planning a process, ensure that all the people involved in the process are represented.

200

- You will need flipchart paper, pens, post-it notes (square for decision boxes, rectangular for tasks, shadow boxes and sausages), a pencil, blu-tack and sellotape.
- Make sure you have plenty of wall space. Deployment flowcharts get very big so fix two sheets of flipchart paper one above the other allowing half a sheet across per person or department involved in the process.

2. Identify the start and end of the process. There may be more than one start and end. If this is being done as part of a project, use the project remit for guidance.
3. List the people or departments involved in the process across the top. Put in order but do this on post-it notes to allow for rearrangement.
4. Ask 'What happens first?' Write this as concisely as possible on a rectangular post-it note and place it under the appropriate person or department.
5. Keep asking 'What happens next?'
   - Place the post-its vertically where activities occur under one person or department and horizontally where they transfer to another.
   - Don't go into too much detail too soon. Use shadow boxes to hide detail and if necessary construct separate flowcharts for these later.
   - Where there are decisions, these should be phrased so that the answer is 'yes' or 'no'. As an example, you would not have a decision box with 'what colour is it?' but several with 'is it red?' – yes/no, 'is it green?', yes/no, and so on. Follow the most common answer and then return to complete the other exit.
6. Continue the process right through to the end and check that both exits have been completed for all decision boxes. Only at this stage should you begin to draw in the flowlines and even now only use a pencil.
7. Ask someone to talk through the process to ensure it makes sense. Tidy it up as you go along.
8. Finally, draw the flowlines in ink and draw vertical lines in a different colour to separate the people or departments and sellotape down the post-it notes.
9. Decide if the flowchart needs to be formally presented or desk top published. If you think you're going to be doing a lot of flowcharting, consider buying some specialist software.

How much detail?

✔ It is hard to determine the level of detail required on a deployment flowchart in advance. This will emerge once the group begins. Three levels of detail are often used:
   (1) *System*: High level overview – no detail.
   (2) *Process*: Medium level.

201

(3)   *Task*: Low level – lots of detail.

Deployment flowcharts are most appropriate for process level although it sometimes helps to start off by constructing a system-level chart to get an idea of how the process works.

✔   If in doubt about how much detail to go into:
   ● Consider the context. If it is part of a project, consider the remit. What level of detail do you need in order to accomplish what you want to?
   ● If the necessary level of detail is still not clear, use shadow boxes for the time being. Once the flowchart is complete, review it. You can always go back and expand shadow boxes. It is more difficult to undo detail once completed.

Tips

✔   There is no 'right way' to draw a deployment flowchart – they are all different. Use these guidelines as far as possible but remember that success is determined by how well those who create it understand and use it.

✔   When flowcharting an existing process, it is important to flowchart the process as it actually works and not how it would work if all the existing procedures were followed.

✔   Only one person at any one time should work on the deployment flowchart. This should be the Quality Adviser if you have one.

✔   Important side issues often emerge while the flowchart is being constructed – have an issue park (see Chapter 21) for these. Record them as they arise for further work.

✔   It can sometimes be useful to physically walk round the process from desk to desk or location to location to get a clear picture of what happens.

ANALYSING YOUR DEPLOYMENT FLOWCHART

Once the deployment flowchart has been completed it is necessary to spend some time analysing, drawing conclusions and identifying ideas for improvement. It is suggested that the group looks at each of the following in turn and list any ideas as they come up:

● things going wrong
● duplication
● unnecessary work

- many people involved in simple activities
- unnecessary waiting
- differences between procedures and actual practice
- differences between the way individuals work
- differences between the way different departments or locations work
- any other inconsistencies
- inefficient work layout
- alternative methods
- any dead ends.

USING YOUR DEPLOYMENT FLOWCHART TO ESTABLISH MEASUREMENT POINTS

A deployment flowchart is an excellent tool for establishing where to measure how a particular process or part of it is performing. The sort of things you might want to measure are 'how quickly', 'how many', 'how often' and so on. Some places to try are:

- At the start and end of a process to establish time from start to finish.
- At decision points to count how many go each way.
- At customer–supplier interactions, between people, departments or organizations.
- Wherever obvious.

KANO MODEL

DESCRIPTION

The Kano model is a tool for the analysis and classification of customer needs. They can then be prioritized so that improvement efforts and resources can be concentrated where they will have the most effect.

WHEN TO USE THE KANO MODEL

- during analysis of customer needs
- following customer research.

HOW TO USE THE KANO MODEL

1. List on post-it notes all customer needs that have been identified.
2. Classify them as follows:
   - *Basic, also known as must be present.* These needs are expected by the

203

customer. As they are usually taken for granted, the customer will often not specifically ask for these. If basic needs are completely fulfilled, the customer will not be particularly satisfied. If basic needs are not met, the customer will be dissatisfied. As an example, if an airline were to ask you as a customer what you would like to see them provide, safety is unlikely to be on your list. This is a basic requirement and you would not expect to have to ask for it. A housing example might be a roof that doesn't leak. A tenant will not thank you for providing a roof but would be quick to complain if it starts to leak.

- *Performance, also known as more is better.* These needs have a direct relationship with customer satisfaction. The more efficiently the need is met, the happier the customer is. The poorer the need is met, the more unhappy the customer. Speed of answering the telephone is a good example – a couple of rings and you're quite impressed, four or five is nothing special, six and above you're beginning to tap your fingers. Another housing example would be the length of time taken to complete a repair to a property.

- *Distinctive, also known as delighters.* These are features which distinguish your service or product, often an unexpected extra touch. Distinctive features are a pleasant surprise for the customer but do not cause dissatisfaction when not present. Some supermarkets, for example, have started to pack up your shopping for you at the checkout.

3. Identify next steps. This will depend on the circumstances in which you are using the model. A good starting place is always to ask the team what they think they should do next. This might be to prioritize efforts or allocate resources.

Tips

✔ Using the Kano model helps focus on issues that really are important to the customer. It is often tempting to tinker with distinctive features when basic needs have not been met. The customer does not think highly of you if you try this! Identify basic needs first, then work on improving performance and finally look at distinctive features. What good is bag packing at a supermarket when you can't get the goods you want and have just spent 20 minutes queuing at the checkout?

✔ Beware: distinctive features will soon slip into the performance category and performance into basic as customer expectations change. Remote control on television sets was once distinctive – it is now basic. Trolley refreshment services on InterCity trains, once distinctive, are now performance – 'how long until the trolley gets here?'

✔   The analysis of customer needs is an extremely complex subject. A quick and easy method of using the Kano model has been described which will stand you in good stead in most situations and enable you to get a good grip on a difficult subject. Where crucial decisions need to be made, consider employing an experienced customer research agency.

WHY KANO?

The Kano model was devised by Noriaki Kano. Kano initially studied chemistry, then engineering and completed his doctorate under the supervision of Kaoru Ishikawa. Like Ishikawa, he was active with the Japanese Union of Scientists and Engineers and has consulted and lectured in dozens of countries.

MEASLES DIAGRAMS

DESCRIPTION

The measles diagram, sometimes called the concentration diagram, is a pictorial tool which enables analysis of where and how often something is happening (see Figure 18.4).

WHEN TO USE MEASLES DIAGRAMS

●   To find out where a particular incident is happening and what the concentration is compared to other locations.
    An example might be instances of vandalism on a housing estate.

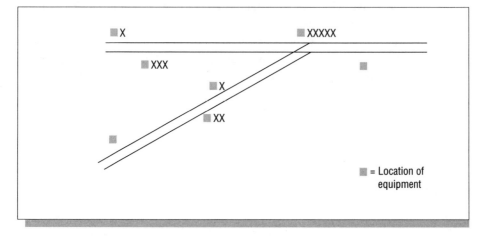

Figure 18.4 Measles diagram – Incidents of vandalism to equipment

● Measles diagrams can also be used in administrative processes. For example, if a particular form is being incorrectly completed, keep one as a master copy and mark all occurrences.

HOW TO USE MEASLES DIAGRAMS

1. Draw a diagram of the physical location under study.
2. Identify the location of an occurrence and mark with an 'x'.
   Identify the next location. If it is the same, put the 'x' as close as possible to the first. Continue until all occurrences have been charted.
3. Identify the areas of highest concentration and focus resources here.

Tips

✔ Use different colours or shapes if you want to show more than one type of effect on a single measles diagram.

✔ Beware of moving a problem from one location to another. Anticipate unexpected side-effects.

SOME BACKGROUND

Professor Measles was a member of the Japanese Union of Scientists and Engineers. Only joking. An early example of the use of this tool, popularized by Joseph Juran, was by Dr John Snow during a cholera epidemic in London in 1854. By marking the occurrence of deaths from cholera on a map, Dr Snow was able to identify a concentration around the Broad Street pump. Further investigation confirmed that those who had died had been getting drinking water from the pump and the source was isolated.

There is another story that, prior to introducing their own small cars, Japanese motor manufacturers purchased second-hand Minis and analysed the occurrence of corrosion so that they could design weaknesses out of their own vehicles.

19 Tools for evaluation and decision making

The tools for evaluation and decision making will help in evaluating ideas, assessing progress and making decisions.

WORKING WITH GROUPS OF PEOPLE

All of these tools are aimed at groups of people working together. Five basic guidelines apply once again:

- Make certain the people involved in the subject under study are present.
- Ensure everyone knows the purpose of the tool.
- Run through how to use the tool beforehand.
- Make sure the room is appropriately arranged.
- Make certain that there is only one person leading at any one time although 3-2-1 voting and traffic light assessment may require the whole group to be working at the flipchart at the same time.

WORKING ALONE

Although the tools have been written from the point of view of working in a group setting, it is certainly possible to use helps and hinders, traffic light assessment and the evaluation matrix when working alone.

HELPS AND HINDERS

DESCRIPTION

Helps and hinders is a simple tool for evaluation through the identification of positive and negative factors.

WHEN TO USE HELPS AND HINDERS

- At the close of a meeting to evaluate effectiveness.
- To identify positive and negative factors for any idea.
- When one of a number of options has to be chosen – produce a helps and hinders sheet for each option to identify the optimum choice.

HOW TO USE HELPS AND HINDERS

1. Divide a sheet of flipchart paper into two columns headed 'helps' and 'hinders' or '+' and '–'.
2. Work around the group in rotation asking each person for a hinder. 'Pass' is allowed. You may go around as many times as is necessary although once is usually enough when evaluating a meeting.
3. Do the same for helps.
4. Record any action items arising or use the list to aid a decision.

3-2-1 VOTING

DESCRIPTION

3-2-1 voting is a tool for reaching a group decision regarding preferences or priorities.

WHEN TO USE 3-2-1 VOTING

- When one of a number of options has to be chosen.
- When there is a list to be prioritized.

HOW TO USE 3-2-1 VOTING

1. Write up the list of options on a sheet of flipchart paper.
2. Explain the process to the group and give each individual a flipchart pen.
3. Each person can award points to their preferred option. They do this by writing their points directly onto the sheet of flipchart paper. Three points for the top option, two for second choice and one point for third choice. No points are awarded to the other options.
4. Add up the scores. The highest score is the chosen option.
5. Have a round robin (see Chapter 21) to ensure the group is happy with the result. If they're not, try the option with the second highest score or another tool.

Tip

✔ 3-2-1 voting is a quick and easy method for prioritization. It is generally better to use helps and hinders to evaluate ideas and it should be borne in mind that there is no substitute for data collection. However, 3-2-1 voting is useful when a quick decision needs to be reached.

TRAFFIC LIGHT ASSESSMENT

DESCRIPTION

Traffic light assessment is an excellent tool for evaluating the current status of an issue or the enthusiasm of a group for a number of options.

WHEN TO USE TRAFFIC LIGHT ASSESSMENT

- When you need to assess relative progress in a number of different areas.
- When you need to get a picture about what both individuals and the whole group think about particular ideas.

HOW TO USE TRAFFIC LIGHT ASSESSMENT

1. Write up the list to be evaluated onto flipchart paper. You will need red, yellow or orange, and green flipchart pens for the group.
2. Either as a whole group or individually, mark each item with a coloured cross. Green means fine or good. Yellow means okay. Red means not happy or poor. Decide on the coding in advance and make sure everyone is clear about this.
3. Examine the resulting patterns. Look for concentration of colours for agreement, different colours for differences of opinion and odd ones out.

Tips

✔ When it would be useful to know who thinks what, have each individual mark their opinion with their initials rather than a cross.

✔ This is a good way to evaluate how happy and confident a group is with a specific methodology. This was used by the steering group at Liverpool Housing Trust to evaluate the steering group methodology. There were many green initials in the early stages so we concentrated our input on the later stages.

EVALUATION MATRIX

DESCRIPTION

The evaluation matrix is a tool to use when you have a number of options which you wish to evaluate against more than one criterion (see Figure 19.1).

WHEN TO USE THE EVALUATION MATRIX

- When you need to decide between a number of different options.
- When you have multiple criteria against which you wish to compare options.

	Option 1	Option 2	Option 3	Option 4	Option 5
Criterion 1	10	10	5	3	5
Criterion 2	10	10	10	5	0
Criterion 3	5	10	10	0	0
Total	25	30	25	8	5

Figure 19.1 Evaluation matrix

HOW TO USE THE EVALUATION MATRIX

1. Write up the list of criteria against which you wish to evaluate the options. Examples might be cost, ease of implementation or speed.
2. Write up the list of options you wish to consider.
3. Draw up a matrix on flipchart paper showing the options along the top and the criteria down the side.
4. Decide how you will score each box. A points system is probably best. Ten points might mean excellent against this criterion, zero might mean it doesn't meet the criterion at all.
5. Score each box and then total to determine the best option.
6. Debate to ensure that the group is happy with the decision.

Tips

✔ Don't be tempted to use a high, medium or low scoring system. This gets confusing when evaluating criteria such as cost where a low cost leads to a high score.

✔ Strive for consistency in your scoring. Refer back to previous scores for comparison if necessary. The Quality Adviser can perform a useful role in keeping an eye on this.

✔ If certain criteria are less important than others, you may want to reduce the scores accordingly. Instead of ten points being the maximum score, this might drop to five for those criteria which are of secondary importance.

20 Tools for data display and analysis

If what follows are tools for analysis then why aren't they in Chapter 18? Good question. The difference between this set of tools and the tools for analysis in Chapter 18 is that these are for the graphical display of numerical data. The principle behind the tools for data display and analysis is to take numerical data and present it in a visual manner so that it becomes easier to understand. Use of one of these tools will normally mean that analysis of the data is quite simple – the resulting patterns and pictures tell you what is going on. You will find more about the tools in context in the data collection, display and analysis methodology (Chapter 13). However, these are tools that you can start to use immediately in your day-to-day work to better see and understand how things are doing.

USING COMPUTERS

Most people today have access to spreadsheet software of one form or another. These will normally convert your spreadsheet into graphical form in a few easy steps. Beware a couple of pitfalls:

✖   Because software is so sophisticated today, it often defaults to the option that looks the best. This is rarely the most useful. In particular, beware of three-dimensional graphs.

✖   Scales are usually automatically determined by the software on the basis of filling the page. Override the automatic scale especially when producing graphs which will be compared.

DRAWING GRAPHS BY HAND

Tips

✔ Use graph paper for accuracy, a pencil in case you make a mistake and a ruler for neatness.

✔ Think carefully about the scales first – it may be worth doing a rough draft to see what it looks like.

✔ Make sure you have a title for the graph and a label for each axis. You may also need to date it or indicate the time period.

A REMINDER ABOUT VARIABLE AND ATTRIBUTE DATA

Variable data occurs on a continuous scale and can be given a precise numerical value. It is often variable over time. Examples are speed of processing, weight and number of widgets produced each day. Attribute data can be counted in single units. Attribute data compares different things – red, blue or green, apples, oranges or pears. There is more on this in Chapter 13 under 'Establish the data type'.

WORKING WITH GROUPS OF PEOPLE

The tools discussed here are not designed to be used by groups of people – at least, not in their production. However, once a chart has been produced, it is very useful to have a group analysis session where opinions and theories are bounced around. This is particularly true where project teams are concerned. Second, the data display tools can cut out a lot of opinion and argument as the facts will speak for themselves.

BAR CHARTS

DESCRIPTION

Bar charts are used to display attribute data – the number of times something occurs. They are a simple way of visually displaying and bringing meaning to numerical data. The data is displayed as a series of columns or bars in a graph (see Figure 20.1).

WHEN TO USE BAR CHARTS

● Whenever you have a set of numbers against some sort of attribute. For example, number of faults listed by cause, income listed by product.

Where the data is time related, a run chart is more appropriate. For variable data, which occurs on a continuous scale such as shoe size, use a histogram.

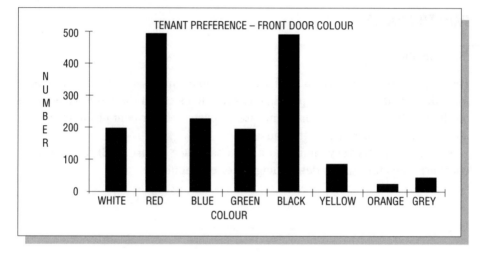

Figure 20.1 Bar chart

HOW TO USE BAR CHARTS

● Prepare a graph with the vertical axis showing the quantities or number of occurrences and the horizontal axis showing the category.

Tips

✔ If you wish to compare one bar chart with others, make certain that the same scale is used on the vertical axis.

✔ You can 'stack' bar charts using different colours or shadings as a code. In the example above you might want to split the preference by area and use a number of colours stacked one above the other to show this.

HOW TO INTERPRET YOUR BAR CHART

Look for the following:

● patterns
● highest and lowest values

- surprises
- any bars that stand out noticeably from the others – much bigger or much smaller
- confirmation of theories
- also examine stage 4 of the data collection, display and analysis methodology in Chapter 13.

PARETO ANALYSIS

DESCRIPTION

Pareto analysis is based upon the Pareto principle which separates the 'vital few' from the 'useful many'. This principle is sometimes called the 80–20 rule based on the fact that when most problems are analysed, 80 per cent of the trouble is attributable to 20 per cent of the causes.

A Pareto chart is very similar to a bar chart (see Figure 20.2), but a Pareto chart arranges the bars in descending order of magnitude.

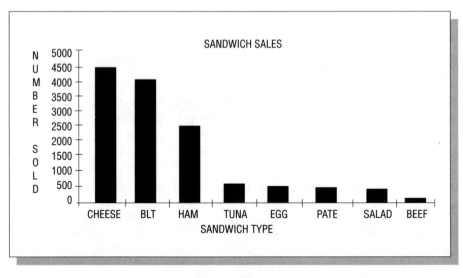

Figure 20.2 Pareto chart

WHEN TO USE PARETO ANALYSIS

Whenever there are a large number of factors at play and you wish to identify the 'vital few'.

216

HOW TO USE PARETO ANALYSIS

1. Consider carefully the measurement you are going to use. In the above example the use of 'number of sandwiches sold' might give a different result to 'income per sandwich type'. Sometimes you might want to do both.
2. Prepare a graph with the vertical axis showing the number of occurrences or quantities and the horizontal axis showing the category as for a bar chart but arrange the bars in descending or ascending order.

Tips

✔   If you are looking for improvement over time, construct successive Pareto charts, maybe showing data for one month at a time, to show how the situation is changing.

✔   A Pareto chart is a good tool to use following the production of an Ishikawa diagram to show the relative importance of each factor.

HOW TO INTERPRET YOUR PARETO CHART

● From the completed chart, identify the 'vital few'. Depending on the situation, these might be areas for further investigation, action or allocation of resources.
● Sometimes a Pareto chart fails to identify a vital few contributors. In this case it is worth considering producing another chart using a different criterion for measurement.
● Look also for highest and lowest values, surprises and confirmation of theories.

THE PARETO PRINCIPLE

The principle behind the Pareto chart is as important as the chart itself. The Pareto principle is simply the differentiation between the 'vital few' and the 'useful many' whether we are talking about problems, complaints, costs, customers, suppliers, projects, key players in a given situation and so on. This differentiation enables the appropriate focus of effort and resources.

Don't be fooled by the apparent simplicity of this principle. It is certainly simple but it is also powerful and frequently overlooked.

WHY PARETO?

Vilfredo Pareto was an eighteenth-century Italian economist who discovered that 80 per cent of the wealth in the country was owned by 20 per cent of the

217

population. The use of the Pareto principle in quality improvement was popularized by Joseph Juran.

RUN CHARTS

DESCRIPTION

A run chart is a graph plotting performance over time (see Figure 20.3).

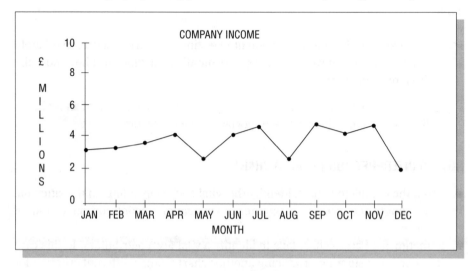

Figure 20.3 Run chart

WHEN TO USE RUN CHARTS

- Whenever you have data about performance over time.
  For example, number of faults each day for a month, income each week over a year.
- When you want to look for trends and patterns over time.

HOW TO USE RUN CHARTS

- Prepare a graph with the vertical axis showing the performance and the horizontal axis showing time.

Tips

✔ If you wish to compare one run chart with another, make sure that the same scales are used.

✔   Calculate the mean or average value and add this in as a line to give the eye a reference point.

✔   You can plot more than one set of data on a run chart. This is particularly useful where you have two sets of data that you wish to compare. This might be current year and previous, or production line A and production line B. Beware, however, of over-complicating the finished chart.

✔   Another way of comparing graphs, especially if you are making a presentation, is to produce them on acetate for an overhead projector and then lay them on top of each other.

HOW TO INTERPRET YOUR RUN CHART

Look for:

● trends – upwards, downwards, cyclical (related to another variable), seasonal
● highest and lowest values
● what might happen next
● surprises.

CUMULATIVE RUN CHARTS AND HOW TO USE THEM

A cumulative run chart differs from an ordinary run chart in that instead of plotting each individual value, you add them up as you go along to give a running total. These are particularly useful when you wish to compare performance against plan over a given period of time or compare two totals. A cumulative run chart is an excellent way to keep track of expenditure against budget (see Figure 20.4).

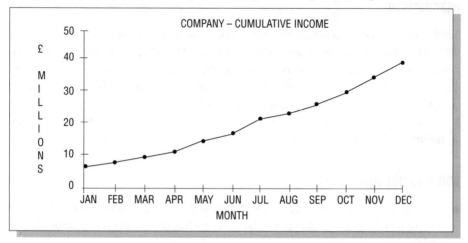

Figure 20.4 Cumulative run chart

Tip

✔ If you wish to compare performance against plan, add in the planned results as an extra line and then plot actual results on an ongoing basis.

CONTROL CHARTS

A control chart is a run chart with an arithmetic mean, and upper and lower control limits added. The control limits are calculated using standard deviations from the mean. There are a number of different types of control chart dependent upon the nature of the data being plotted. The calculation of control limits is outside the scope of this book as the intention here is you should be able to read and do.

However, the principle is a simple but important one. Walter Shewhart was the inventor of the control chart. He discovered that in any process there are two types of variation – common and special cause. Common cause variation is always present. Special cause variation results from something unusual and unexpected taking place. You can often spot special causes using a run chart and your eye. Control charts are a bit more reliable!

The implication is that where a special cause is present, the nature of the action that you need to take is likely to be very different than if only common causes are present. To find out more about control charts, try reading *The Deming Dimension* by Henry Neave (see 'Further Reading' on page 273).

HISTOGRAMS

DESCRIPTION

Similar to a bar chart, a histogram is a simple way of visually displaying numerical data. The data is shown as a series of columns or bars in a graph and used to display the frequency of occurrence of variable data (see Figure 20.5). The main difference between a bar chart and a histogram is that a histogram has a continuous scale on the horizontal axis whereas the items shown on the horizontal axis of a bar chart could be placed in any order. Histograms are sometimes called frequency distributions.

WHEN TO USE HISTOGRAMS

● Whenever you wish to display the frequency of occurrence of a variable. For example, number of matches per box, days a house stands empty before being re-let.

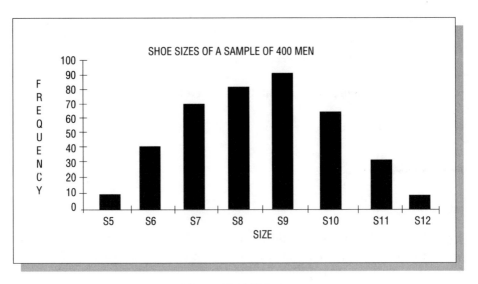

Figure 20.5 Histogram

● As extra information to support a run chart.

When you wish to show how a process is performing over time, a run chart is more appropriate. For attribute data, use a bar chart.

HOW TO USE HISTOGRAMS

● Prepare a graph with the vertical axis showing the number of occasions or frequency of a particular value and the horizontal axis showing the value.

Tips

✔ If you wish to compare one histogram against another, ensure that the same scale is used.

✔ Produce a progression of histograms over time so that you can see if the situation is changing. You might, for example, produce a histogram of a particular situation each month.

HOW TO INTERPRET YOUR HISTOGRAM

Look for the following:

● The shape and how this changes over time.

221

- Patterns.
- Highest and lowest values and the spread. The spread is the difference between the highest and lowest value. Does the spread also change over time?
- Surprises.
- Any bars that stand out noticeably from the others – much bigger or much smaller.
- Confirmation of theories.

PIE CHARTS

DESCRIPTION

A pie chart is a diagram which divides a circle into the different parts of a whole group to show the proportional relationship of each (see Figure 20.6). Actual figures may be used although it is more usual to see percentages applied.

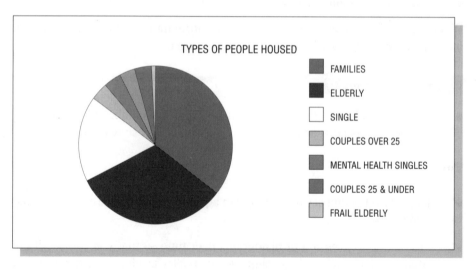

Figure 20.6 Pie chart

WHEN TO USE PIE CHARTS

It is better to use a Pareto chart or bar chart than a pie chart. A pie chart can actually hide information. The pie chart is mentioned here so you can interpret one that might be presented to you and ask questions about the information that might be hidden.

HOW A PIE CHART IS CONSTRUCTED

A pie chart is constructed by calculating the relative value of each of the component parts of a whole group. A circle or pie is divided up into slices to represent the relative value of component based upon the 360 degrees in a circle.

1. For percentage value pie charts, one per cent is equal to 3.6 degrees.
   For each slice multiply the percentage value by 3.6.
2. For actual value pie charts, divide the 360 degrees by the total value.
   For each slice, multiply the resulting figure by the actual value. For example, if you have a total value of 3000 and the first slice is 500, the calculation would be (360 ÷ 3000) x 500 = 60 degrees.

A COMMON MISTAKE

Because the total value of a percentage pie chart is always 100 per cent, it is common to show pie charts intended for comparison as circles of the same size. Although the circles might be the same size, the actual values might be very different. Always make sure that you know the total actual value of pie charts you are comparing. Ideally, pie charts should be constructed of different sizes so that the total area is proportionate to the total values.

21 Techniques for group work

The technique most often used by groups is to sit around a table and talk. Sometimes this is described as 'debate' or 'discussion' but participation is rarely balanced and often the structure used is inadequate. Most people chairing a meeting or Quality Advisers helping out will make bold attempts to ensure that contribution is even but there are some simple structural techniques that will greatly help.

These techniques have the added bonus of varying the format and pace of a meeting. This should help reduce the levels of fatigue in long meetings and keep energy levels high.

Some groups can be quite resistant to some of the techniques that they might find strange or unfamiliar. Always bear in mind the culture you are working in and start with the safe ones!

DISCUSSION AND DEBATE

Discussion and debate needs careful chairing. Before starting, be sure what is being debated and what the outcome should be. This might be, for example, that everyone has a common understanding of the issue, a decision is reached, a way forward is agreed, an option is chosen or a policy is decided.

ISSUE PARK

If there are many issues circulating in a discussion, list them on a sheet of flipchart paper as they emerge. At the end of the discussion, go through the list to check that each issue has been dealt with or determine a way forward to ensure that it is dealt with.

This is also useful in closing down circular arguments or recurring issues. Once the particular issue has been written up on flipchart it is much easier to move on.

PAIRWORK

Put people in pairs with a specific and structured remit to discuss. Each pair then reports back to the group and key issues are noted on the flipchart. Each pair can address the same issue or alternatively different remits can be set in order to cover more ground.

This technique overcomes 'contagion' in a group. One person says something and other group members latch onto it without having given the matter much thought. In pairs each individual is forced to put some thought into the subject and discuss it with their partner. The similarity or difference between pairs at report back is also useful in assessing how much agreement or disagreement there is in the whole group.

PRESENTATION

An extremely underused technique is presentation. A formal presentation, even if short, using a few visual aids is an excellent way to get across a great deal of information. It is particularly useful for updating project progress, making proposals, briefing in new developments and policies.

Questions should usually be taken at the end. If the presentation is likely to provoke considerable debate, an option is to follow up with some pairwork to share impressions and come up with areas for clarification and questions.

QUESTION AND ANSWER SESSION

Useful when an individual or team has to make a presentation or proposal or is the expert in a subject on the agenda. Can be preceded by pairwork to generate the questions.

ROUND ROBIN

A technique that never lets you down. Simply go once round the room to hear an opinion from each participant in turn. No interruptions allowed. Applicable in a number of situations:

- When there is an uneven level of contribution in a group. This applies when there are one or two individuals dominating a discussion as it enables everyone to get a say. It also applies when there are one or two very quiet people in the group as it offers them an opportunity to speak when otherwise they might remain silent: 'Let's go once round the room and hear what everyone has got to say on this issue.'

● When you want to offer everyone the opportunity to ask a question.
  'Let's go once round the room and see if anyone has any questions.'

● When a lot of ground has been covered and you want to assess where everyone is.
  'Let's go once round the room and see where people are on this issue.'

● When an important decision has been made and you want to ensure that everyone is on board.
  'Let's go once round the room and hear what people now think about this decision.'

SNOWBALL

A very useful technique for reaching consensus if the group needs to come to a joint decision. Each individual spends a few minutes making notes on their opinion and position. Then the individuals come together into pairs or threes and reach a common viewpoint. Then the pairs or threes join with another pair or three and so on until finally a group decision is reached.

A snowball can also be used when producing policy statements. It will help identify areas of agreement and difference between individual group members. In this case it is sometimes useful to debate any items that get 'knocked out' following the snowball.

SYNDICATE WORK

Particularly useful for large groups. Split people up into appropriate groups of between three and six people. Sometimes it is appropriate to split people randomly to ensure a balance between the syndicate groups. On other occasions it is better to deliberately mix people. The final option is to split people into their natural work groups.

The syndicates address a specific and structured remit and report back to the main group. Make sure you tell the syndicates how much time they have got and, if possible, monitor progress occasionally – you don't always get the timing right.

TAKE A BREAK

There are two types of break, planned and unplanned. Depending on the length of your meeting, you should plan 15 minutes for tea and coffee in both the morning and afternoon. Allow 45 minutes to an hour for lunch. Avoid working lunches – these might create an illusion of making the best use of time but you'll suffer in terms of tiredness and reduced concentration later. It's much better to get people outside for some fresh air. Finally, watch out for what you put on the agenda immediately after lunch. People will become naturally less attentive as their digestive processes kick in! Aim for something lively and preferably participative.

As far as unplanned breaks are concerned, take a five-minute stretch break when people look weary, before or after a particularly arduous session, or when you get stuck.

USE THE FLIPCHART

The use of a flipchart may seem obvious but it is rarely practised. Useful for capturing key points, summarizing and focusing a debate. Recording issues on the flipchart will make sure they are not lost and can be tackled in a structured manner. If you don't have a flipchart, get your stationery catalogue out now and order one for your office or meeting room. Two may well be more useful than one – one can have prepared material for input and the other can be used for anything that comes up as you go along.

VARY THE ROOM LAYOUT

Most meetings take place in a 'boardroom' layout – around the four sides of a rectangular table. This can be quite a cramped layout and it is difficult to see all the participants around the table. My favourite room layout is a 'U-shape'. This allows a flipchart and overhead projector to be placed at the head of the U and is particularly useful when there are presentations. It is also much easier to see all the participants.

A further option, when you are looking for something a bit different and there are no papers involved, is to do away with the tables completely.

Finally, if you intend to do pair or syndicate work, make sure you use the whole of the room and have other rooms or work areas available if necessary.

WARM UPS

Warm ups can be used in a number of situations and for a number of purposes:

- At the start of a meeting as a form of introduction to each other.
- Ongoing as part of a project so that people get to know each other better.
- As an energizer when energy levels in a group are beginning to drop.
- As a means of switching off from the work people have left behind and focusing on the task in hand.

There are many and varied warm-up exercises. You need to judge carefully the appropriateness of a particular exercise bearing in mind the situation, why you want to use a warm up, the people present, and their maturity as a group. Bear in mind my word of warning at the start of this chapter. Some people love warm ups, some hate them! You can pair people, put them in small teams or ask them to do the warm up individually taking turns or at random.

Here are a variety of my favourites:

- Name, job, what you think you can contribute to this project.
- Name, job, three things about yourself one of which must be a lie. The rest of the group must decide which the lie is.
- Hopes and concerns.
- Any brain teasers you might know.
- CV exercise. Put people in pairs to write up a CV for their partner on a sheet of flipchart paper. Then introduce your partner to the rest of the group.
- Gargle that tune. Small groups gargle a tune. The others say what the tune is.

22 Effective meetings

Effective meetings are one of the keys to getting things done, running good projects and managing more effectively. How well a meeting goes is determined by several factors:

- The methodology adopted or the structure of the agenda.
- The behaviours of the people involved.
- Tools and techniques used.
- Logistical issues.

Getting all of the above right is not an easy task. It is very easy to trip up by forgetting some simple logistical issues at the planning stage. This chapter provides some practical techniques for the logistical aspects of meetings. They apply to any type of meeting.

PURPOSE AND PEOPLE

Plan the meeting well in advance and consider the following:

- What is the purpose of the meeting?
- Will this be the only meeting or will it be the first or part of a series?
- Do I need a Quality Adviser to help?
- Who needs to attend to make sure there is informed input to all the agenda items?
- If decisions need to be taken, will the people with the relevant authority be present?
- Is there anyone attending who might not have a role or any input to make?

THE AGENDA

Make sure you issue an agenda in advance of the meeting. If there are many potential items, put them on post-it notes and use chronological clustering (see Chapter 17) to put them in a logical order. You can also use must-should-could (see Chapter 17) to prioritize potential agenda items.

- Be clear about what you want from each agenda item – this might be debate, a decision or an update.
- Show who is in the lead or who is to report against each agenda item.
- Estimate the time for each item to determine the length of the meeting. Show the timings on the agenda.
- Consider distribution of the agenda.
  How soon will it need to go out to make sure people have a chance to look at it?
  Do any supporting papers need to be distributed along with it?
- Programme regular breaks particularly before or after tough topics.

SOME 'STANDING ITEMS' FOR AGENDAS

- Introductions for guests and newcomers.
- Warm up.
- Review the actions from the previous meeting.
  Beware of spending a big chunk of every meeting reviewing the notes from the last meeting. A good habit is to review only key action items from the previous meeting. Any that are likely to consume a fair amount of time should become a separate agenda item. It is always worth checking with the person responsible for the action when you are compiling the agenda. Find out what progress has been made and what they want out of the meeting.
- Arrangements for the next meeting.
- Meeting review. Use helps and hinders (see Chapter 19) at the end of each meeting. You will be able to discover what people have liked and disliked so you can improve for the next time round.

THE NOTES

Someone should be appointed to take the notes, but not the chairperson or Quality Adviser. Include the following:

- Meeting title and date.
- Who attended.

- Action items, who and by when.
- Decisions made.
- Arrangements for the next meeting.
- Results of the meeting review although this is optional. It is more important for the chairperson and Quality Adviser to keep the sheet of flipchart paper for their review meeting.

Notes need to be circulated promptly, ideally next day, certainly within the week. If you have access to one, it is possible to use a portable personal computer to record notes as they happen during the meeting. It's also a good idea to review the format of the notes after a couple of meetings.

SOME COMMON IRRITATIONS

✖ Interruptions. These come in several forms – messages being brought in, pagers and mobile phones ringing. Make arrangements for messages before the meeting. At the start of the meeting, ask if anyone is expecting any important messages and ask people to switch off the mobile phones and pagers.

✖ People don't start their actions until they get the notes. Make it clear at the start of the meeting that people are responsible for keeping a record of their own actions. The notes then become a check-list and reminder.

LOGISTICS CHECKLIST

1. Where will the meeting be held and who will book the venue?
2. What layout is suitable?
   Boardroom, U-shape, with or without tables.
3. What equipment is needed?
   Flipchart, pens, blu-tack, overhead projector, video.
4. What are the 'quorum' rules?
   Who must attend for the meeting to go ahead?
   What happens if either the chairperson or Quality Adviser can't attend?
5. In what circumstances will guests attend?
6. Do any special arrangements need to be made to ensure release of attendees from their usual jobs?
7. If someone is delayed or unable to attend, who should be notified, how and when?
8. How often will the meeting take place?

9. What are the start and finish times?
10. Are refreshments or meals required and who will arrange? Does anyone have any special dietary requirements?
11. Will smoking be allowed?
12. Who will take the notes?
13. How will the notes be circulated and how soon after the meeting?

23 Tools and techniques in action

This chapter is on the tools and techniques in action. The examples are intended to show that tools and techniques can be very potent when pulled out of the hat in all sorts of situations. Here are some examples highlighting their use.

TPN AT GAMBIER TERRACE

Sometimes, although you may well be following one of the methodologies, there is a sudden moment when you see the light. This is often when a specific tool or technique clears the fog for you. This is a letter I received from Maggi Howard who is the Development Officer at Liverpool Housing Trust. Maggi had one of those moments.

Dear Richard,

I think I've got just the story you need for illustrating TPN analysis and the general planning principle of identifying key players for your book. Do you remember the first Development department quality training day back in December two years ago? I was insistent on using a real life project rather than a pretend scenario. Jayne and I applied TPN analysis to our 'for sale' project at Gambier Terrace. I was new in my job. My old role had been to identify and manage refurbishment projects at properties already in the Trust's ownership. It irritated me to carry out works at properties that weren't as bad as the derelicts next door. This project gave me the opportunity to spend £1.25 million on purchase and refurbishment of derelict houses – just what I'd always wanted to do and just what I'd always criticized 'them' for not doing. I had always said 'they ought to do something about that building'. Frighteningly, 'they' turned out to be me.

I had £550 000 of grant to commit by 9th March the following year. All I needed was to exchange contracts to purchase four properties. I felt wholly responsible for making this happen and hadn't recognized how important it was to identify the key players and get them all on board with the project. I felt I wasn't going to achieve the deadline. In these days of shrinking grants, it is a cardinal sin not to spend grant funds. To lose grant to another association or worse to another region was not an option for me.

I recognized that unless I was able to instil a sense of urgency into the Estates Department of the City Council I would not be able to deliver. Although terms had

235

been agreed with the existing lease holders, the freeholds remain in the ownership of the City Council. TPN analysis identified what was within my control, what was not within my control and what was partially within my control. It was when we shifted the 'key player' post-its from the N section to the P section that I realized I could influence the outcome, even if I couldn't control it. As a direct result of the training day, I arranged a meeting that incorporated a visit by the key players, including my solicitor, the city solicitor and city estates surveyor, to the site. This meeting tipped the balance. The key players acknowledged their role in making the project happen. A failure to deliver on their part would result in a huge missed opportunity for the city (which needs all the opportunities it can get!), the potential residents, the buildings, LHT and for Merseyside as a whole. The commitment of my solicitor was outstanding (she did most of the city's documentation for them) and, at the eleventh hour, we exchanged contracts on the four properties on 9th March. Not only did we exchange but we have since finished the building work and the flats are sold.

In answer to your question about the tools: was it easy? Yes, with the right tools. Without them it would not have happened.

Maggi Howard

There is an important lesson in this story. You can never predict which tool or technique is going to be most important in any project. Nor does the methodology always tell you when to use one. When I am working as a Quality Adviser with a group of people and they are struggling or are stuck, I can't claim that I always know what to do so I suggest 'why don't you try tool x on it?'. If they look blank, then I suggest tool y. Ninety-nine times out of a hundred this works.

TOOLS IN TENANT PARTICIPATION

This is a piece that Leonie Lupton, Tenant Liaison Manager at South Yorkshire Housing Association, wrote for me. It is particularly interesting from two points of view. First, there is no formal quality initiative in SYHA and Leonie is the only person in the organization who has had any training in the methodologies, tools and techniques. Second, the tools and techniques have found a new forum. Leonie's job involves working with groups of tenants and they are finding the tools and techniques as useful as any workplace group. Leonie writes:

BACKGROUND TO SOUTH YORKSHIRE HOUSING ASSOCIATION

SYHA has been in existence for 25 years and manages 3 000 homes for rent throughout South Yorkshire. 1 000 of these homes are bed spaces in residential care for people with special needs. There is no formal quality initiative at the moment. There are future plans to pursue a Charter Mark or Investors in People. Hardly anyone knows what Total Quality Management is, and people who have come across it are pretty sceptical. So now is a good time to start talking about me!

LEONIE DISCOVERS TQM

I previously worked for Liverpool Housing Trust as a Tenant Participation Adviser and was trained with their first batch of Quality Advisers. For me the training was life changing in all sorts of ways. It revolutionized the way I did my job and gave me a real sense of achievement. A big part of my job was training and facilitating tenant groups and I became a much more effective (and interesting) trainer as a result. As for the tools and techniques, I took to them like a duck to water and was soon flowcharting and clustering everywhere. One of the best results of my new-found skills was winning a contract through competitive tender from the Department of the Environment to organize a national conference for consultants involved in promoting tenant management. The tools and techniques really got me through. I began by spending a Sunday evening constructing a huge planning grid on my living room floor. This got me and the other people through to the day, which was a great success. I know that because of the questionnaire I designed and the bar charts I produced of what attendees thought about all the various aspects of the conference. The 85–15 rule about processes and people made complete sense and I became a much better manager as a result. I never blame people before fully considering the processes by which they get their job done.

This new and wonderful belief that I could achieve most things career wise using a combination of the right tools and techniques and the planning methodology meant that I felt I was ready for a promotion. Just over a year ago I was successfully interviewed by SYHA for their new post of Tenant Liaison Manager. I was sad to leave the quality initiative in LHT but this was a really good opportunity and I left to start a new life in Sheffield. On my first day at SYHA I blew the dust off the office's only flipchart stand (I'm not joking) and ordered a stack of post-it notes. Now I was ready to take the organization by storm with Quality Adviser training ... well not quite.

APPLYING THE TOOLS AND TECHNIQUES AS AN INDIVIDUAL

At first it was really difficult to keep working by the principles I had learned at LHT. I underestimated the impact of the new quality culture in LHT and how that had made applying my training not only easy but expected. At SYHA I began by going for an overly holistic approach. 'Oh ... how interesting' people said unconvincingly. But I also organized my workload using must-should-could and clustering and following the planning methodology. As a result I met the vast majority of my annual targets within my first year. And other staff noticed that I wasn't just using post-it notes for telephone messages! I ran some training for both staff and tenants associations on the key tools of brainstorming, clustering and Ishikawa diagrams. People were enthused but I didn't really see many of them using the tools in action.

The key moment for me was when SYHA needed a new approach for collecting rent arrears. I sat in a meeting where people talked about taking on extra staff and having performance rewards for those staff who got their arrears down first. Dr Deming had always been spoken about in almost reverent terms and while it had been interesting it had never really sunk in. Now I could see with Damascus-like clarity that the approach we were taking was far too people based and didn't tackle any of the underlying processes. At the next meeting I chaired. I decided we were going to do an Ishikawa diagram to get people thinking in terms of processes. We did it and it was brilliant – the best one I've ever facilitated and people were so enthusiastic. It was really noticeable that the blame culture completely disappeared and people were really focused on solutions. Now a small project group are considering all of the ideas on the diagram. Perhaps even better than this was that yesterday I went into a meeting room and there on the wall someone had begun a new Ishikawa diagram.

APPLYING THE TOOLS AND TECHNIQUES TO TENANT PARTICIPATION

The quality principle of 'involve the workers' has a direct parallel with 'involve the tenants' and I've had a lot of success, and fun, with using these techniques with tenants groups. I think this is because the tools are all so participative and they really make things move much quicker than just discussion. Things like Ishikawa diagrams are also highly visual and they really focus people and give them a sense of achievement. I've only just started learning about Quality in the Community. It's a very exciting way of bringing communities together that is working successfully in America and I'm sure it's going to be a big thing in Britain too.

Now for a few practical examples. The first is from my work in Liverpool where I was working with a tenants organization who wanted to manage their own estate. They were confident they could deliver and manage better repairs than their council landlords. We used an Ishikawa diagram to look at all the elements of a good repairs service and then we arranged the ideas using TPN. This was then the basis of their repairs policy and procedure.

The second example follows some training on meeting techniques that I ran for tenants associations in May last year. One group particularly loved clustering. A day later I received a call from our Rotherham office wanting to know why Dalton Brook Tenants Association wanted a pad of flipchart paper and some post-it notes! The next time I went to one of their meetings they brainstormed and clustered loads of suggestions for improving their estate. One of the local councillors, who was usually very negative about their ability to do anything, could not believe how many good ideas they had. That group now feel a lot more empowered and are expressing an interest in exploring the possibility of getting more involved in managing the estate.

The final example which springs to mind is about the planning grid. These are just brilliant as action plans for tenants associations. I used to spend half a meeting agreeing an action plan with a group. Then it would get typed up and after another few meetings completely forgotten. Now we do all our action plans as a planning grid which we leave on sheets of sellotaped together flipchart paper. This is brought to every meeting and the post-it notes are moved about if people haven't managed to do what they said. This really focuses people on the task. You try ignoring an action plan that's four feet tall!

A word about names. It just doesn't work to call Ishikawa diagrams by their Japanese name when working with community groups. I've tried but it's just meaningless jargon. I call them by their plain and descriptive name of cause-and-effect diagrams. I've discussed this with Richard but he's a purist.

AND FINALLY...

My advice to anyone reading Richard's book who thinks 'this is interesting stuff, but I don't have a Quality Adviser or Champion so it's not going to work for me' is yes it will! Try using some of the tools and techniques on your own first to look at some individual projects. Then have a go at introducing some of the tools in meetings. Helps and hinders and round robins are good ones to start with. Then you can go on to Ishikawa diagrams and maybe even a deployment flowchart. You might feel strange standing up and facilitating these at first (have a rehearsal on your own and give everyone a copy of the rules) but these techniques are infectious and they really do work. Good luck.

Leonie Lupton

ISHIKAWA AT THE CLUB

Here is another letter I received in reply to a request for examples. This one is from Phil Bennett who is Plant Controller with Greater Manchester Waste at their Stockport Reclamation Site. Phil was trained as a Quality Adviser at GMW and found an unusual application outside work for some of the tools.

Dear Richard,

Hi! It seems ages ago now since I first met you and John at Alsager on your three-day course. I was there by default as someone else had dropped out at short notice and I hadn't a clue what to expect and that's the way it was from session to session throughout the course, fast and furious and pretty good fun. When I returned home I remember thinking to myself, was all that quite real and, if it was, how was I going to use it? Little did I know, I'd just seen the tip of a very large iceberg.

When we next met you may recall I told you how I had quite amazed myself regarding events in connection with my local club. At the time I was acting chairman of the club and a member of the bar and finance committee. It was the task of this sub-committee to prepare a comprehensive job description, in advance of interviews, for the post of club steward. It had previously been decided by full committee that the club was due for refurbishment and it was obvious that the same sub-committee was going to be dealing with this matter in the not too distant future, so bearing the above in mind, where were we going to start?

Well we started by someone saying let's look at the cellar duties first. The result? You've got it – chaos! Stock control in the cellar is tied with stock control in the bar, is tied with what's on order, is tied in with cash at hand, is tied with and on it went and that's what was happening from any start point. Now at this juncture, I don't know how it happened, but quite spontaneously I'd got each member of the group in turn saying what they thought was right and then wrong regarding anything to do with the club whilst I jotted it down. No post-its and no flipchart, but there we were without fully realizing it – brainstorming.

From the above we generated an enormous list and it wasn't until this was complete did anyone deem to ask, where is all this leading? That's when I had to put my thinking cap on. To keep things flowing I got the group to break the list down by clustering which was quite easy. The finished clusters suggested their own titles – facilities, bar prices, decor and so on. It was now I needed my Quality Advisers Manual. The group had run with me thus far, what would they make of Ishikawa? More to the point, what would I make of Ishikawa?

We reconvened our meeting the following evening and I was at least a little more prepared. Still no post-its but I had rewritten all the suggestions made the previous evening onto little strips of paper and prepared two sheets of wallpaper backing, both with a fishbone diagram and in the effect boxes nothing more simple than 'positive' and 'negative'. Add to this a small roll of sellotape and with fingers, arms, legs and anything else that could be crossed, crossed I was ready. Were the rest of the group?

I couldn't believe how easily they accepted what I was proposing and shortly after a brief introduction to Ishikawa we were well on our way to completing our diagrams. The headings we used for the main arrows were adequately covered by those suggested in the Quality Advisers Manual – methods, equipment, people, environment and materials. Now what really amazed me was, for the first time I saw this group working together as a team. We now had after two brief sessions all the information required and in a format that we all understood to be able to put together a comprehensive job description for the post of club steward, but not only that. We now have all the information at hand which just needs prioritizing and costing when we start discussing refurbishment. In this case a little knowledge went a long, long way.

I'm happy to say that things have developed and the more we've met the more I've learned and hopefully I'm a little more professional in my approach now than I was then. I recently had some success with a snowball! Well it is that time of year.

Phil Bennett

THE BIGGEST CHRONOLOGICAL CLUSTER IN THE WORLD?

Here is a piece that Peter Strachan, Director Railtrack Midlands, wrote. This is an important example as it illustrates that chronological clustering is not only useful in small or medium-sized projects, but equally powerful in very complex situations. In this case the use of the tool also provided an excellent point around which other issues could be addressed.

BACKGROUND

The late 1990s saw the biggest structural change in UK railways since nationalization in 1948. In preparing for privatization of the system, British Rail was divided into 100 individual components. Train Operating Companies would run trains and provide the end user product to passengers. Infrastructure Service Units would undertake day-to-day maintenance and renewal of the network. Rolling Stock Companies would act as leasing companies for the locomotives and coaches. Embracing the whole system would be Railtrack, the 'infrastructure controller', responsible for track, signalling, stations and other fixed infrastructure and for facilitating access to the track to allow passenger and freight trains to run. Railtrack is effectively the heart of the network.

THE CHALLENGE

In March 1993 I was asked to become Railtrack's Director for the Midlands and set up one of ten Zones, the management structure by which Railtrack would run its business. Maps showed the embryo Railtrack Midlands as a vast swathe of middle England and mid-Wales: Aberystwyth in the West to Skegness in the East and down to Gloucester and London. Throw in the West Midlands conurbation, the East Midlands, over 100 signal boxes and around 1200 staff ... A month later I had a secretary, some project accommodation in old railway offices in Derby and was rapidly recruiting key people to help in the task of getting Railtrack Midlands up and running by 1st April 1994.

Although work had been done on the outline organizational structure much of this was pretty rough and ready and was based on concepts rather than those essential to making the railway run at 3 o'clock in the morning. It soon became obvious that the range of activity needed some focus and structure if we were to have any chance at all of achieving the vesting date the following April.

By September there were about 15 of us. Many had been involved previously in British Rail reorganizations or in multi-million pound capital investment projects, but this was on a different scale – I am often quoted as saying that 'this one was three times more difficult in half the time – if we get it 60 per cent right we'll have done well'. Being familiar with project-by-project, an approach which had worked well in the past for a number of us, we knew that any plan must have its roots there. But there seemed so many tasks, across so many dimensions: within Railtrack, with new customers and suppliers, with old 'dying' BR organizations and externally through local authorities, opinion formers and the media. And all by 1.4.94?

BRINGING THE PROJECT TEAM TOGETHER

I also wanted to build some team spirit so in mid-September I took the whole team of 17 away for two days to a secret venue in rural Staffordshire. As well as team building we got down to the business of scoping, planning and preparing to implement the Zone.

My project team had been recruited with individual skills against my very early mental picture of both the project requirements and the sort of skill mix I would need in the new team when we actually had to run the outfit. Although some people joined the team for the first time at the event itself, most had been around for a few weeks and were already trying to get their minds around their own specialities. Some of these were hard tasks: detailed consultation with staff representatives, populating the new organization with everyone from signallers to train planners, securing sufficient accommodation and – critically – satisfying the safety validation requirements without which we would not 'go live'. Other tasks were softer and were mostly about working relationships both inside and outside Railtrack. Splitting the BR family to go our own separate ways created new tensions which had to be addressed.

THE APPROACH

We decided to rely on our own knowledge and skills and, on several pads of post-it notes, we individually jotted down what had to be done on a 'one task to one post-it' basis. Then taking a sheet of flipchart paper for each of the six months that remained until vesting we considered every post-it and tried to best place its task on the relevant month's flipchart. Of course there were overlaps and considerable debate went on in the team as to precisely what was meant by a particular item and was it the same as the one we dealt with four post-its ago? But we were careful not to rationalize or reduce too much for fear of losing a vital task. Eventually, we had six very full flipcharts and significantly a seventh sheet holding items which did not need to be addressed before 1st April but could wait until after we went live.

WHAT DID WE SEE?

Not surprisingly there was quite a lot of bunching as we attempted to force tasks to fit 'just-in-time'. That gave us some clues about starting to do things earlier than we had originally intended – the immense job of recruiting people was brought forward as a result. January was the worst month and we tried to move out some of the tasks to less busy periods. We also flushed out a number of interdependencies: final organizational design *before* safety validation could be complete, which led to more movement in the plan. A large cluster of a number of diverse tasks suggested that we needed significantly more people in some areas of the project team than we had first scoped. We were also able to juggle the plan to give tired people an opportunity to refresh over the Christmas holiday!

WHAT HAPPENED NEXT?

Immediately after the event my project manager responsible for project planning converted the flipchart chronology into a proper project plan with bars, milestones and accountabilities. We updated it regularly and it formed the basis for running the project from then all the way through to live running.

GOING LIVE

As I visited signal boxes on Saturday 1st April 1994, handing out commemorative Railtrack mugs, few people would have known we got there by way of clustered post-it notes, flipcharts and … a lot of hard work.

Peter Strachan

Part V
More about Quality Advisers

24 How to select Quality Advisers

The selection and training of Quality Advisers is a critical step in a quality initiative. Quality Advisers as individuals and as a group will probably have the single largest impact of any step you take. Following this the success of your project teams will be heavily dependent upon the methodology they follow, the tools they use and the effectiveness of their teamwork. All of these will be largely influenced by their Quality Adviser. It follows, therefore, that you need to put a lot of thought into how you select your Quality Advisers.

HOW MANY, HOW QUICKLY?

The answers to the questions 'How many?' and 'How quickly?' are largely determined by logistical issues tied up with your quality initiative and organization. Twelve to 15 is a good start for an organization. This is mainly because it's a good number to have on the training course and a good number to have as a coherent group afterwards. How quickly will be determined by how soon you want to set up some projects. If you're serious about adopting the project-by-project approach this needs to be as soon as possible.

WHERE DO QUALITY ADVISERS COME FROM?

Quality Advisers are not usually full-time jobs but people with potential in line positions from across the organization. Potential is the most important word here. Selection as a Quality Adviser as part of a quality initiative is an excellent developmental opportunity. This chapter has been written to assist managers identify potential Quality Advisers. It may be used as initial guidelines to stimulate ideas on possible candidates or to short-list people who have volunteered. All the organizations I have worked with have preferred to pick potential Quality Advisers rather than advertise for volunteers. This is partly because the role is additional to existing workload, partly because it involves no extra payment but

245

mainly because the managers concerned have had a good idea about the sort of people they have been looking for. That is not to say they have always got it 100 per cent right, and I will cover dropping out later.

LOGISTICS

Logistical issues are the starting place in the selection of Quality Advisers. If a person is unable to satisfy these logistics they should be discounted. Quality Advisers must be able to participate in:

1. An initial residential training course lasting three days.
2. Further training as necessary with each project team they are allocated to. As an example, a quality improvement team would normally receive two days' training.
3. Regular meetings for each project team.
4. Further training and development as a Quality Adviser, maybe a full day every three months.

PERSONAL ATTRIBUTES AND BEHAVIOURS

Unlike the logistical issues above, which are generally yes or no answers, this section is subjective and relies on the good judgement of the user. Wherever possible, think what actions might be associated with the attribute. For example, 'the person has demonstrated an interest in quality' might mean that they have volunteered for courses, borrowed and read books or actively enjoyed participation in a project. It may be useful to verify your judgement by asking a colleague whether or not they agree with your opinion. The characteristics have been split into essential and desirable. If the essential characteristics are not met, then the individual should not be selected. The desirable characteristics are icing on the cake.

ESSENTIAL

5. The person has demonstrated an interest in their job or the organization.
6. The person has demonstrated an interest in quality, customer service or improving the job.
7. The person has demonstrated an interest in learning or self-improvement.
8. The person has demonstrated respect for colleagues and their views.
9. The person is articulate.

10. The person is numerate.

DESIRABLE

The person has shown that they:

11. Give adequate preparation to tasks and are generally well organized.
12. Can stick with a task despite difficulties.
13. Have the respect of their colleagues.
14. Can understand the contribution of both theory and practice.
15. Contribute at meetings.
16. Enjoy a challenge.
17. Are able to make a point in a constructive manner.
18. Are not overbearing.
19. Do not easily lose their temper in an argument.
20. Are prepared to ask for help when they get stuck.
21. Have the ability to make presentations.
22. Have conducted training sessions.

WHAT NOT TO CONSIDER

Do not discount anyone for the following reasons:
- grade or seniority
- gender, race, disability
- current role
- shift worker
- not a white-collar worker
- length of service (short, medium or long)
- age.

DROPPING OUT AND TOPPING UP

No matter how carefully you choose your Quality Advisers there will always be some people who drop out. Sometimes this happens straight after the initial training. This is simply because they just don't fancy the role. Some people drop out because they don't get given a project for one reason or another and feel too rusty to have a go later. The main reason for loss of Quality Advisers in the longer term, however, tends to be that they move on to bigger and better things. Remember that this is not wasted effort. Even those Quality Advisers who drop out straightaway will use their new-found skills in their everyday work. Those people who get promoted often do so because these skills dramatically improve their personal effectiveness.

This means that an organization will have to top up the numbers at some stage. If it does not make sense to train an extra dozen or so people, this means there are two options for topping up. The first option is to have conversion training for people who have already received some training in quality skills. This normally takes a day. Alternatively, people can attend an open course with delegates from a mixture of organizations.

FULL-TIME QUALITY ADVISERS

Full-time Quality Advisers are a rare breed. As Quality Manager for InterCity West Coast I had a small team of Quality Improvement Managers working for me who were the closest to full-time Quality Advisers I have seen. These people also had other duties apart from acting as Facilitator (the railway industry prefers this term to Quality Adviser) to project teams. The other main tasks were designing and running training courses in all aspects of quality, facilitating regular management meetings of one sort or another, running one-off planning events and providing consultancy support to line managers. One of the Quality Improvement Managers was also responsible for running the regular network meetings for part-time Facilitators.

As this was a full-time job with an appropriate training programme associated with it, the requirements were different from those for a part-time Quality Adviser. These posts were advertised within the industry and a full interview held. This included questions based upon the person specification shown, a presentation and written work to test numeracy and literacy. No previous experience was required, potential being the main factor. This approach stood me in good stead and led to excellent appointments. The person specification is shown in Figure 24.1 in case you are considering this option.

	Essential	Desirable
Skills	Ability to articulate both verbally and in writing Basic numeracy Ability to learn	Presentation skills Training skills Facilitation skills Awareness of group dynamics
Knowledge	None	Importance of the customer Why facilitation is important Quality philosophy Organizational structure
Qualifications	None	None
Experience	None	Project work Research Attended meetings Been in a quality improvement team Attended a quality course

Figure 24.1 Person specification for Quality Improvement Manager

25 How to train and develop Quality Advisers

During my own training and development I attended quite a few courses that were called Facilitator Training or similar, aimed at developing Quality Adviser skills. I used to receive many calls from people asking me to recommend courses and I set up several using outside consultants. As our experience of working with project teams grew and grew, we became far more discerning about what worked and what didn't. Eventually, I decided that we could do it better and the team set about designing an in-house course. This chapter is the latest development of this early work.

INITIAL TRAINING

DURATION AND VENUE

Initial training needs to be of three days' duration and run on a residential basis. Three days is the best option for a number of reasons. Two days is too short to cover the essentials. Although it would easily be possible to fill four or five days, three allows coverage of all the vital material but people are pretty full up at the end of it. I doubt if there would be any capacity left for further learning after this period of time. The residential aspect is especially important where this is a course run for an organization in the early days of a quality initiative as the group of Quality Advisers will be vital to success. It allows reflection and conversation in the evening and provides an opportunity for the Quality Advisers to bond together. There are also the advantages of being off-site, no interruptions and an opportunity to work hard without distraction.

THE STYLE

Quality Adviser training needs to be very practical but offer something to suit all learning styles. There needs to be a mixture of theoretical underpinning, some real examples and practical exercises with the opportunity to practise new skills. It needs to be hard work at quite a pace but allow time for reflection and relaxation to allow the learning to sink in.

WHO ATTENDS?

It is fairly obvious that all the people you want trained as Quality Advisers need to attend. It is also a very good idea for the senior manager who is leading the initiative to attend. There are a number of reasons for this. First, they too need to develop these skills. Second, they will be the figurehead of the Quality Advisers network and have an important leadership role to play both during the initial training and subsequently. Third, they can provide specific organizational input that the people running the course can't. They may be able to answer specific questions there and then but it is also likely they will go away with a long list of things to sort out or think about. Lastly, if they don't attend, they won't know what's gone on at a pivotal point in their initiative. To return to the examples we talked about earlier, both Dave Power of Liverpool Housing Trust and Sue Ormrod of Greater Manchester Waste set this example and attended the training. There is another category of people you might want to attend. These fall into the category of unlikely to ever carry out the role formally but are either very interested or important enough to want on your side. Think about this one carefully.

CONTENTS

The following needs to be incorporated into your Quality Adviser training:

- an overview of the history of quality
- key principles
- overview of the project-by-project approach
- the methodologies
- effective meetings
- introduction to processes, why they are important and how to improve them
- tools and techniques and how to lead groups through them
- what to look for in groups
- key models of group dynamics
- how to make an intervention in a meeting.

PUBLIC COURSES

Public courses are open to anybody. They may not be advisable at the first stage in a quality initiative, but public courses are essential for very small organizations or when you need to top up the numbers of your Quality Advisers. Public courses need to incorporate all the contents listed above. What is lost in a public course is a lot of the specific organizational issues. What is gained though is an opportunity to hear about other people's work environments. Everyone is always surprised at the commonality of problems across both organizations and industries, and they get a lot out of mixing with new people.

NETWORK MEETINGS

Network meetings are vital in maintaining the momentum following initial training. For those who are allocated a project soon after the training, they are an important source of support and provide an opportunity for review and reflection. Not everybody will be allocated a project straightaway and someone will always be last, maybe having to wait over a year for their first opportunity to undertake the role formally. For these people, network meetings are vital so they don't completely forget everything they have learned.

USE THE NETWORK METHODOLOGY

It is a good idea to use the network methodology for your meetings and particularly cover the relevant parts of stage 1 at the first meeting. Now here's a deep question. Do you need a Quality Adviser for a Quality Advisers network meeting? My own advice (having tried it) is no! It's too easy to get caught up in interventions about interventions. You do, however, need to be very clear about who is in the lead at any particular time.

WHAT TO DO AT NETWORK MEETINGS

The network methodology should help you to originate your own ideas, but here are a few:

- Have refreshers about the material covered on the initial training.
- Watch videos about quality, teams or other relevant subjects and debate them.
- Practise using the tools.
- Have round robins (see Chapter 21) about who's done what.
- Organize practising Quality Advisers to do short presentations about what their teams have done, the data they have collected and the tools they have used at key stages of the project.
- Have short training sessions.

● Have a 'surgery' session – a chance to help with difficult issues and problems that teams and Quality Advisers are encountering.

FOLLOW-ON TRAINING AND EDUCATION

Remember that three days' training and a couple of network meetings only really scratch the surface of what a proficient Quality Adviser needs to know. But also remember that you don't know what you don't know and as Quality Advisers start to apply what they have learned they will start to identify areas for follow-on training. Some ideas for this are:

● more about the methodologies and how to adapt them to suit your needs
● data collection, display and analysis
● influencing skills
● advanced group working skills
● upgrade training on the tools and techniques
● change and how to manage it
● quality management and the work of people like Deming, Juran and Ishikawa.

If you have a full day every six months, you have the basis for a good three-year developmental programme. At the end of it you won't just have an excellent Quality Adviser. You'll also have an excellent manager.

CONFERENCES AND VISITS

This idea should come up as part of the network methodology. Consider getting your Quality Advisers to attend conferences where other organizations present how they are approaching quality. Some organizations put on the occasional seminar or may allow you to attend their own Quality Advisers network meetings. These are also opportunities for follow-on training and education.

TRAINING FOR PROJECT TEAMS

Quality Advisers will also attend training with the teams they are allocated to. Although some of this will be repetition of what they have heard before, no-one has complained that it's not worthwhile.

26 Practical tips for Quality Advisers

Perhaps the most daunting step for a Quality Adviser is the first telephone call following their training when they are asked to help out with a meeting or project. The secret to a good start is preparation. This chapter is designed to help you prepare for that initial encounter and your subsequent meetings.

PRE-MEETINGS

A Quality Adviser may well be asked to help out with all sorts of meetings. These might be team meetings, regular management meetings, project meetings and so on. If this is part of a project, the Champion will arrange a pre-project meeting which should follow a fixed agenda. If not, the first thing to do is fix up a pre-meeting with the chairperson. Before going to your pre-meeting, plan an agenda based on the check-lists shown in Figures 26.1 and 26.2. Decide which of the items listed you need to consider. Think in advance about what methodology would be appropriate for the meeting, what sort of things you would expect to see on the agenda and use Chapter 22 on 'Effective meetings' as a refresher.

MY ROLE

- Why do you want a Quality Adviser?
- Is there anything specific you want me to do?
- Explain the three elements of your role and what you will do before, during and after the meeting (see Figure 26.3).
- Agree how you will work together.
  Don't ask, 'What would you like me to do?' Say, 'This is how I would like to work.' Make interventions, lead in the use of tools, conduct a review at the end.

Use this check-list to gather information about the meeting you have been asked to help out with. These are questions to ask the chairperson.

(1) What is the purpose of the meeting?

(2) Is this a one-off or part of a series?

(3) How many previous meetings have there been?

(4) How does it fit in with other meetings?

(5) Who attends? (Look for duplication, anyone missing, inappropriate attendees.)

(6) Can you explain the role of each attendee?

(7) How long have the group known each other?

(8) Have you had problems with the meeting?

(9) What works well?

(10) What are group behaviours like?

(11) Are there any specific people causing you problems? (In what way?)

(12) Are there any specific people who have a key role or who help you a lot? (In what way?)

Figure 26.1 About the meeting check-list

Use this check-list to gather information about the logistics of the meeting. These are questions to ask the chairperson. The questions in brackets you should ask yourself. Also use the full check-list in Chapter 22 for other logistical issues.

(1) What are the start and finish times? (Are they sensible?)

(2) What is the room layout? (Is there a better alternative?)

(3) What is the venue and location? (Are they suitable?)

(4) Have refreshments, lunch and equipment have booked?

(5) Have you planned an agenda? (If yes, review. If no, do you want to plan it now?)

(6) What do you want to get out of each item? (For example, debate, decision, briefing item.)

(7) How are the agenda and papers circulated? (Can you see any problems?)

(8) Who takes the notes?

Figure 26.2 Meeting logistics check-list

256

THINK AHEAD

- Are there any tools or techniques that might be useful?
- Plan a review meeting now.
- If necessary, suggest to the chairperson that you speak to other participants prior to the meeting to gather more information.

PRE-PROJECT MEETINGS

If this is a pre-project meeting and you will be working with the Project Leader on an ongoing basis see the relevant sections elsewhere in the book. Note especially stage 8 of the steering group methodology (see Chapter 6) and stage 0 of each of the planning, quality improvement team, problem-solving or network methodologies (see Chapters 9, 10, 11 and 12). Also make sure you are well up on what to look for in the project remit. This is in stage 5 of the steering group methodology.

BEFORE, DURING AND AFTER THE MEETING

MAKE CERTAIN THAT YOU HAVE WITH YOU

- Post-it notes – oblong and square.
- Blu-tack.
- Flipchart pens.

ON ARRIVAL

- Make sure you're there in good time.
- Check the room layout is as planned and that any equipment needed is there, the flipchart in a suitable position and overhead projector focused.
- Decide where you want to sit. Consider where the chairperson will be sitting and find a good vantage position.

DURING THE MEETING

- Work with the chairperson according to your pre-arranged ground rules.
- Ensure the agenda is followed. Watch out for the discussion going off at a tangent or too much detail.
- Observe the group dynamics and take notes about what you see:
  Levels of contribution – who says a little, who says a lot.
  Poor meeting behaviours – side debates, interruptions, arguments.

- Make interventions as necessary.
- Watch for decisions. Encourage the use of tools and data for decision making. Ensure decisions are clearly understood and recorded.
- If a tool is to be used, make sure everyone is clear about the purpose and rules. You should lead so that the chairperson and team can contribute.
- Keep an eye on the time. If agenda items are over-running, draw this to the attention of the chairperson.

AT THE END OF THE MEETING

- Conduct a meeting review – use helps and hinders (see Chapter 19). Contribute any personal observations you might have.

AFTER THE MEETING

- Hold a review with the chairperson. Share any observations you might have. Ask for feedback on how you did.
- If you will be working with the group again, make notes about what to do the same, what to do differently, and what to watch out for next time.

THE BALANCE

Thinking about the three responsibilities of a Quality Adviser, it is useful to have an idea about the balance between them before, during and after the meeting so you can be clear about where to focus your attention (see Figure 26.3).

| *Responsibility 1:* Helps the Project Leader and team plan and follow the methodology by which they will work. | *Before:* Plan it. | *During:* Keep the group on track. | *After:* Review. |

| *Responsibility 2:* Advises which tools and techniques are appropriate at each stage of the project and helps apply these. | *Before:* Identify suitable tools and plan their use | *During:* Lead the group in the use of the tools. Suggest techniques for group work. | *After:* Review. |

| *Responsibility 3:* Observes and helps with team dynamics and the effectiveness of meetings. | *Before:* Anticipate problems. Plan techniques. | *During:* Make interventions as appropriate. | *After:* Review. |

Figure 26.3 The balance before, during and after

259

27 Quality Advisers in action

It has been quite difficult to separate the material in this chapter from that in 'Methodologies in action' and 'Tools and techniques in action' because of the obvious overlaps between the three areas. What I have tried to do here is address some specific issues, such as how Quality Advisers have been selected in practice and running network meetings. You'll also find contributions from practising Quality Advisers. This should convey what it feels like to be a Quality Adviser and what it's like to try and use the tools and techniques.

SUE ORMROD SELECTS

I asked Sue Ormrod at Greater Manchester Waste how she selected her Quality Advisers.

SUE:

I went for people who I thought would be interested, a mix of people who would do it and sell it. This included what you might call a political element in the form of trade union representatives. I took the view that, if out of the first 15, ten actually made it then that would have been a success and I've supplemented the number since. Even if someone doesn't make a good Quality Adviser, they're then an excellent potential team member. I also went for different levels of the organization right from senior manager to heavy goods vehicle driver.

How did the training go?

SUE:

Very well. It was easy to understand and non-threatening. A lot of people are frightened of training. The nature of the topic suited an off-site venue and I would say that the residential aspect is essential. I got a lot of stick in the bar in the evenings which is one of the reasons I was there. Some have dropped out since partly because I've not been able to give them projects but that doesn't matter because they're using their skills elsewhere.

Have you seen any spin off benefits?

SUE:

Yes, we've had a very short pay-back period. There were lots of intangible benefits quite quickly. People have had an attitude change about the way they approach work. There's more interaction between groups and departments. If they are on a course or in a team together, they tend to pick up the phone and sort things out. People think before they act. They stop and think about the processes involved in something. They'll think 'if we do that, what are the implications elsewhere?'. There's been a big increase in confidence levels in people who were once quite timid – they're now prepared to take senior management to task. The Quality Advisers have become a network of people who know and enjoy each other's company and there's a sense of belonging in terms of multidisciplinary groups. People also look at the individuals in a different manner. You hear things like 'she's really good at what she does'. The Quality Advisers cut through the traditional 'them and us' barriers both between managers and workers and different groups of staff and I think it's engendered a feel of corporate belonging, something we've not had before.

JANET TAYLOR

Janet wrote this piece for me. It's an interesting story with some specific examples and some general observations.

I was assigned to one of the first quality improvement teams to be established in Liverpool Housing Trust – improving the hand-over process. We had a good choice of team members across departments. This worked well within the team and also improved interdepartmental links generally. I stuck rigidly to the quality improvement team methodology in the manual. One of the things I learned from the experience was that the requirements of each project vary slightly from the strict methodology but I would still always follow this as a guide. It took an age to complete the deployment flowchart. This was due to lack of experience and I can now do one with my eyes shut! I think a lot of teams have found this difficult simply because of the complexity of some of our processes. We got a bit stuck on data gathering but I've since had training and learned from analysing the data how to do it better next time.

I have also had some involvement in project steering groups. I am currently Quality Adviser to two project steering groups – the Core Services Review and the St Domingo Strategy steering group. The Core Services Review has a remit to develop a customer-focused housing service for the future. The role of the steering group is to direct the overall project and coordinate sub-groups looking at specific areas. St Domingo is a problem area suffering from low demand for homes, high crime and houses in poor condition. The steering group was established to coordinate and implement a strategy to improve social, environmental and physical conditions. The scope of the project is wide and three sub-groups have been established. In both projects the leader of each sub-group is a steering group member. So far this approach seems to be working. It allows a lot of people across the Trust to be involved which is necessary because of the subject areas but it also allows the steering groups to keep control of the projects.

As far as tools are concerned I particularly like the Ishikawa diagram when used at the start of a project to generate ideas. We used this tool in the St Domingo Strategy steering group. The head of the 'fish' had 'St Domingo, the perfect place to live' and was done with about 20 people who were all to remain in the steering group or one of the sub-groups. We used brainstorming with people focused on the head. We filled a wall with ideas, some innovative, some obvious. These were then clustered into areas for the sub-groups to work on. Four months on, these are still forming the sub-groups' work. I also use brainstorming and clustering all the time myself. It's a great way to get things moving. Without these, in the past people have struggled to think at the start of projects.

The techniques for group work are also very useful. I used to do warm ups religiously. I now find that I only do them for one-off projects or when the team seem to need lifting a little. Senior managers don't like them but I've started again lately despite this, especially for the 09.30 Monday morning meetings. The tip you gave me about communications for the Core Services Review steering group works very well. Now we do a round robin at the end of each meeting – around the room for two areas each which need to be communicated to the organization. We've had three briefs out so far which I think have contained loads of information. Nobody now says that they don't know what is going on with the review. Whether they like it or not is another matter…

So far all my experiences of quality advising have been good ones! I have been able to build up a good relationship with the Project Leader. This is vital to fulfil your role. You need to have an informal relationship so that you can be honest with each other. I think if I hadn't had this my experiences might not have been so good. You need to be quite active, especially in the early stages, so that team members see the value of having you there. I would say that a Quality Adviser does need some knowledge of the subject area as then you know if the team are going off track. It's difficult to judge when to intervene if you don't know anything about the subject.

As for me, what can I say? It has changed my life! This might sound a bit drastic but it has made a difference. I think more clearly because I think in a structured way. I don't just accept that problems occur now. I try and find out when in the process something has gone wrong. It's also given me a lot more confidence both in work and outside. In my day-to-day work I spend time gathering data in order to identify problems and I plan better now.

Janet Taylor

ANDY BARRETT

Andy is a Housing Manager at Liverpool Housing Trust and one of the first group of Quality Advisers to be trained there.

How did you become a Quality Adviser?

ANDY:

Dave Power selected me. I don't know what criteria he used. I think he chose people who had a bit of a track record of flexible thinking. What I thought at the time was another management guru training course. But when I went on the training not only was it practical but it also made intellectual sense. It provided a practical framework and I came away thinking it was a good idea. To give you an example, I'd seen Ishikawa diagrams many times before the training but I'd never actually done one or seen anyone else do one. The tools made sense in the framework of the philosophy.

What happened after the training?

ANDY:

After the training there was a bit of a gap for me. I think the early quality improvement teams were a bit of a learning curve. We tackled relatively straightforward things, which was a good idea. We were all learning as we went along. Me and the other Quality Advisers were seen as experts, which we weren't. Again, to give you an example, there was a lot of concern about deployment flowcharts and the first few were more about learning than anything else. There was also a bit of a feeling that we were the chosen ones. The people who hadn't been selected were asking 'why wasn't I? – I'd have liked a go at that.' As people got quality training and there were more Quality Advisers this got less and less. Now nearly everyone has been touched by quality and I think it was the right way to go about it.

How have the methodologies worked for you?

ANDY:

A methodology gives a clear framework and imposes a certain amount of rigour. It's a big help, it gives you a clear plan, shows where you want to go to and why and forces you to concentrate on relevant issues. The difficulty can be in the rigidity of the model. Although in the training you said to be flexible it's quite hard to know when we were okay to do this. Once we did we were fine. I think you've got to be careful not to think if you follow the methodology it will deliver the results, especially if you slavishly follow the model when common sense says otherwise. You also need to put some thought into it and I'm more comfortable doing that now.

Have you any advice for future Quality Advisers?

ANDY:

Be open minded. Gurus come and go but the philosophical underpinning of the work of Dr Deming is what gives this approach its strength. The easy thing to do is use post-it notes. The hard thing to do is grasp the philosophy and its implications. Beware the comfort blanket of tools and techniques. These are not substitutes for thought. I'm not saying that I understand it but I do make an effort.

In a way I was surprised I was chosen. I'm quite impatient and like to get things done. This doesn't lend itself to teamwork or rigour and this has been a good discipline for me. There's another danger in wanting to take shortcuts. Because I get a clear idea of what I want to achieve I find the process tiring. Take shortcuts only with caution. What I've found is that answers often present themselves early on but you need to spend time validating them. It would be easy to say let's dispense with that but if you start with a preconception and go forward without checking it out you keep meeting obstacles. Some of the people who are most impatient are senior managers who keep referring you to the real world but in the real, real world projects just don't get finished.

Also don't bog yourself down in unnecessary data gathering. Don't gather tons of data you don't need. Don't forget you can ask the person who does the job.

RAY TASKER AND STEVE ROBINSON REFLECT

Here are a couple more examples from Greater Manchester Waste. Ray Tasker, who I interviewed about his experience as Project Leader on the fleet composition quality improvement team, and Steve Robinson reflect on how the Quality Adviser training affected them personally and some of the changes they have seen.

Ray Tasker

Attending the course and being trained as a Quality Adviser has given me a better way of running the job. I don't just mean projects, just in my day-to-day work. We might have had a good laugh on that course but we didn't stop working. It's given me better methods, I'm more organized and absolutely more confident in doing a presentation or working the flipchart. That used to be very, very daunting to me. If you'd given me this project twelve months ago I'd have just jacked and said I can't do that. Before the training I was very, very sceptical. I remember you coming and doing a briefing before the training and afterwards I was saying to people 'he didn't answer one question, that bloke'!

Steve Robinson

I've always been of the opinion that you should ask the person who does the job. The person doing the sweeping up runs their own home, runs their own bank account, has hobbies and isn't an idiot. People used to say 'they never ask us'. That's changing, we are being asked. I'm not saying we get it right all the time but the more we include people like that the better.

The Quality Adviser training gave me confidence. I came out feeling that I wanted to control a meeting rather than sit back. Previously, I never really went to many meetings but I can remember going to one where everyone was talking in little groups. You don't get that now. The quality of meetings has really improved. People get dragged back to the topic where before they'd be allowed to ramble and they're stopped from talking in small splinter groups.

Looking back at the training it was a brilliant three days. Being residential it just worked. I met other people in the company who I'd only heard about and didn't know. At the end of the day you saw the other side of people and I've never heard anybody say anything negative about it. Although we worked long days there was the right balance between practical stuff and listening and no-one was watching the clock.

I was Shift Charge Engineer for Bolton Incinerator when I went on the training. Now I'm Safety Officer for the company and I'm still finding my feet in my new job but I've seen good results from the project teams. In my own job I'm using bar charts and pie charts on accident figures and this has been helpful in highlighting areas for improvement. As an example, our Health and Safety Committee is working on the introduction of head protection throughout our sites at the moment, after the figures highlighted this as an area we could improve on.

JAYNE MASON

Jayne Mason is another of the Quality Advisers at Greater Manchester Waste. Her current job is as Operational Administration Manager and she has been working as Quality Adviser to the load optimization quality improvement team. I asked her some questions about how things were going.

How were you chosen to be a Quality Adviser?

JAYNE:

I suspect I was chosen at random. A few likely candidates were chosen but I don't know what criteria are used. I think the aim was for a good cross-section. I wasn't in my current post then, I was an admin assistant at the time.

What sticks out most in your memory about the training?

JAYNE:

The methodologies, tools and techniques especially brainstorming, clustering and Ishikawa is a big favourite – I love that. It's really easy to do an Ishikawa diagram. You can see it building up and you can see the patterns straightaway. I also remember the camaraderie and it was great fun. Also how we felt when we came back, still attached to the group.

What happened after the training?

JAYNE:

Not a great deal initially. A couple of months later myself and Carol were given a couple of projects to quality advise. We were among the first to be given projects. But I felt different, mentally organized. It felt weird, almost like a brainwashing.

Can you tell me about the project you were given?

JAYNE:

It was to do with load optimization; it's about making sure each journey made by a vehicle conveys the optimum load especially in terms of weight. Graham the Champion, Pat the Project Leader and myself looked at each area affected and picked someone for the team. We tried to select a good cross-section of people. We aimed to produce recommendations at the end relating to capital expenditure on equipment and improvements on loads going out. We've already done a lot of that but the project is still ongoing.

How did you work with the Project Leader?

JAYNE:

Very well. It helped that we'd worked together before I think. We were very cooperative. We planned before and moved the group along between us and I could shut him up as well if needed. Luckily I didn't have to do that very often. It was useful that we'd been on the Quality Adviser training together and that certainly helped with a totally new concept.

What was the most difficult bit?

JAYNE:

The first meeting I think. Although you understand your role it's difficult to get it across. It's initially daunting getting up in front of them when they're sitting there thinking, 'what's she going to do?'. But this disappeared quickly.

And what was easiest?

JAYNE:

Using the tools and techniques made things really easy, which is I suppose what they're designed to do.

How did the methodology work?

JAYNE:

We followed the quality improvement team methodology and stuck reasonably closely to it. It's helpful to have something to look at before a meeting and work through with Pat and it's something to refer back to. Initially we referred to it a lot, later it became easier. I'd say we stuck to it about 80 per cent of the time. My most important job was to keep the team moving in the right direction and we had one or two strong members who I had to keep in check but they were still very positive.

Have you used your skills elsewhere?

JAYNE:

Yes. Shortly after the course I organized a system for myself. I did a mini-Ishikawa diagram and then prioritized it. I think much more methodically especially when I'm prioritizing something. I may not have made the effort before.

BALI MAMAN

This is a piece by Bali Maman who works for Mediation Sheffield. What is particularly interesting in this example is that Bali works in an organization of just two part-time workers. No matter how good you are at team selection, this presents a problem when establishing project teams. Bali reflects first on her training spent with people from very different organizations, and then on how she is applying her new skills.

Mediation Sheffield

MESH is a voluntary organization which uses trained volunteers to mediate in neighbourhood disputes. MESH is a registered charity and is run by a voluntary management committee which meets every six weeks. Day-to-day operations are managed by two paid, joint coordinators of which I am one, each employed on a part-time basis for 30 hours per week. MESH currently supports 35 volunteer mediators.

Why I was interested in Quality Adviser training

A friend who had an understanding of the work I am involved in suggested the course to me. I was particularly interested in the programme because there was a balance between looking at processes and practical applications of the methods using tools and techniques. The course was directly relevant to my main areas of responsibility such as developing plans and strategies to achieve MESH objectives and developing and implementing further funding strategies. I was particularly interested in learning about methodologies. I also had a personal interest in attending the course as I felt it would contribute to my own personal development in terms of group work and using tools and techniques.

The course

When I arrived, most of the delegates were from organizations very different to my own such as Railtrack and Greater Manchester Waste. I was initially concerned that the training was going to be dominated by issues related to their areas of work and we would have little in common. I did find it a bit cliquey at first because people who came in a group were sitting together and shared the same background. Of course I was guilty of doing the same thing by homing in on people with a similar background to me! Quite often when you go away to a conference or training course where everyone is from a similar background you end up talking shop. People love to sit around drinking coffee, smoking cigarettes and moaning about their jobs! I actually found it useful to be with people who were able to offer a different perspective on common problems. It was nice to hear from other people on the course that they were experiencing the same sort of problems in a completely different work setting. The residential aspect was brilliant and it made a massive difference to the energy everybody was putting into the course because we didn't have to think of those oh so boring things like cooking and cleaning.

How I've used the skills

Well, I just couldn't wait to get hold of a load of post-its and start clustering and planning! In fact it was easy to start using the tools and techniques straightaway. I used brainstorming and a chronological cluster initially to plan and manage my day-to-day responsibilities in work. This worked really well and gave me an overview of what and who was involved in the work that I did. I have since used the planning methodology to look at the priorities for MESH. This has been useful in allowing the organization to identify the immediate as well as long-term priorities. More recently, I have referred back to the manual to look at the project-by-project approach to quality and tools for display and analysis to help me address specific problems in my work.

I have used the techniques for group work a number of times. This has worked very well in situations where I have a clear facilitatory role but is much more difficult when this role has not been defined and I am an 'equal member' of the group.

Conclusion

I think the voluntary sector has to accept the challenge of the nineties by becoming more professional in its planning, implementation and delivery of service. In a society which expects high quality – whether it is a service or a product – the voluntary sector has to prepare itself for change and move on. It is no longer acceptable to muddle along with knee-jerk reactions to crises. I am still learning about the project-by-project approach but the Quality Adviser training has given me a set of skills that will help MESH achieve these improvements.

MAKING INTERVENTIONS

The third role of a Quality Adviser is to observe and help with team dynamics and the effectiveness of meetings. The subject of group dynamics, observing what is going on, drawing conclusions and acting upon them through making interventions and giving feedback is outside of the scope of this book. However, it is possible to give a few tips about making interventions in a meeting situation which will stand you in good stead. These go with the word of warning that they are no real substitute for some proper training. My thanks to my business partner John MackMersh who wrote this contribution for me.

Reflecting on the role of interventions I would offer the following thoughts. When you make an intervention in a group working in or towards a project-by-project approach the purpose of an intervention is primarily to allow the structure of the methodology to continue working effectively – not to improve teamwork because 'that is a good thing'. This mainly involves guiding the energies of the people in a meeting away from 'survivalist urges'.

Survivalist urges are shaped by people's past experience of meetings as battlegrounds rather than tools with a clear function. So people learn to argue rather than look at data. They learn to keep reiterating their point because they know it has nowhere else to go and if it isn't dealt with 'here and now' it will never get dealt with. People learn to accept making snap decisions because the need for a decision suddenly presents itself out of nowhere.

Many interventions at meetings with groups working in the project-by-project approach are simply a case of pointing out when the survivalist perspective is present and promoting project-by-project behaviours. These are the most common situations in which I find myself making interventions during a meeting.

Common situations

Be ready to get the group to do the following:

- Defer – the issue will be dealt with but in the right place.
- Stick to the point – only work on one relevant issue at one time.
- Balance the contribution – no one person should dominate, no one person should be quiet all the time.
- Keep discussion at the right level of detail.

Promote the principles

A second type of intervention is aimed at promoting the principles of the project-by-project approach:

- 'Let's make sure everyone is clear what needs to be done today.'
- 'Have we got the right people to resolve this issue?'
- 'Can I suggest we try this tool now?'
- 'Do we need to collect some data about that?'

FACILITATORS NETWORK

This is a contribution from Tony Finnegan. There are two aspects to look out for. First, Tony provides some tips on operating a network for Facilitators. Second, there are some interesting lessons about running any type of network meeting.

Purpose of the network

If you've read the book and are wearing the T-shirt, you'll know the purpose of networks; people doing similar things in different parts of the organization sharing information and adopting best practice. There are more specific reasons for a network of this kind:

- You've had a few days' training.
- You're expected to help in a change of culture in the way your organization works.
- People are looking to you for the answers.
- You are at best apprehensive, at worst scared.
- You need support from people who understand your problems.
- You need coaching from those who know more than you.

Background

I was promoted to a new job which had as part of its responsibilities the development of a Facilitators network. The network had previously been established by a very capable and skilled colleague, Sylvia Cotton. Her sigh of relief and dancing on the desk at hand-over did give me some cause for concern and with good reason.

Logistical problems

Many a nervous twitch and outbreaks of deleted expletives were experienced for the following reasons:

- Network members based over a large geographical area.
- Different departments involved.
- People who worked shifts.
- Continuous reorganizations, people moving around, keeping mailing lists up to date.
- Last minute cancellations due to operational necessity.

It was a frustrating and difficult task but nearly always worthwhile and satisfying. A good measure of success was the high number of Facilitators who attended regularly. One of the most disappointing aspects of the meeting was the low number of projects available for people to apply their newly acquired skills. Even so, it was noticeable that even those people who never got to facilitate a sizeable project enjoyed the experience and developed their skills. If the meetings were to be successful then the content had to be good enough to stimulate their attention and hold their interest.

Meeting composition

To have some idea about the contents of the meetings, a colleague and I brainstormed ideas with the heading of 'the effective Facilitator' followed, of course, by clustering. From this we devised the main body of the meeting. Some examples are:

- Warm ups – experimenting with new warm ups, asking attendees if they could suggest any and trying them out.
- Facilitators update – a round robin of projects we had been doing, what worked well, what problems we had, what tools we'd used, what data we'd collected.
- Videos – anything based no matter how loosely around quality which would stimulate debate.
- Book review session.
- Tools – introducing new ones, developing skills.
- Guest speakers – Directors, Project Leaders, team members, interesting people.

Benefits

'If you want to know the cost of training, just look at the balance sheet and there it is. The benefits you'll never know.' – Dr Deming. (Don't quote this if you're ever interviewed for a training job.) The moral? I have much anecdotal evidence and believe that projects run more efficiently and with better results with training and a Facilitator, but I think you need to try the method yourself and see what it does for you.

Further reading

This is not a bibliography but a list of books that I have found interesting and useful.

The Deming Dimension
Henry R. Neave
SPC press, Knoxville, Tennessee, USA
ISBN 0-945320-08-6

I would recommend this book highly if you want to know more about the work of Dr Deming. Written by Britain's leading authority on the great man and founder of the British Deming Association.

Profiles in Quality: Learning from the Masters
Louis E. Schultz
Quality Resources, White Plains, New York, USA
ISBN 0-527-76238-5

Shewhart, Deming, Tribus, Juran, Sarasohn, Ishikawa and Kano. You'll find a chapter about each of these and six other quality 'masters' in this easy to read book by Louis Schultz. Each chapter comprises a brief history of the individual, a summary of their thinking and their key models.

Fourth Generation Management : the New Business Consciousness
Brian L. Joiner
McGraw-Hill Inc., New York, USA
ISBN 0-07-032715-7

A great book that bridges the gap between cultural issues and practical application. Littered throughout with stories that get the points across.

Self-assessment for Business Excellence
David Lascelles and Roy Peacock
McGraw-Hill Book Company, Maidenhead
ISBN 0-07-709186-8

The best book I have come across about the European Business Excellence Model and self-assessment.

The Team Handbook (2nd edition)
Peter R. Scholtes, Brian L. Joiner and Barbara J. Streibel
Joiner Associates Inc., Madison, Wisconsin, USA
ISBN 1-884731-11-2

The Team Handbook is similar in approach to the book above but is more about team working issues and less about projects. Manages to combine theoretical underpinning with useful techniques to bring about change.

Index

The Essentials of Project Management

Dennis Lock

Project management skills are no longer just required by project managers, but by most of us in the natural course of our working lives. *The Essentials of Project Management* is a practical primer drawn from Dennis Lock's comprehensive and highly regarded textbook *Project Management*, which is now in its 6th Edition and has sold tens of thousands of copies. In order to specifically answer the needs of the non-specialist, the content has been carefully selected and organized to form an accessible introduction to the subject.

The result is a concise but well-rounded account of project management techniques, concentrating on the key tasks of project definition, organization, estimating, planning and control, and paying special attention to the role of purchasing. With the aid of examples and illustrations, the book describes the essential project management procedures and explains how and when they should be used.

This is an ideal introduction for anyone for whom project management is part of their professional role (or who would like it to be), or for students for whom it is a component within a broader course.

Gower

Gower Handbook of Project Management

Second Edition

Edited by Dennis Lock

The first edition of this handbook was published in 1987 under the title *Project Management Handbook*. With its uniquely authoritative and comprehensive coverage of the subject, it quickly established itself as the standard work.

For this new edition the text has been revised and updated throughout to reflect recent developments. Eight entirely new chapters have been added dealing with such diverse topics as the impact of the European Community, project investment appraisal and environmental responsibility. More than twenty individuals and organizations have pooled their knowledge and experience to produce a practical treatment which ranges from first principles to some of the most advanced techniques now in use.

It is difficult to imagine anyone concerned with industrial or commercial projects who would not profit from a study of this Handbook.

Gower

ISO 14000 and ISO 9000

Brian Rothery

This is a practical 'hands-on' description of how companies can implement a comprehensive system to meet the requirements of the ISO 14000 Environmental Management Standard and the ISO 9000 Quality Management Standard, in addition to the Health and Safety regulations, and other public and product safety and general liability requirements. Written by the leading authority in this field, it anticipates the Phase Two revisions of ISO 9000 and provides complete sets of generic documentation including a Quality Manual and all the environmental registers and manuals.

The author also takes account of the 'backlash' against the ISO 9000 certification process which uses checklists of documents to please inspectors rather than implementing real quality improvement schemes. Throughout the book, advice is given on introducing good, comprehensive systems rather than producing sets of bureaucratic documents.

By presenting an integrated approach to the standards covering quality, health and safety and environmental issues, Brian Rothery has once again provided managers with an important reference and guide.

Gower

Project Management

Sixth Edition

Dennis Lock

Dennis Lock's bestselling book covers the project management process from initial appraisal to closedown, using methods that range from simple charts to powerful computer systems. The relevant techniques can be applied with profit whether the project is worth £1000 or £100m. Every aspect is explained in detail with the aid of illustrations and examples. The projects described are drawn from many different industries, so that the book will appeal to the widest possible range of readers.

For this sixth edition the text has been thoroughly revised and extended to reflect current practices and technology. New case studies have been added, all the computer examples have been reworked and there is increased emphasis on the precedence system of networking.

This is a book that will continue to be the standard work on the subject for managers and students alike.

Gower

Right Every Time

Using the Deming Approach

Frank Price

Over the five years since the publication of Frank Price's book *Right First Time* the business landscape of the Western World has undergone an upheaval - a Quality Revolution. This explosion of interest in the management of quality has not just affected the manufacturing sector but has influenced all areas of industry; and with diverse effects. In *Right Every Time* the author not only examines the content of quality thinking, the statistical tools and their application to business processes; he also explores the context, the cultural climate, in which these tools are put to work, the environment in which they either succeed or fail. The core of the book consists of a critique of Deming's points - which the author refers to as the new religion of quality - and an examination of the pitfalls which act as constraints on quality achievement.

This is more than a 'how to do' book, it is as much concerned with 'how to understand what you are doing', and the book's message is applicable to anybody engaged in providing goods or services into markets where 'quality' is vital to business success.

There can be no doubts concerning the benefits of quality control, and in this important and highly readable text Frank Price reveals how such visions of excellence may be transformed into manufacturing realities.

Gower

Right First Time

Using Quality Control for Profit

Frank Price

This remarkable book combines simplicity of treatment with depth of coverage and is written in a refreshingly original style. Dispelling the mystique which so often surrounds the subject, and without indulging in complex mathematics, the author explains how to achieve low scrap rates, zero customer rejections and the many other benefits of systematic quality control.

The twin themes of the book are the need for quality to be an integral part of the manufacturing process and the importance of commitment throughout the workforce. Thus it deals not only with QC concepts and techniques but also with the human and corporate relationships whose effects can be critical.

Gower